A TROUBADOUR READER

A Troubadour Reader

William D. Paden

THE MODERN LANGUAGE ASSOCIATION OF AMERICA

NEW YORK

2025

© 2025 by The Modern Language Association of America
85 Broad Street, New York, New York 10004
www.mla.org

To order MLA publications, visit www.mla.org/books. For wholesale and
international orders, see www.mla.org/bookstore-orders.

The MLA office is located on the island known as Mannahatta (Manhattan) in
Lenapehoking, the homeland of the Lenape people. The MLA pays respect to the
original stewards of this land and to the diverse and vibrant Native communities that
continue to thrive in New York City.

Introductions to Older Languages 6
ISSN 1099-0313

Library of Congress Cataloging-in-Publication Data

Names: Paden, William D. (William Doremus), 1941- author.
Title: A troubadour reader / William D. Paden.
Description: New York : The Modern Language Association of America, 2025.
Series: Introductions to older languages, 1099-0313 ; 6 | Includes bibliographical
    references and index.
Identifiers: LCCN 2024030335 | ISBN 9781603296960 (paperback)
Subjects: LCSH: Provençal language—Readers. | Provençal poetry.
Classification: LCC PC3225 .P33 2025 | DDC 849/.1208—dc23/eng/20241028
LC record available at https://lccn.loc.gov/2024030335

CONTENTS

ACKNOWLEDGMENTS

I am grateful to the members of the informal Occitan Reading Group who met at Northwestern University from 2010 to 2016: Christopher Davis, Joseph Derosier, Annalese Duprey-Henry, Rebecca Fall, Scott Hiley, Barbara Newman, Frances Paden, Stephanie Pentz, Raashi Rastogi, Barbara Rosenwein, Elizaveta Strakhov, and William West. I provided the group with texts glossed on the page. At each meeting, we translated one poem. As we worked together, we engaged with the text in conversation ranging from fine points of translation to broad issues of historical and poetic understanding. We tried to make sense, full and present, of this poetry from long ago and far away. Many of those texts are now in the present volume.

Christopher Davis and Wendy Pfeffer read sample texts and gave me their advice, for which I am also grateful.

Thanks to the editorial team at the MLA for its expertise, dedication, and patience throughout the process of publication.

I hope that this volume will prove helpful to individuals or small groups who use it to discover, explore, and enjoy the poetry of the troubadours and trobairitz.

A *Troubadour Reader* is intended as a supplement to the author's *Introduction to Old Occitan* (henceforth *Old Occitan*), which presents a systematic grammar of the language with readings and a complete glossary. The *Reader* provides glosses to the side of each line and notes after each stanza, enabling the student to work through the Occitan text without constant reference to the back of the book. This volume relies on *Old Occitan* for explanation of grammatical structures. It duplicates none of the readings in *Old Occitan* but adds more poems by women, others that were written early (nos. 1–3) and late (nos. 28–30), some that are linguistically diverse (see index, Occitan in contact with other languages), and some that are more challenging (nos. 8–10, 18–19). These readings enable the student to appreciate more fully the range and wealth of medieval Occitan lyric poetry.

WHAT IS A TROUBADOUR?

For the purposes of this book, a troubadour was a medieval lyric poet who expressed himself or herself in the Occitan language. Lyric poetry is understood as poetry in stanzas, unlike narrative poetry in couplets. The Occitan language was and remains one of the Romance languages that developed from Latin, like its neighbors Italian, Catalan, and French. Occitan was a native language in the South of France, surrounded on every side by these sister languages.[1]

The troubadours included poets born in the South of France (the Midi), Catalonia, and Italy. The corpus of Occitan poetry in the Midi begins with a ninth-century charm (no. 1), a tenth-century stanza of love poetry (no. 2), and a religious hymn (no. 3). The classic troubadours appear around 1100 with Guilhem IX, duke of Aquitaine and count of Poitiers. They continue through the twelfth and thirteenth centuries and into the early fourteenth. In Catalonia poets adopted Occitan for lyric compositions from the thirteenth century to the

---

1. For a map, see *Old Occitan*, pp. 7–8.

fifteenth, although prose writers used their native Catalan. In Italy some poets used Occitan in the thirteenth and early fourteenth centuries, although more of them wrote in their native Italian. The troubadours generally composed for musical performance; musical notations survive for about ten percent of their works.[2]

CONTENT OF THE VOLUME

The *Reader* provides a diverse selection of medieval lyric poems in Occitan. It presents each one with glosses to the side, notes after each stanza, and a brief introduction. The section "Elements of Occitan" introduces the basic grammar. The section "Manuscripts" explains their abbreviations and provides web addresses so that readers may consult them online. An index characterizes the readings.

Each Occitan text is presented in an edition based insofar as possible on one medieval source. The manuscripts used are available on the web.[3] The interested student is encouraged to access the manuscript and compare what it says with the version in the *Reader*. The scholarly tradition of troubadour study has often focused on multiple versions of a poem, represented in various manuscripts that give differing readings. Some editors have combined versions into a single edition presented as authoritative; others have normalized orthography. The *Reader* adopts a selected medieval source as the base for each poem and presents it with reference to other manuscripts as needed to produce an acceptable text. It hews closely to the base, making minimal corrections. In orthography, consonantal *j* is distinguished from vocalic *i*, and consonantal *v* is distinguished from vocalic *u*. When *c* represents a sibilant before *a, o, u,* it is spelled *ç*. In meter, elision of a vowel is made explicit: *cailla e* in the manuscript, constituting two syllables, is edited as *caill'e*. So is hiatus of a vowel: *reina* in the manuscript, counting three syllables, appears as *reïna*. If the manuscript text is garbled, the *Reader* corrects it, referring to other manuscripts as needed, on the assumption that the troubadour intended to mean something. Conjectures are bracketed with the symbols [ ] and listed in the section "Corrected Readings." The result is a text that takes the medieval base as its authority. Other manuscripts of the same text could have provided other editions. The *Reader* does not claim to present a single, original, authoritative version of each poem. In the view taken here, any such claim is illusory.

Although the manuscripts commonly end each verse line with a point or period, most do not make lines of different syllabic length visually distinct. The

---

2. On troubadour music, see Aubrey, *Music. Old Occitan* offers musical examples (scores) for the poems included there (560–77) and an audio CD with performances of five of them by Aubrey, who introduces the CD ("Music"). Poems in this *Reader* that have music are nos. 2, 3, 6, 7, and 13. The headnotes identify musical editions.

3. The manuscript of no. 3, on the web earlier, was not accessible when the book was submitted to the press. Hopefully it will be available again at the time of publication.

Reader does so by indenting shorter lines, thus making the metrical structure of the text visible. It enables the student to confront the medieval source of this edition directly on the web, to recognize its prosodic shape, and to decipher what it means.

HOW TO USE THIS BOOK

The texts are presented chronologically but may be read in any order. Inexperienced students may first read over the section "Elements of Occitan," then continue with the Comtessa de Dia (nos. 14–15), Guilhem IX (no. 4), and Bernart de Ventadorn (no. 12), in that order. These readings provide grammar reviews designed to help assimilate the "Elements." Students may then turn to short readings (nos. 1–2, 24, 27–28). They may find others that appeal to them by consulting the index, which lists themes and other notable matters. Eventually they may tackle more difficult texts (nos. 8–10, 18–19). As they work through the Occitan, they may refer to *Old Occitan* for explanation of grammatical structures.

TRANSLATIONS

The goal of this book is to engage readers directly with the Occitan text. Full translations are not provided, because they might distract from such engagement. Nevertheless, translation can be an act of insight and love that illuminates the original. The following poets, among others, have translated readings in this book:

> Ezra Pound, *Poems*, nos. 13 (402), 18 (502 and 515), 19 (1118 and 1126), and 27 (1190);
> W. D. Snodgrass, nos. 13 (Kehew 66) and 17 (Kehew 96);
> Paul Blackburn, nos. 4 (12), 5 (19), 17 (97), 18 (166), 22 (173), and 25 (269);
> Sally Purcell, no. 11 (39); and
> Claudia Keelan (translated the trobairitz), nos. 11 (41), 14 (68), 15 (82), 20 (90), 23 (102), and 25 (128).

In *Troubadour Poems from the South of France*, William D. Paden and Frances Freeman Paden translated many of the texts closely and with an attempt to capture poetic effects. The earlier editions listed in the headnote for each reading provide translations by the editors. On varieties of translation from the troubadours into English and French, see Roy S. Rosenstein, "Translation."

Spelling. Medieval Occitan, like other vernacular languages at the time, lacked standardized spelling. An Occitan word may be spelled more than one way within a single line of verse. Readers must learn to cast aside the expectation of standard orthography.

Stress. In general, words ending in a consonant were stressed on the last syllable: *cantár* 'to sing'; *senhór* 'lord.' Words ending in a vowel were stressed on the syllable before the last one: *cánta* 'he sings'; *dómna* 'lady.' In notes to the texts, the *Reader* provides generous indications of the stressed syllable (´).

Sounds. The vowels *e* and *o* had two varieties, one called close (with the tongue higher in the mouth, reducing the aperture) and the other called open (with the tongue lower, increasing the aperture). The open varieties could be written as a single vowel or a diphthong. Open *e* alternated with *ié*; open *o* alternated with *uó* or *ué*. The consonants *n* and *l* had palatal varieties that merged with yod (the first sound in Eng. *you*). Palatal *n*, now conventionally written *nh* as in *senhor* (Sp. *señor*), was also spelled *gn* or *ign*. Palatal *l*, now conventionally written *lh* as in Occitan *melhor* 'better' (It. *migliore*), was also spelled *ill*.

Verbs. Verbs were conjugated for tense, person, and number. They carried more information about the structure of the sentence than nouns did.

The most frequent type of infinitive in Occitan ended in *-ar*. Latin *cantare* 'to sing' gave Italian *cantare*, Occitan *cantar*, Spanish *cantar*, and French *chanter*. Other infinitive types ended in *-ir* (*partir* 'to leave'), *-er* (*aver* 'to have'), or unstressed *-re* (*perdre* 'to lose'). Verbs were conjugated for eight tenses. The tenses fall into three groups, as may be seen in the third person singular forms of *cantar*:

PRESENT GROUP, BASED ON THE ROOT
(CANT-) WITH ENDINGS FOR TENSE:

Present Indicative: *cánta* (cant- + -a) 'she sings'
Present Subjunctive: *cant* (cant- + -zero) 'that he sing'
Imperfect: *cantáva* (cant- + -áva) 'she was singing'

FUTURE GROUP, BASED ON THE INFINITIVE
(CANTAR-) WITH ENDINGS FOR TENSE:

Future: *cantará* (cantar- + á) 'he will sing'
First Conditional: *cantaría* (cantar- + ía) 'she would sing'

PAST GROUP, BASED ON THE ROOT (CANT-) WITH AN INFIX
(-É-) FOR THE GROUP AND ENDINGS FOR TENSE OR PERSON:

Preterit: *cantét* (cant- + -é- + -t for third person singular) 'he sang'
Past Subjunctive: *cantés* (cant- + -é- + -s for past subjunctive) 'that she sang'
Second Conditional: *cantéra* (cant- + -é- + -ra for second conditional) 'he would have sung'

The indicative expresses a fact, the subjunctive an emotion, the conditional a hypothesis. The subjunctive is often subordinate to an indicative verb, as in *Amors vol c'om cant* 'Love wants a person to sing' or, more literally, 'Love wants that a person sing.' In this sentence "Love wants" is presented as a fact; what Love wants (that a person sing) is produced by Love's desire. *Vol* is independent; *cant* is subordinate.

In each tense, six forms expressed the first, second, or third person in the singular or plural. In the process of reading, some of these forms are encountered more frequently than others, so they are more important for students to recognize. The most frequent endings of *cantar* are these:

PRESENT INDICATIVE

1 sg. *cant* (root + -zero) 'I sing'
3 sg. *cánta* (root + -a) 'she sings'
3 pl. *cántan/cánton* (root + -an/on) 'they sing'

PRESENT SUBJUNCTIVE

1 sg. *cant* (root + -zero) 'that I sing'
3 sg. *cant* (root + -zero) 'that he sing'
3 pl. *cánton* (root + -on) 'that they sing'

PRETERIT

1 sg. *cantéi* (root + -é- + -i) 'I sang'
3 sg. *cantét* (root + -é- + -t) 'she sang'
3 pl. *cantéron* (root + -é- + -ron) 'they sang'

In the present indicative, the contrast between first person singular and third person singular occurs frequently: first person singular *cant* 'I sing' versus third person singular *cánta* 'he sings.' So does the contrast between present indicative and present subjunctive for third person singular: indicative *cánta* 'she sings' (a fact) versus subjunctive *cant* 'that he sing' (a wish).

A distinction may be made between "*ar* verbs" and "non-*ar* verbs," the latter including all verbs with infinitives that do not end in -*ar*. This distinction underlies further overlaps and contrasts in conjugation, as in *partir* 'to leave':

PRESENT INDICATIVE

1 sg. *part*
3 sg. *part*
3 pl. *párton*

PRESENT SUBJUNCTIVE

1 sg. *párta*
3 sg. *párta*
3 pl. *párton*

PRETERIT

1 sg. *partí/partís*
3 sg. *partí/partít/partíc*
3 pl. *partíron*

A fundamental pattern may be seen in the forms for third person singular:

	PRESENT INDICATIVE			PRESENT SUBJUNCTIVE
Ar verbs: -*a* (*canta*)	-*a*	-Ø		*Ar* verbs: -Ø (*cant*)
Non-*ar* verbs: -Ø (*part*)	-Ø	*a*		Non-*ar* verbs: -*a* (*parta*)

These patterns may seem intricate, but actually they are simple. In the readings, the forms of nouns and verbs are identified in glosses and notes after the stanzas.

Nouns. Nouns were declined for case and number. The nominative case was used for the subject of a sentence. The most frequent type of masculine nouns used final -*s* for the nominative singular, but no ending (-zero) for the nominative plural. The other case, called the oblique, was used for the direct object and the object of a preposition. A masculine noun like *jorn* 'day' had four forms:

	SINGULAR	PLURAL
Nominative	*jorns*	*jorn*
Oblique	*jorn*	*jorns*

The oblique forms were declined as in Modern English: the singular had no ending, the plural had *-s*. Nominative forms had the reverse distribution of *-s* (singular) and *-*zero (plural), contradicting the expectations of speakers of Modern English. Most feminine nouns, however, did not distinguish the two cases: singular *dómna* and plural *dómnas* (stressed as in the singular) were either nominative or oblique.

Declension in two cases was observed regularly in twelfth-century manuscripts; after that time the system became simpler.[4] Nominative forms gradually ceased to be used; oblique forms extended to all functions. (Only the originally oblique forms continue in Modern Occitan.) Therefore, if a twelfth-century poem transmitted in a later chansonnier shows a divergence from normal declension, the divergence is probably due to transmission, not the troubadour, so it is emended here. Exceptionally, however, if the manuscript is the only one that contains music (as is the case in nos. 6, 7, and 13), its version gains special authority as the only one that makes a poem into a song, so this edition respects any anomalies it may have. Each reading provides glosses on the declension of individual words, and nos. 1, 2, 29, and 30 include a more general "Note on Declension."

For more on all the above, see *Old Occitan* (10–16 and following). Full tables of verb and noun forms also may be found in *Old Occitan* (349–52).

---

4. The two-case system always had limits. Proper nouns never declined consistently. Sometimes declension operated on a noun but not an adjective modifying it. Lat. neuter nouns that became masc. in Oc. could take nom. sg. *-s* or not. There were regional variations such as the "Limousin sibilant" (see no. 3, note 16). See *Old Occitan* (281 and 290); Paden, "Declension."

adj.	adjective
BEdT	Asperti, *Bibliografia elettronica dei trovatori*
BN	Bibliothèque Nationale (Paris)
BT	Boutière et al., *Biographies des troubadours*
Cat.	Catalan
col(s).	column(s)
DBT	Guida and Larghi, *Dizionario biografico dei trovatori*
DOM	Selig and Tausend, *Dictionnaire de l'occitan médiéval*
Eng.	English
fem.	feminine
FEW	Wartburg, *Französisches etymologisches Wörterbuch*
fol(s).	folio(s)
Fr.	French (Modern)
fut.	future
indic.	indicative
It.	Italian
Lat.	Latin
masc.	masculine
nom.	nominative
obl.	oblique
Oc.	Old Occitan
OFr.	Old French
Old Occitan	Paden, *Introduction to Old Occitan*
part.	participle
PD	Levy, *Petit dictionnaire provençal-français*
pl.	plural
prep.	preposition
pres.	present
pron.	pronoun
r	recto

sg.	singular
Sp.	Spanish
subj.	subjunctive
v	verso
v., vv.	verse(s), line(s) of poetry
1, 2, 3	first, second, third person
>	becomes
°	marks a glossed word in the text

cobla	stanza
coblas doblas	stanzas that use given rhyme sounds in pairs of stanzas
coblas singulars	stanzas that use given rhyme sounds in only one stanza
coblas unissonans	stanzas that use the same rhyme sounds throughout a song
tornada	short final stanza that typically imitates the scheme and rhymes from the corresponding last lines of the preceding full stanza
$(-1), (+1)$	one syllable lacking (-1) or extra $(+1)$
'	an unstressed final syllable, not counted in the meter

Texts

Tomida femina

One manuscript: Clermont-Ferrand, Bibliothèque communautaire et interuniversitaire (Bibliothèque du Patrimoine), MS 201, ninth or tenth century. The charm was added after the manuscript had been written. Facsimiles: Bischoff (plate IV); Meneghetti (plate 8); Paden and Paden (*Troubadour Poems* 14); Lauranson-Rosaz (254).
Major editions: Bischoff (261–68); Hilty (25–29); Meneghetti (164–67); Lazzerini (*Letteratura medievale* 11–15); Paden ("Before the Troubadours" 513–15); Paden and Paden ("Swollen Woman").

This birthing charm, recorded perhaps about 975, is the first poem in Occitan. The *tomida femina* 'swollen woman' is pregnant (Paden and Paden, "Swollen Woman"). The speaker is a midwife who helps her patient give birth. She refers to birthing instruments of wood and iron, some of which still exist today.

The language is archaic, between Latin and the Occitan of the troubadours. The first and last lines are nearly identical to Latin. Some words between them are Latin, but others are not (see glosses). The metrical form is not that of the troubadours and trobairitz, who began to sing more than a century later, but neither is it plain prose. It is free verse, that is, "poetry without a combination of a regular metrical pattern and a consistent line length" (Cooper 522).

The charm was written upside down in the bottom and side margins of a Latin legal treatise. It is not lineated. This edition divides it into lines as defined by rhymes or slant rhymes and indents the lines, as throughout this book, according to the number of syllables they contain.

Clermont-Ferrand, MS 201, fol. 89v.

Tomida° femina°	a swollen; woman
in tomida via° sedea°;	a road; was sitting
tomid'infant°	child
in falda° sua tenea°;	her lap; she was holding
5 *tomid[a]s mans°*	hands
et tomid[e]s pes,°	feet
tomidas carnes°	bodies
que est colbe° recebrunt°;	this blow; that will receive
tomide fust°	wood
10 *et tomide fer°*	iron
que [est] colbe done[runt]°.	that will strike
Exsunt° en° dolores°	go out; from them; pains
d'os° en polpa°,	from bone; to flesh
[de polpa en curi°,]	to skin
15 *de curi in pel°,*	to hair
de pel en erpa°.	to grass
Tærra madre° susipiat° dolores°.	mother earth; let receive; pains

---

(1) *Tómida.* Attested only in this text (*DOM, tomide*); Lat. *tumida.* Masc. obl. sg. *tomide* (vv. 9, 10), *tomid'* (v. 3), obl. pl. *tomid[e]s* (v. 6); fem. nom. sg. *tomida* (v. 1), obl. pl. *tomidas* (vv. 5, 7). See the note on declension below.

(1) *fémina.* Lat. Cf. Oc. *fémena, femna.*

(2) *sedéa.* Imperfect 3 sg. of *sezer,* between Lat. *sedébat* and Oc. *sezía.*

(3) *infant.* Obl. sg., between Lat. *infantem* and Oc. *enfant.*

(4) *falda.* Oc., from Gothic **falda* 'lap' (reconstructed form); refers here to the womb by synecdoche. Cf. Lat. *gremium, sinus.*

(4) *tenéa.* Imperfect 3 sg. of *tener,* between Lat. *tenébat* and Oc. *tenía.*

(5–8) 'Swollen hands and swollen feet, swollen bodies that will receive this blow.'

(5) *mans.* Obl. pl. of Oc. *man,* from Lat. *manus.*

(6) *pes.* Obl. pl. of Oc. *pe,* from Lat. *pedes.*

(7) *cárnes.* Obl. pl. of *carn* 'flesh, body.' Lat. *carnes* is identical in archaic Oc. Pl. referring to mother and child.

(8) *cólbe.* Obl. sg. of Oc. *colp/colbe,* from Late Lat. *colaphus.*

(8) *recebrúnt.* Fut. 3 pl. of Oc. *recébre.* Cf. Lat. *recipient.*

(9–11) 'Swollen wood and swollen iron that will strike this blow.' Birthing instruments.

(9) *fust.* Oc., from Lat. *fustem.*

(10) *fer.* Oc., from Lat. *ferrum.*

(11) *est.* Oc. masc. obl. sg., from Lat. *istum.*

(11) *donerúnt.* Fut. 3 pl. of Oc. *donar* 'to strike [blows]' (*PD, DOM*). Cf. Lat. *donábunt.*

(12) *Éxsunt.* Pres. indic. 3 pl. between Lat. *éxeunt* (from *exire*) and Oc. *éison* (from *eisir*).

(12) *dolóres.* Lat. *dolóres,* nom. pl. of *dolor.* Cf. Oc. *dolórs.*

(13) *os.* Oc. obl. sg. = Lat. accusative.

(13) *polpa.* Oc. obl. sg., from Lat. *pulpam.*

(14) *cúri.* Obl. sg., between Lat. *cúrium* and Oc. *cuér.*

(15) *pel.* Oc., from Lat. *pellem.*

(16) *erpa.* Lat. *herbam,* Oc. *erba.*

(17) *Tærra.* Nom. sg. of *terra* (Lat. = Oc.). The Lat. diphthong *ae* (in other words) merged with short *e.*

(17) *madre.* Nom. sg., between Lat. *mater* and Oc. *maire.*

(17) *susípiat.* Lat. *suscípiat,* pres. subj. 3 sg. Oc. *soiséba.* Subj. expressing a wish.

(17) *dolóres.* Obl. pl. (cf. v. 12).

Form

Seventeen rhythmic lines of varying meter with recurring rhymes or assonances (**b, c, d, e**).

SCHEME

a	b	c	b	c	d	d	e	e	f	e	d'	g	h	i	j	d

RHYMES OR ASSONANCES

'-ina 'ea ant 'ea ans es '-es unt ust er unt '-es 'olpa 'uri el 'erpa '-es

METER

4″ 8′ 4 7′ 4 5 4′ 7 4 5 8 5′ 3′ 5′ 5 4′ 10′

Fémina (v. 1) has two unstressed syllables after the stress, a pattern that occurs in Medieval Latin rhymes but not in those of the troubadours.

Note on Declension

The case of *mans, pes, carnes* (vv. 5–7) and *fust, fer* (vv. 9–10) is oblique, like the Latin accusative in exclamations (*Aquilam!* '[I see] an eagle!') and the Occitan oblique after words meaning "Behold!" (Jensen, *Syntax* 19–20).

Corrected Readings

(5) *tomid[a]s.* Clermont-Ferrand, MS 201: *tomides* (modifies *mans,* fem.).

(6) *tomid[e]s.* Clermont-Ferrand, MS 201: *tomidas* (modifies *pes,* masc.).

(10) *tomide.* Clermont-Ferrand, MS 201: *tomides.*

(11) *[est].* Clermont-Ferrand, MS 201: *istae.*

(11) *done[runt].* Clermont-Ferrand, MS 201: *done-* followed by erasure.

(14) Lacking in Clermont-Ferrand, MS 201; conjectured by parallel to vv. 13 and 15–16.

Las, qu'i non sun sparvir, astur

One manuscript: London, British Library, Harley MS 2750. The stanza was added in a late-eleventh-century hand. Facsimiles: Bischoff (plate V); Meneghetti (plate 12); Haines (208).

Major editions: Bischoff (266–69); Lazzerini ("A proposito" 125); Paden ("Before the Troubadours" 522–25). Music: Haines (208–09).

The stanza may have been composed circa 1050 as a complete poem (an anticipation of the genre of the *cobla*) or part of a longer one. It echoes Poitevin, the speech of Poitou, which resembled but differed from both French and Occitan (see note for (2) *voler*, (3) *imbracher*, (4) *baser*). Poitevin also left traces in Guilhem IX and Richard Lionheart, counts of Poitiers (nos. 5 and 21).

The manuscript was written in Germany by a German scribe (Lazzerini, "A proposito" 125), which helps account for the spellings *buch, schi, sintil*. Germany and Poitou had direct connections. Agnes, daughter of Guilhem V, duke of Aquitaine and count of Poitiers, married Emperor Henry III in 1043. Singers accompanied her from Poitou to the wedding at Ingelheim am Rhein (Meneghetti 190–91). Later she became an aunt of Guilhem IX.

Harley 2750, fol. 94v.

Las°, qu'i non sun° sparvir, astur°,	alas; that I'm not; a sparrow-
	hawk (or) a goshawk
qu'i podis° a li° voler°,	so I could; to her; fly
la sintil° imbracher°,	the noble [woman]; embrace
se buch° schi duls° baser°,	her mouth; so sweet; kiss
5 *dussiri° e repasar° tu dulur°.*	sweeten; soothe; all pain

(1) *sun.* Oc. *son,* pres. indic. 1 sg. of *éser.* Poitevin *soi, sui* (Boucherie 255); OFr. *sui.*

(1) *sparvír.* Oc. *esparvier,* OFr. *espervier.* The sparrowhawk was regarded as inferior to the larger, more powerful goshawk.

(1) *astúr.* Oc. *austor,* OFr. *ostor.*

(2) *podís.* Past subj. 1 sg. of *poder.* Closer to Poitevin 3 sg. *poguist* (Boucherie 56) than Oc. 1 sg. *pogués* or OFr. *peüsse.*

(2) *voler,* (3) *imbracher,* (4) *baser.* Poitevin (all three words) or OFr. (*voler*), but not Oc. The Lat. infinitive ending *-are* produced *-er* in Poitevin. In OFr. it yielded *-er* in *voler* but *-ier* in *embracier, baisier,* after the palatal consonant. In Oc. it gave *-ar* in *volar, embrasar, baizar.*[i]

(3) *sintil.* Oc. and OFr. *gentil.*

(4) *buch.* Oc. *boca,* OFr. *boche,* Poitevin *bouche* (Boucherie 357).

(4) *schi.* Oc. and OFr. *si.*

(4) *duls.* Oc. *dols,* OFr. *dolz.*

(5) *dussiri.* Oc. *doucir,* OFr. *doucier.*

(5) *repasar.* Closer to Oc. *repauzar* than OFr. or Poitevin *reposer* (Boucherie 70).

(5) *dulur.* Oc., OFr., and Poitevin *dolor.*

Form

One stanza of five lines.

SCHEME

a b b b a

RHYMES

ur er er er ur

METER

8 7 6 6 10

Note on Declension

The German scribe did not record case endings carefully. In verse 1, *sparvir* and *astur* are predicate nominatives in the oblique, contrary to the norm in Latin and Occitan, which called for the nominative. In verse 5, *dulur* is feminine, so one expects *tuta/tute,* not *tu.*

Corrected Reading

(2) *voler.* Corrected in Harley 2750 from *vorer.*

---

i. On these endings in Poitevin, see Pignon (1: 190). For endings in Occitan, see Avalle (22–23, 49–50, 55–56); Guilhem IX (ed. Pasero 333). For French endings, see Pope (163–64). Poitevin texts edited by Boucherie.

O Maria, Deu maire

One manuscript: Paris, Bibliothèque Nationale, lat. 1139. This section was written in 1096–99 (Chailley 111).
Major editions: Thomas (199–200 and 239–42). Music: Haines (216–21).

This liturgical song may have been written about 1050. It sets an Occitan text to the melody from a ninth-century Latin hymn, *Ave maris stella* (*Hail, Star of the Sea*) (Raby 94–95). The musical notation continues throughout but differs in detail from one stanza to another. Troubadour melodies may have varied similarly, although they are almost always notated for only the first stanza.

The term *versus* in the title was used for "a particular kind of Latin sacred song popular from the 11th century on" (Crocker 504). The term and concept may have been adapted by the troubadours in their *vers*.

BN lat. 1139, fols. 49r–50r.

Versus sancte Marie
'A *versus* for Saint Mary' (Lat.)

I

O Maria, Deu maire°,	mother of God
Deu[s] t'es° e fils° e paire°;	God is for you; both son; and father
domna, preia° per nos	pray
4 *to fil° lo glorios°.*	to your son; glorious

(1) A noun for a person in the oblique (*Deu*) can express possession by being juxtaposed with another noun (*maire*).
(2) The song addresses the Virgin as *tu*.
(3) *préia*. Imperative 2 sg. of *pregar*.

II

E lo pair'° aissamen°	to your father; also
preia per tota jen°;	people
e c'el° no nos socor°,	if he; does not help us
8 *tornat° nos es a plor°.*	turned; weeping

---

(7) *socor.* Pres. indic. 3 sg. of *socorre.*

(8) *tornát.* Past part. of *tornar.* '[Everything] for us has turned to weeping.'

III

Eva creet° serpen°,	obeyed; a serpent
un a[n]gel resplanden°,	shining
per so° nos en vai° gen;	which is why; it goes well for us
12 *Deus n'es om veramen°.*	truly

---

(9) *creét.* Pret. 3 sg. of *creire.*

(10) *resplandén.* Pres. part. of *resplandir.* The reference is to Lucifer.

(11) *vai.* Pres. indic. 3 sg. of *anar.*

(11–12) Original sin was a 'happy fault' (Lat. *felix culpa*) because it led to the Incarnation.

IV

Car de femna° nasquet°,	of a woman; he was born
Deus la femna salvet;	
e per quo nasquet hom,	
16 *que garit° en fos° hom.*	saved; would be

(13–14) 'Because he was born of a woman, God saved that woman.'

(13) *nasquét.* Pret. 3 sg. of *náiser.*

(14) *salvét.* Pret. 3 sg. of *salvar.*

(15–16) 'And that is why [God] was born as a man, so that man would be saved.' In both lines *hom* means 'a human being, person, man,' like Lat. *homo.*

(16) *garít.* Past part. of *garir*, masc. nom. sg. One expects nom. sg. *garitz*, but final *-t* here represents the "Limousin sibilant," a regional reduction of *-tz* that also occurs in *tot* (v. 36), *crot* (v. 38), *tert* (v. 39), and *aut* (v. 41) (Paden, "Declension" 71–74).

(16) *fos.* Past subj. 3 sg. of *éser.*

V

Eva, moler Adam°,	wife of Adam
quar° creet lo Setam°,	because; Satan
nos mes° en tal afan°	put us; such grief
20 *per qu'avem° set° e fam°.*	that we have; thirst; hunger

---

(17) *móler.* Nom. sg. of *molér* (shifting declension). The phrase *móler Adám* indicates possession expressed by juxtaposition, as in *Deu maire* (v. 1).

(18) *lo Setám.* The definite article was used with proper names, especially biblical ones.

(19) *mes.* Pret. 3 sg. of *metre.*

(20) *avém.* Pres. indic. 1 pl. of *aver.*

VI

Eva mot° foleet° greatly; committed folly
quar de queu frut° m[an]jet° that fruit; she ate
que Deus li devedet° forbade to her
24 *e cel° que la creet.* to him

---

(21) *mot.* That is, *molt.*
(21) *foleét.* Pret. 3 sg. of *folejar.*
(22) *m[an]jét.* Pret. 3 sg. of *manjar.*
(23) *devedét.* Pret. 3 sg. of *devedar.*
(23–24) Eve ate of the fruit 'that God forbade to her and to him (Adam) who obeyed her.'

VII

E c'el° no la.n crees° if he; had not obeyed her
e deu fruit° no manjes°, that fruit; had not eaten
ja no° murira° hom ja no, never; would a person die
28 *chi ames° nostre don° . . .* who loved; lord

---

(25) *creés.* Past subj. 3 sg. of *creire.*
(26) *deu.* Equivalent to *de + lo.*
(26) *manjés.* Past subj. 3 sg. of *manjar.*
(27) *muríra.* Second conditional 3 sg. of *morir.*
(28) *amés.* Past subj. 3 sg. of *amar.*

VIII

Mas° tan fora° de gen but; there would have been so many
ch'aner'° a garimen°, who would have gone; to salvation
cil chi° perdut° seran° those who; lost; will be
32 *ja° per re° no foran.* ja . . . no, never; at all

(29–32) 'But there would have been so many people who would have been saved [that] those who will be lost would never have been [lost] at all.'
(29) *fora.* Second conditional 3 sg. of *éser.*
(30) *aner'.* That is, *anera,* second conditional 3 sg. of *anar.*
(31) *perdút.* Past part. of *perdre,* masc. nom. pl.
(31) *serán.* Fut. 3 pl. of *éser.*
(32) *fóran.* Second conditional 3 pl. of *éser.* Imperfect rhyme: *-an* is stressed in v. 31 but unstressed in v. 32.

IX

Adam menjet° lo fruit ate
per que° fom° tuit perdut°; because of which; we were; all lost
Adam no creet Deu,
36 *a tot nos en vai° greu°.* for us all it goes; badly

---

(33) *menjét.* Pret. 3 sg. of *manjar* with variant vowel in the root.
(34) *fom.* Pret. 1 pl. of *éser.*

(34) *túit.* Masc. nom. pl. of *tot.*

(36) *tot.* Equivalent to *totz,* masc. obl. pl. of *tot* (see v. 16 note on *garit*).

X

Deus receubt° per lui° mort°	received; because of him; death
e la crot° a gran tort°	on the cross; with great injustice
e resors° al tert dia°,	rose again; third day
40 *si cum o dii Maria.*	

(37) *receúbt.* Pret. 3 sg. of *recebre.* God died because Adam fell.

(38) *e ... crot.* Equivalent to *en crotz* (see v. 16 note on *garit*).

(39) *resórs.* Pret. 3 sg. of *resórzer.*

(39) *tert.* Equivalent to *tertz* (see v. 16 note on *garit*), obl.; normal Oc. *-z* is part of the stem.

(40) 'As Mary said it.' Mary Magdalene told the apostles that Christ told her he would rise again (John 20.18).

(40) *dii.* Pret. 3 sg. of *dire.* Perhaps a Latinism (*dixit*) reduced to one syllable.

XI

Aut apostols° cumtet°	to the apostles; she spoke
e dis° c'ap Deu° parlet°,	said; with God; she talked
qu'eu° poi° de Galilea	on the; hill
44 *viu° lo verem° angera°.*	alive; we will see him; again

(41) *Aut.* Equivalent to *autz* (see v. 16 note on *garit*), Lat. *ad illos.*

(41) *cumtét.* Pret. 3 sg. of *comtar.* The subject is Mary Magdalene (v. 40).

(42) *dis.* Pret. 3 sg. of *dire.*

(42) *Deu.* Christ.

(42) *parlét.* Pret. 3 sg. pf *parlar.*

(43) *eu.* Equivalent to *en el.*

(43) *Galiléa.* Jesus foretold that after he rose again, he would reappear to the apostles at Galilee (Matt. 26.32, Mark 14.28).

(44) *verém.* Fut. 1 pl. of *veire.*

(44) *angéra.* Imperfect rhyme with *Galiléa* (assonance on *é-a*).

XII

Vida°, qui mort° aucis°,	life (i.e., Christ); death; killed
nos donet° paradis;	gave
gloria° aisamen°	glory; also
48 *nos do Deus° veramen°!*	may God give us; truly

(45) *aucís.* Pret. 3 sg. of *aucire.* Jesus said, "Omnis qui vivit et credit in me, non morietur in aeternum" 'Everyone who lives and believes in me will never die' (*Bible,* Latin Vulgate Version, John 11.26).

(46) *donét.* Pret. 3 sg. of *donar.*

(48) *do.* Pres. subj. 3 sg. of *donar,* expressing a wish.

Form

Twelve *coblas singulars* of four lines.

SCHEME
>   a   a   b/a   b/a

The rhyme scheme, elsewhere **aabb**, is **aaaa** in stanzas III, V, VI.

RHYMES

I	*áire*	*áire*	*os*	*os*
II	*en*	*en*	*or*	*or*
III	*en*	*en*	*en*	*en*
IV	*et*	*et*	*om*	*om*
V	*am*	*am*	*an*	*am*
VI	*et*	*et*	*et*	*et*
VII	*es*	*es*	*om*	*on*
VIII	*en*	*en*	*án*	*óran*
IX	*úit*	*ut*	*éu*	*éu*
X	*ort*	*ort*	*ía*	*ía*
XI	*et*	*et*	*éa*	*éra*
XII	*is*	*is*	*en*	*en*

Some lines assonate instead of rhyming (*an/am, om/on, án/óran, úit/ut, éa/éra*).

METER
>   6'/6   6'/6   6/6'   6/6'

The meter is six syllables masculine or feminine; an unstressed seventh syllable (') appears in stanzas I, VIII, X, and XI.

Corrected Readings

(2) *Deu[s]*. BN lat. 1139: *Deu*.

(10) *un a[n]gel*. BN lat. 1139: *una gel*.

(15) *per*. Reading in BN lat. 1139 uncertain, read as *pre* (Thomas 199) or *pro* (Thomas 239).

(20) *qu'avem*. BN lat. 1139: *qua vem*.

(22) *m[an]jet*. BN lat. 1139: -*an*- lacking; *miet* 'she ate' (as in Haines 217 and 219; a questionable interpretation); *m[en]iet* (Thomas). Cf. *manjes* (v. 26), *menjet* (v. 33).

Guilhem IX of Aquitaine

Molt jauzïons mi prenc amar

Two manuscripts: *C, E. BEdT* 183.8.
Major editions: Pasero (213–40); Bond (32–35 and 74–75).

Guilhem IX, duke of Aquitaine and count of Poitiers (as Guilhem VII), inherited about a third of modern France. He was born in 1071 and died in 1126. The chansonniers identify him as *Coms* or *Comte de Peiteus* 'count of Poitiers'; historical sources say the count who composed poetry was Guilhem IX. He laid claim to Toulouse as his wife's inheritance and participated in two Crusades, one to the Holy Land that ended in disaster (1101) and another to Spain (1120). He is the first troubadour whose name we know and whose works we have.

E, pp. 115, col. 2–116, col. 1, with reference to *C*, fol. 230r, cols. 1–2.

Comte de Peiteus
Cómte. Obl. sg.; cf. nom. sg. *coms.*

I

Molt jauzïons° mi prenc° amar	very joyful; I begin
un joi don° plus° mi vueill° aizir°,	that; more; I want; to enjoy
e pos° en joi vueill revertir°	since; to return
ben dei°, si puesc°, al mei[l]s° anar°,	I must; I can; to the best; go
5 *qu'a[l meils] or° n'an°, estiers cujar°,*	now; I go; without doubt
c'om° puesca° vezer° ni auzir°.	one; could; see; hear

(1) *jauzïons.* Masc. nom. sg. *-s.*
(1) *prenc.* Pres. indic. 1 sg. of *prendre* (reflexive); *-k* (spelled *-c*) marks pres. indic. 1 sg. of some non-*ar* verbs.
(2) *plus mi vueill aizir.* 'I want to enjoy more.'

(2, 3) *vuéill*. Pres. indic. 1 sg. of *voler*. Root *vol-* + yod for pres. indic. 1 sg. Yod marks pres. indic. 1 sg. of some non-*ar* verbs. Open *o* > *ué*. *L* + yod > *-lh*, spelled *-ill*.

(4) *déi*. Pres. indic. 1 sg. of *dever*. Root *de-* + yod for pres. indic. 1 sg.

(4) *puésc*. Pres. indic. 1 sg. of *poder*. Root *posc-* + -zero for 1 sg. Open *o* > *ué*. On *-sk*, see *Old Occitan* (168).

(5) *an*. Pres. indic. 1 sg. of *anar*. No ending for 1 sg.

(6) *om*. Masc. nom. sg. Cf. obl. *óme*.

(6) *puésca*. Like *puesc* (v. 4) + -*a* for pres. subj. 3 sg. of non-*ar* verbs. Subj. after superlative *a[l meils]* (v. 5).

II

Eu°, so sabetz°, no.m dei° gabar°	I; you know; must not; boast
ni de grans laus° no.m sai° formir°,	praise; nor do I know how; provide
mas s'anc° negus jois° po[c]° flurir°,	if ever; any joy; could; bloom
10 *aquest° deu° sobre totz° g[r]anar°*	this one; must; beyond all [others]; bear seed
e part° los autres° esmerar°,	more than; the others; improve
si com sol° brus jorns° esclarzir°.	as does; a dark day; brighten up

(7) *sabétz*. Pres. indic. 2 pl. of *saber*. Root *sab-* + -*étz* for 2 pl.

(7) *déi*. As in v. 4.

(8) *grans laus*. Masc. obl. pl. because of the -*s* in *grans*. *Laus* is invariable (cf. v. 42).

(8) *sái*. Pres. indic. 1 sg. of *saber*. Root *sa-* + yod for pres. indic. 1 sg. of a non-*ar* verb.

(9) *negus jois*. Masc. nom. sg. -*s*.

(9) *po[c]*. Pret. 3 sg. of *poder*; -*k* (spelled -*c*) marks pret. of some non-*ar* verbs.

(10) *déu*. Pres. indic. 3 sg. of *dever*. Root *dev-*; no ending for pres. indic. 3 sg. of non-*ar* verb; made final, -*v* > -*u*.

(10) *totz*. Masc. obl. pl. -*s/z*.

(12) *sol*. Pres. indic. 3 sg. of *soler*, to be accustomed (impersonal). Root *sol-* + -zero for 3 sg. of non-*ar* verb.

(12) *brus jorns*. Masc. nom. sg. Cf. obl. *brun jorn*.

III

Anc mais nom° poc hom faisonar°	never; imagine
cors° en voler° ni en dezir°	[such a] body [as hers]; wish; desire
15 *ni en pensar° ni en consir°.*	thought; reflection
Aitals jorns° non pot° par°	such a day [as this]; cannot; equal;
t[r]obar°,	find
e qui° be.l volria° lauzar°	if someone; wanted; praise
d'un an° no.i poiri'° avenir°.	in a year; could; succeed

(13) *nom*. That is, *non* 'not.' The -*m* anticipates *p-* in *poc*.

(13) *hom*. Equivalent to *om* (v. 6). The initial *h-* is a Latinate spelling (*homo*).

(16) *Aitals jorns*. Masc. nom. sg. Cf. obl. *aital jorn*.

(16) *pot*. Pres. indic. 3 sg of *poder*. Root *pod-* + no ending for pres. indic. 3 sg. of non-*ar* verb; made final, -*d* > -*t*.

(17–18) 'And if someone wanted to praise it (i.e., this day), he could not succeed in a year.'

(17) *qui.* When lacking an antecedent, *qui* means 'if someone.'

(17) *volría.* First conditional 3 sg. of *voler.* The infinitive reduces to root *volr-* + *-ía* for first conditional.

(18) *poirí'.* That is, *poiría*, first conditional 3 sg. of *poder.* The infinitive reduces to root *poir-* + *-ía* for first conditional.

IV

Totz jois° li° deu humeliar°	every [other] joy; to her; bow
20 *e tot'autr'amors° obezir°*	every other love; obey
midons° per° son bel° acuillir°	milady; because of; pretty; welcome
e per son bel douset° esgar°,	tender; glance
e deu hom mais° sent tans° durar°	more (longer); a hundred times; live
qui.l joi de s'amor° pot sazir°.	her love; possess

(19) *Totz jois.* Masc. nom. sg. Cf. obl. *tot joi.*

(20) *tot'autr'amors.* That is, *tota autra amors*, fem. nom. sg. Cf. obl. *amor.*

(21) *midons.* Fem. invariable (always -s), here obl. for object of *obezir.*

(23–24) *hom ... qui.* 'A man who.'

V

25 *Per son joi pot malaus° sanar°*	a sick man; be cured
e per sa ira° sas° morir°	anger; healthy [man]; die
e savis° hom enfolezir°	wise; go mad
[e belhs° hom sa beutat° mudar°]	beautiful; beauty; lose
e.l plus cortes° vilanejar°	most courtly; become peasantlike
30 *e.l totz vilas° encortezir°.*	completely peasantlike; become courtly

(25) *Per son joi.* 'Because of the joy of it,' that is, of her love (*s'amor*, v. 24).

(25) *maláus.* Masc. nom. sg. -s. Subject of *pot*, like *sas* (v. 26), *savis* (v. 27), *belhs* (v. 28), *cortes* (v. 29), and *vilas* (v. 30).

(26) *sas.* Masc. nom. sg. -s. Cf. obl. *san.*

(27) *sávis.* Masc. nom. sg. -s. Cf. obl. *sávi.*

(28) *belhs hom.* Masc. nom. sg. -s. Cf. obl. *belh ome.*

(30) *totz vilás.* Nom. sg. -s/-z. Cf. obl. *tot vilan.*

VI

Pos° hom genser° non pot trobar°	since; nobler; cannot find
ni hueils° vezer° ni boca° dir°,	eye; see; mouth; say
a mos obs° la vueill retenir°	for my needs; keep
per lo cor° dedins° refrescar°	my heart; inside [me]; refresh
35 *e per la carn° renovelar°,*	my flesh; renew
que no puesca° enveillezir°.	so that I cannot; grow old

(31) *génser.* Etymologically nom., vs. obl. *gensór.* Declension simplified, however, and both etymological forms came to express either case (Jensen, *Syntax* 38; *Old Occitan* 288). No need to correct *genser* in both MSS to *gens[o]r*, as major editors do.

(32) *huéils.* Nom. sg. *-s;* cf. obl. *olh.* Initial *h-* is purely orthographic; open *o* > *ué; -il-* spells *-lh-.*
(33) *mos obs.* Obl. pl. *obs* is invariable (Classical Lat. *opus*).
(34–35) *lo cor ... la carn.* The definite article expresses possession: 'my heart ... my flesh.'
(36) *puésca.* Pres. subj. 1 sg., identical to 3 sg. (v. 6).

VII

Si.m vol° midons° s'amor donar°,	wants; milady; give
pres soi° del penre° e del grazir°	I am ready; for the taking; the thanking
e del celar° e del bendir°	the hiding; the blessing
40 *e de sos plazers° dir e far*	her pleasures
e de son pretz° tener en car°	her reputation; hold dear
e de son laus° enavantir°.	her praise; advance

(37) *midons.* Cf. v. 21.
(37) *vol.* Pres. indic. 3 sg. of *voler.* Root *vol-* + no ending for 3 sg. of non-*ar* verb.
(38) *del penre.* The *-l* cannot be the masc. pronoun *lo* reduced to *.l* 'it,' referring to *amor,* because *amor* is feminine (cf. *amor certana,* no. 12, v. 43). The *-l* is a definite article introducing *penre,* normally a verb but used here as a noun: 'the taking.' The same is true of *del grazir, del celar* (v. 39), and *del bendir* (v. 39).
(40) *sos plazers.* Obl. pl. Cf. obl. sg. *son plazer.*
(41) *pretz.* Obl. sg., invariable.
(42) *laus.* Obl. sg., invariable.

VIII

Ren per autrui non l'aus mandar	
tal paor° ai c'ades° s'azir°,	fear; at once; she might get angry
45 *ni ieu mezeis,° tan tem° faillir°,*	I myself; I fear; to fail
non l'aus m'amor fort° asemblar°;	strongly; declare
mas ela.m deu mon meils° triar°,	my best; choose
pos sap° c'ab lieis° ai a guerir°.	she knows; with her; I must be saved

(43) 'I don't dare send her anything by [way of] anyone else' (i.e., as a messenger).
(43) *aus.* Pres. indic. 1 sg. of *auzar.* No ending for pres. indic. 1 sg.
(44) 'I have such fear that she might get angry at once.'
(44) *azir.* Pres. subj. 3 sg. of *azirar.* No ending for pres. subj. 3 sg. of *-ar* verbs.
(45) *iéu.* Equivalent to *éu* (v. 7). Open *e* > *ié.*
(45) *tem.* Pres. indic. 1 sg. of *temer.* No ending for pres. indic. 1 sg.
(45) *faillir.* The *-ill-* spells *-lh-* (*falhir*).
(47) *meils.* The *-il-* spells *-lh-* (*melhs*).
(48) *sap.* Pres. indic. 3 sg. of *saber.*
(48) *ab liéis ai a guerir.* Aver *a* + infinitive implies an obligation or necessity, like Fr. *avoir à* + infinitive: *J'ai à travailler* 'I must work.'
(48) *liéis.* That is, *léis.* Open *é* > *ié.*

Grammar Review

Masculine nouns and adjectives
Nom. sg. -*s/z*: *jauzïons* (v. 1), *brus jorns* (v. 12), *aitals jorns* (v. 16), *totz jois* (v. 19), *malaus* (v. 25), etc.
Obl. sg. -zero: *un joi* (v. 2), *son joi* (v. 25)
Obl. pl. -*s/z*: *grans laus* (v. 8; *laus* invariable cf. v. 42), *totz* (v. 10), *sos plazers* (v. 40)

Nouns of shifting declension (stress pattern shifts from nom. sg. to obl. sg.)
Masc. nom. sg.: *coms* vs. obl. *cómte* (in rubric), *hom/om* (vv. 13, 28) vs. obl. *óme*

Infinitives in -*ar*

PRESENT INDICATIVE
1 sg. -zero: *aus* (v. 43)

PRESENT SUBJUNCTIVE
3 sg. -zero: *azir* (v. 44)

Infinitives in non-*ar*

PRESENT INDICATIVE
1 sg.
   -zero: *an* (v. 5), *tem* (v. 45)
   -*k*: *prenc* (v. 1)
   -*sk*: *puesc* (v. 4)
   -*yod*: *vueill* (vv. 2, 3), *dei* (v. 4), *sai* (v. 8)
3 sg. -zero: *deu* (v. 10), *pot* (v. 16)

PRESENT SUBJUNCTIVE
1 sg. -*a*: *puesca* (v. 36)
3 sg. -*a*: *puesca* (v. 6)

FIRST CONDITIONAL (-RÍA)
3 sg. -*ría*: *volria* (v. 17), *poiri'* (*poiria*) (v. 18)

PRETERIT
3 sg. -*k*: *poc* (v. 9)

Form

Eight *coblas unissonans* of six lines.

SCHEME

a b b a a b

RHYMES

ar *ir* *ir* *ar* *ar* *ir*

METER

8 8 8 8 8 8

Corrected Readings

(4) *mei[l]s. E: meins.*
(5) *qu'a[l meils]. E: quar molt.*
(9) *s'anc. E: si anc* (+1).
(9) *po[c]. E: per*, corrected to *por* (or *poc*?) by the scribe of *E*; *C: poc.*
(10, 16) A historiated initial at the beginning of the next poem, on the following page, has been cut out (*E*, p. 116, col. 2). The excision barely touched this poem on p. 115, col. 1, removing the *-r-* of *g[r]anar* (v. 10) and partially removing the *-r-* of *t[r]obar* (v. 16). Both words are confirmed in *C*.
(14) *voler.* So *C*; *E: volver.*
(17) *qui.* So *C*; *E: quil.*
(28) Line omitted in *E*; supplied from *C*.

Guilhem IX of Aquitaine

Ar voill que auzon li plusor

Five versions in four manuscripts: *C, D, E,* and two versions in *N. BEdT* 183.2.
Major editions: Pasero (159–86); Bond (24–28).

Guilhem IX here uses occasional Poitevin forms, as the author of the Harley
lyric had done (no. 2), and as Richard Lionheart would do (no. 21).[ii]

D, fol. 198r, cols. 1–2, with reference to *C,* fol. 230v, cols. 1–2; and *E,* pp. 113,
col. 2–114, col. 1.

Peitavin
Peitavin. 'A Poitevin': the scribe recognized the regional effect.

I

Ar° voill° que auzon° li plusor°	now; I want; to hear; everyone
un verset° de bella color°	small *vers* (v. 6); [rhetorical] color
que ai trait° de mon obrador°,	taken from; [notary's] office
qu'eu port° d'aqest mester° la flor°;	win; trade; prize
5 *et es vertaz°!*	truth
lo vers en [puesc] tra[ir]'° ad auctor°	I can cite; as authority
quant er° finaz°.	it will be; finished

(1) *vóill.* Pres. indic. 1 sg. of *voler.*
(1) *áuzon.* Pres. subj. 3 pl. of *auzir.*
(4) *mestér.* Also in vv. 23, 39, 48. Poitevin form (Boucherie 2); cf. Oc. *mestier* in *C* and *E.*
(5–6) *vertaz . . . vers. Vertaz* in line 5 is a pun on *vers* in line 6.

ii. The rhyme *-er* is Poitevin (stanzas VII–IX, as in no. 2, vv. 2–4 note), as is *-ain,* rhyming
with *-á* and *-an* (see v. 36 note on *certain*). Within the line, so are the words *mester* (v. 4 note,
vv. 23, 39, 48) and *vousist* (v. 43 note). On Poitevin rhymes see no. 2, footnote 5.

(6) *vers*. Masc. (invariable); 'poem,' 'song.' General term for a lyric composition before genres became specialized late in the twelfth century.

(7) *er*. Fut. 3 sg. of *éser*.

(7) *finaz*. Past part. of *finar*.

II

Ben conosc° sen° e folor°	I know; sense; folly
et ancta° conosc et honor°,	shame; honor
10 *et ai ardiment° e paor°;*	eagerness; fear
e si.m partes° un joc° d'amor,	offer; match
no son tant faz°	foolish
q'eu no tries° ben lo meillor°	I would not choose; the better
vers° lo malvaz°.	over; the bad

---

(8) *conósc*. Pres. indic. 1 sg. of *conóiser*.

(11) *partés*. Pres. indic. 2 pl. of *partir*.

(12) *faz*. Masc. nom. sg. of *fat*.

(13) *triés*. Past subj. 1 sg. of *triar*.

(14) *vers*. Poitevin form (Boucherie 21) of *vas* 'toward,' 'against.'

III

15 *Ben conois qui° mal° me di°*	if someone; bad [thing]; tells
e qui ben° me di atressi°,	good [thing]; too
e conois ben celui° qe.m ri°;	someone; who laughs at me
e si.l pro° s'azautan de mi°,	worthy; are amused by me
conois assaz°	quite well
20 *qu'[atressi]° dei° voler lor fi°*	likewise; I should; friendship
e lor solaz°.	company

---

(15) *di*. Pres. indic. 3 sg. of *dire*.

(17) *ri*. Pres. indic. 3 sg. of *rire*.

(18) *pro*. Masc. nom. pl. of *pro*.

(18) *azáutan*. Pres. indic. 3 pl. of *azautar*.

(20) *déi*. Pres. indic. 1 sg. of *dever*.

IV

Ben aia° cel que°.m noiri°,	may he have; he who; raised me
que° tant bon mester m'eschari°;	since; he gave me
et anc° de re° no.i mesfailli°,	anc ... no, never; anything; I fell short
25 *q'eu sai° jogar° sobra coissi°*	I know how; to play; on a pillow
a toz tocaz°—	at every move [in a game]
mas° [en] sai [de] nuill mon vezi°,	more; any neighbor of mine
qal qe°.m veiaz°.	just as; you see me

---

(22) *áia*. Pres. subj. 3 sg. of *aver*, expressing a wish.

(22) *noirí*. Pret. 3 sg. of *noirir*.

(23) *escharí*. Pret. 3 sg. of *escarir*.

(24) *mesfaillí*. Pret. 1 sg. of *mensfalhir*.

(28) *qal qe*. Form of *cal que*. Cf. *tal . . . que* 'such as' (*Old Occitan* 481).

(28) *veiáz*. Pres. subj. 2 pl. of *véire*; subj. after indefinite *qal qe*.

V

Lau° en° Deu e saint Julian,	I praise; for it
30 *tant ai apris° del juoc° dolzan°*	learned; game; sweet
que sobre toz° n'ai bona man°;	more than all [others]; skill
e cel qui° conseill° me qera°	if someone; advice; will seek from me
noi.ill er vedaz°,	refused
ne ja° negus° non tornera°	ja . . . non, never; anyone; will go away
35 *desconseillaz°.*	without counsel

(29) *Lau*. Pres. indic. 1 sg. of *lauzar*.

(29) *saint Julián*. Perhaps Julian the Hospitaller, patron of travelers.

(30) *aprís*. Past part. of *aprendre*.

(30) *juóc*. Joc with open *o* > *-uó*.

(32) *qerá*. Fut. 3 sg. of *querre*.

(33) *vedáz*. Past part. of *vedar*. 'It will not be refused to him.'

(34) *tornerá*. Fut. 3 sg. of *tornar* (*-ar* reduced to *-er*).

(35) *desconseilláz*. Past part. masc. nom. sg. of *desconselhar*.

VI

Eu ai nom° maistre certain°,	am called; a sure master
e ja donn'° anuoiz° no m'aura°	a lady; at night; will have me
que no.m voill'° aver cent deman°,	want to have me; forever
q'eu son d'aqest mester, zo.m van°,	I boast
40 *tan enseignaz°*	[well] taught
qe ben sai° guazaignar° mon pan°	I know how; to earn; my bread
en toz mercaz°.	all markets

(36) *Eu ai nom*. Literally, 'I have a name.'

(36) *certain*. Poitevin form (Boucherie 56); cf. Oc. *certan*. Rhymes with *aurá, deman, van, pan*, as in Poitevin (no. 21, v. 25 note to *am*).

(37) *aurá*. Fut. 3 sg. of *aver*.

(38) *voill'*. That is, *voilla*, pres. subj. 3 sg. of *voler*. Subjunctive (marked by yod + *a*) because of indefinite antecedent *donn'* 'any lady' (v. 37).

(38) *cent deman*. Literally, 'a hundred tomorrows.'

(39) *van*. Pres. indic. 1 sg. of *vanar* (reflexive).

(42) *toz mercaz*. Masc. obl. Pl.

VII

E pero°, si.m vousist° gaber°,	yet; if she had wanted; to mock me
toz en fui° ta usaz° l'autrer°	I was; so used up; the other day
45 *q'eu jogava° a un juoc grosser°,*	I was playing; a game with high stakes

e fo° tant bos° al cap° primer°,	it was; so good; start; first
tro° fo taulaz°!	until; put on the board
e quant garde[i]° no m'ac mester°,	when I looked; it did me no good
si.m fo chanzaz°.	it was so changed

(43–47) 'And yet, if she had wanted to mock me, I was so exhausted the other day when I was playing for high stakes, and [the game] was so good at the first start, until it was put on the board' (as for backgammon). The sentence is exclamatory: he was so exhausted, etc., but he does not say what resulted until v. 49.

(43) *vousíst.* Past subj. 3 sg. of *voler*, Poitevin form (*volsist*, Boucherie 33n).

(43) *gaber.* Poitevin form of Oc. *gabar.*

(44) *fúi.* Pret. 1 sg. of *éser.*

(44) *usáz.* Past part. of *uzar.*

(44) *l'autrér.* Poitevin form of Oc. *l'autrier.*

(45) *jogáva.* Imperfect 1 sg. of *jogar.*

(45) *grossér.* Poitevin form of Oc. *grosier.*

(46) *fo.* Pret. 3 sg. of *éser.*

(46) *bos.* Masc. nom. sg., modifying implicit *juocs* (obl. *juoc*, v. 45).

(46) *primér.* Poitevin form (*premer*, Boucherie 39) of Oc. *primier.*

(48) *gardé[i].* Pret. 1 sg. of *gardar.*

(49) *chanzáz.* Past part. masc. nom. sg. of *camjar.*

VIII

50 *Mas ela.m dis un reprocher°:*	insult
"Don°, vostre dat° son menuder°,	Sir; dice; tiny
et er° revidatz° a dobler°!"	so now; come back to life; doubled
Fis m'eu°, "Qi.m dava° Monpenser,	I said; If someone gave me
non er laissaz°."	I won't be left behind
55 *Et ai li levat lo tauler°,*	I raised her [backgammon] board
e'npeinz° los daz°.	I threw; the dice

---

(50) *reprochér.* Poitevin form of Oc. *repropchier.*

(51) *dat.* Masc. nom. pl.

(51) *menudér.* Poitevin form of Oc. *menudier*, masc. nom. pl.

(52) *revidátz.* Imperative 2 pl. of *revidar.*

(52) *doblér.* Poitevin form of Oc. *doblier; a doblier* 'in abundance.'

(53) *Fis.* Pret. 1 sg. of *faire.*

(53) *dáva.* Imperfect 3 sg. of *dar.*

(53) *Monpensér.* Poitevin form of Montpensier (Puy-de-Dôme). MSS C and E read *Monpeslier* 'Montpellier' (Hérault).

(54) *laissáz.* Past part. masc. nom. sg. of *laissar.*

(55) *levát.* Past part. of *levar.*

(55) *taulér.* Poitevin form of Oc. *taulier*, backgammon board (not Fr. *tablier* 'apron,' since the Fr. is not attested until the sixteenth century).

(56) *e'npéinz.* That is, *e enpeinz* 'and I threw.' *Enpeinz*, pret. 1 sg. of *empénher.*

(56) *daz.* Masc. obl. Pl.

IX

E fi.ls° fort ferir° al tauler,	I made them; strike
58 *E fo jogaz°!*	it was won

---

(57) *Fi.* Pret. 1 sg. of *faire* (alternative to *Fis*, v. 53). 'And I made them strike the board hard.' Backgammon players roll dice to determine how far they can move; the dice must land on the board (Semrau 68).

(58) *jogaz.* Past part. masc. nom. sg. of *jogar*, modifying implicit *juocs*, as does *bos* (v. 46). *Jogar* 'to win' (Semrau 82; Bond 70).

Form

In *D*, eight *coblas doblas* of seven lines with one *tornada* of two. The sixth line of three stanzas lacks one syllable (vv. 6, 20, 27). Other manuscripts insert a first *tornada* of four lines.

SCHEME

a	a	a	a	b	a	b

RHYMES

I–II	*or*	*or*	*or*	*or*	*atz*	*or*	*atz*
III–IV	*i*	*i*	*i*	*i*	*atz*	*i*	*atz*
V–VI	*an/ain*	*an/á*	*an*	*á/an*	*atz*	*á/an*	*atz*
VII–VIII	*er*	*er*	*er*	*er*	*atz*	*er*	*atz*
IX						*er*	*atz*

METER

8	8	8	8	4	8	4

Corrected Readings

(6) *lo vers en [puesc] tra[ir]' ad auctor.* *D*: *lo vers en trac ad auctor* (−1); *C*: *e.n puesc en trair lo vers auctor*; *E*: *e puesc ne trair lo vers auctor.*

(20) *qu'[atressi] dei voler lor fi.* *D*: *qu'eu dei ben voler lor fi* (−1); *C*: *qu'atressi dey voler lor fi*; *E*: *atressi dei voler lur fi.*

(27) *mas [en] sai [de] nuill mon vezi.* *D*: *mas no sai nuill mon vezi* (−1); *C*: *mais en say que nulh mo vezi*; *E*: *mas no sai de nuill mon vezi.*

(47) *tro fo taulaz.* *D*: *tro fo dau taulaz* (+1); *C, E*: *tro fui entaulatz*; Pasero, Bond: *tro fo taulatz.*

(48) *garde[i].* *D*: *garde*; *C, E*: *gardei.*

Jaufre Rudel

No sap cantar qui.l so no.m ditz

Seven manuscripts: *C, E, M, R, a,* and two versions in *e. BEdT* 262.3. *R* gives the
melody over stanza I.

Major editions: Pickens, *Songs* (234–36; version 1-b); Wolf and Rosenstein
(134–37); Chiarini (55–63). Music: van der Werf (see Wolf and Rosen-
stein, plates 9–10); van der Werf and Bond (220*).

Jaufre Rudel was styled *princes* 'prince' of Blaye (Gironde), north of Bor-
deaux, in his *vida*. His name appears in a document written after 1120. He par-
ticipated in the Second Crusade (1148), according to an allusion by Marcabru
(no. 9, vv. 38–39 note). He was no longer alive in 1164. The *vida* gives a romantic
account of his life (*Old Occitan* 16–17; *BT* 16–19).

The version of this song in *R* lacks two stanzas present in other manuscripts
and revises others. It has some irregular rhymes and other anomalies that proba-
bly arose in transmission. It diverges from standard declension (see v. 5 note and
further references there). This edition respects the idiosyncrasies, which most
editors normalize, and hews closely to the only source that gives the melody,
thus making the poem into a song. The text in *R* illustrates the creative trans-
mission that Jaufre Rudel welcomed (see vv. 31–32 note).

R, fol. 63r, col. 2.

Jaufre Rudelh
Jaufré. Oc. form of OFr. *Geoffroi*, Eng. Jeffery.

I

No sap° cantar° qui.l so° no.m ditz°,	know how; to sing; melody; perform
ni.l vers° trobar° qui.ls motz° no fay°,	poem; to compose; words; make

ni no sap° de rima° co.s vay,°
si razo° non enten° en si°;
5 *mais° lo mieu chant° comens° aisi°—*
com pus l'auziretz, mais valra.

know; about rhyme; how it goes
reason; understand; in himself
but; my song; I begin; this way

---

(1) *sap.* Pres. indic. 3 sg. of *saber.*
(1) *qui ... ditz.* Subject of *sap.* 'He who doesn't perform a melody doesn't know how to sing.'
(1) *ditz.* Pres. indic. 3 sg. of *dire* on the root *ditz-/diz-.*
(3) *vay.* Pres. indic. 3 sg. of *anar* on the root *vai-.*
(4) *entén.* Pres. indic. 3 sg. of *entendre.*
(5) *lo miéu chant.* Obl. for the direct object of *comens*: 'I begin my song.' One may also read *comens'* as 3 sg. *comensa*: 'My song begins'; then *lo mieu chant* is obl. although it is the subject of *comensa*, despite the expected declension, as in vv. 9, 13 (?), 15, and 24 (see notes to these vv.).
(6) 'The more you hear it, the more it will be worth.'
(6) *auzirétz.* Fut. 2 pl. of *auzir.*
(6) *valrá.* Fut. 3 sg. of *valer.* Jaufre claims that because he understands rhyme and reason his song will be good.

II

Nuls hom no.s meravilh° de mi
s'ieu am° so qu'°enquar vist no m'ha,
car d'autra mon cors° joy non a

10 *mais d'aisela° qu'ieu anc non° vi°,*
ni no.m dis° ver° ni no.m menti°,
ni no sai° si ja so fara°.

should be amazed
I love; that which
my body (my heart; my self;
  i.e., I)
the one; never; I saw
she told; truth; she lied
nor do I know; she will ever do
  [so]

---

(7) *meravílh.* Pres. subj. 3 sg. of *meravilhar (de),* expressing a wish.
(8) 'If I love that which (someone who) has not seen me yet.'
(8) *am.* Pres. indic. 1 sg. of *amar.*
(8) *so qu'.* That is, *so que; so* is a neuter pron.
(9) *mon cors.* Subject of *a.* *Mon* is obl.; cf. nom. *mos* in *mos cors* (v. 22). The noun *cors* 'body,' 'self' is invariable, whereas *cor* 'heart' has forms nom. sg. *cors,* obl. *cor.* Either word may be intended here.
(10) *vi.* Pret. 1 sg. of *véire.*
(10) *aisela.* Fem. form of *aicel* 'the one.' Cf. no. 23, v. 42 note to *aicella.*
(11) *dis.* Pret. 3 sg. of *dire.*
(11) *mentí.* Pret. 3 sg. of *mentir.*
(12) *sai.* Pres. indic. 1 sg. of *saber.*
(12) *fará.* Fut. 3 sg. of *faire,* vicarious, representing repetition of *dis* or *mentí* from v. 11.

III

Colp° de joy me fer° que m'ausi°,
e ponha° d'amor que.m sostra°

a blow; strikes me; kills me
a pain; reduces

15 *la carn°, don° mon cors magri[r]a°,*   my flesh; from which; I'll grow thin
     ez anc mais tan greu° no.m fezi°,   disagreeable [thing]; she did
     ni per nulh colp tant non lagui°,   I languished
     ni no.s cove° ni no s'e[s]cha°.   is deserved; is right

---

(13) *Colp.* Masc. obl. sg. 'She [unseen] strikes me a blow of joy,' unless obl. *Colp* is the subject: 'A blow of joy strikes me.'
(13) *fer.* Pres. indic. 3 sg. of *ferir.*
(13) *ausí.* Pres. indic. 3 sg. of *aucire.*
(14) *sostrá.* Pres. indic. 3 sg. of *sostraire.*
(15) *mon cors. Mon* is obl. for subject, as in v. 9.
(15) *magri[r]á.* Fut. 3 sg. of *magrir.* Weight loss was considered a symptom of love sickness.
(16) *fezí.* Pret. 3 sg. of *faire.*
(16) *laguí.* Pret. 1 sg. of *languir.*
(18) *cové.* Pres. indic. 3 sg. of *convenir* (reflexive).
(18) *e[s]chá.* Pres. indic. 3 sg. of *escazer* (reflexive).

IV

     Anc tan suau° no m'adormi°   so softly; I fell asleep
20 *que mos esperitz° no fos° lay°,*   that my spirit; was not; there
     ni tan d'ira° non ac° de sa°   grief; [my spirit] had; here
     mos cors c'ab gaug° no si aisi°;   joy; take its ease
     mais cant mi ressit° lo mati°,   I wake up; in the morning
     tot mon bosaber° si desva°.   pleasure; goes away

---

(19) *adormí.* Pret. 1 sg. of *adormir* (reflexive).
(20) *fos.* Past subj. 3 sg. of *éser.*
(20) *lay.* His spirit was where she was; that is, he thought of her.
(21–22) 'Nor did my body (my heart; i.e., I) have so much grief here [that] it does not take its ease with joy.' The noun *cors*, nom. sg., means either 'body,' from Lat. *corpus*, which produced invariable -s in Oc.; or 'heart,' from Lat. neuter *cor*, which became masc. and took Oc. -s by analogy with other masc. words. The phrase *mos cors* 'my body,' 'my heart' is used as a paraphrase for 'I.'
(21) *ac.* Pret. 3 sg. of *aver.*
(22) *aisí.* Pres. Subj. 3 sg. of *aizinar* (reflexive).
(23) *ressít.* Pres. Indic. 1 sg. of *reisidar* (reflexive).
(24) *tot mon bosabér.* Obl. sg. as subject of *si desva.*
(24) *desvá.* Pres. indic. 3 sg. of *dezanar* (reflexive).

V

25 *Bos° es lo vers, can° no.i falhi°,*   good; since; I did not err
     e tot so que.i es ben esta°,   fits
     e sel que de mi l'apenra°   will learn
     gart° se no.i falha° ni.l pessi°,   should take care; err; break it
     q'aisi° l'auzo° en Lemozi   so that thus; they may hear it
30 *en Bertrans e.l coms° e.l Tolza.*   count

(25) *Bos.* Masc. nom. sg. of *bon.*

(25) *falhí.* Pret. 1 sg. of *falhir.*

(26) 'And all that is in it fits well.'

(26) *está.* Pres. indic. of *estar.*

(27) *apenrá.* Fut. 3 sg. of *aprendre.*

(28) *gart se.* Pres. subj. 3 sg. of *gardar*, expressing imperative. Chaucer, too, urged his scribe to copy his work faithfully in his poem "Chaucer's Wordes unto Adam, His Owne Scriveyn" (Benson 650). Cf. vv. 31–32 note.

(28) *fálha.* Pres. subj. 3 sg. of *falhir*, expressing wish or command.

(28) *pessí.* Pres. subj. 3 sg. of *pesiar.*

(29–30) 'Sir Bertran in the *Lemozí*' (around Limoges) 'and the count in the *Tolzá*' (around Toulouse). Perhaps Jaufre refers to Alphonse Jourdain, count of Toulouse, and his illegitimate son Bertran (Pickens, *Songs* 277).

(29) *áuzo.* Pres. subj. 3 pl. of *auzir.*

(30) *coms.* Nom. sg. of *cómte.*

VI

Bons er° lo vers, e faran y°	will be; they will make for it
32 *calsque motz° que hom chantara°!*	some words; people will sing

(31) *er.* Fut. 3 sg. of *éser.*

(31) *farán.* Fut. 3 pl. of *faire.*

(31–32) On the mobility of troubadour texts (Fr. *mouvance*), see Pickens ("Jaufré Rudel"). Cf. v. 28 note on *gart se.*

(32) *cálsque.* Masc. obl. pl. of *calque.*

(32) *chantará.* Fut. 3 sg. of *chantar.*

Form

Five *coblas unissonans* of six lines and one *tornada* of two. Variant rhymes in stanzas I and IV.

SCHEME

a b b a a b

RHYMES

I	*itz*	*ay*	*ay*	*i*	*i*	*a*
II	*i*	*a*	*a*	*i*	*i*	*a*
III	*i*	*a*	*a*	*i*	*i*	*a*
IV	*i*	*ay*	*a*	*i*	*i*	*a*
V	*i*	*a*	*a*	*i*	*i*	*a*
VI					*i*	*a*

METER

8 8 8 8 8 8

Corrected Readings

(11) *ni no.m dis.* R: *ni* above the line in a later hand.
(12) *ni no.* R: *ni o no* (*o* expunctuated).
(13) *m'ausi.* R: *ausira.*
(15) *magri[r]a.* R: *magrisa.*
(18) *cove.* Pickens read *mue* (see edition in *Songs*), but cf. *co-* in *cors* (v. 15).
(18) *s'e[s]cha.* R: *secha.*
(20) *esperitz no.* R: *esperitz cors no* (*esperitz* in margin, *cors* expunctuated).
(22) *cors c'ab.* R: *cors esperit no fos la cab* (*esperit no fos la* expunctuated).
(26) *esta.* R: *estan.*

Jaufre Rudel

Can lo rossinhol e.l fulhos

Thirteen manuscripts: *A, B, C, D, E, I, K, M, N², R, Sg, a¹, e. BEdT* 262.6. *R* gives
the melody over stanza I.

Major editions: Pickens (*Songs* 84–86; version 3-a); Wolf and Rosenstein (142–
44); Chiarini (111–13). Music: van der Werf (see Wolf and Rosenstein, plates
13–14); van der Werf and Bond (222*).

This edition is based on *R*, the only manuscript with music. *R* was written
in the fourteenth century in Languedoc (see "Manuscripts"). It diverges from
normal declension in verses 1 and 7 (see notes).

R, fol. 63v, col. 1.

Jaufre Rudelh

I

Can lo rossinhol° e.l fulhos°	nightingale; in the leafy [wood]
dona° d'amor e.n quier° e.n pren°	gives; seeks; takes
e mou° son chan jauzen°, joyos°,	starts; joyful; rejoicing
e remira° sa par° soven°,	looks at; mate; often
5 *e.l rieu° son cl[a]r°, e.l prat° son gen°*	streams; clear; meadows; pretty
pe.l° novel deport° que renha°,	because of the; new delight; reigns
mi ven° al cor° grant joy° cazer°.	comes; into my heart; great joy; fall

---

(1) *rossinhól.* Obl. sg., although *rossinhol* is the subject of *dona.*

(2) *dona.* Pres. indic. 3 sg. of *donar.*

(2) *d'amor.* Partitive *de* (*Old Occitan* 388) may be omitted in translation. Literally 'Gives of
 love and seeks of it and takes of it.'

(2) *quiér.* Pres. indic. 3 sg. of *querre.*

(2) *pren.* Pres. indic. 3 sg. of *prendre.*

(3) *móu*. Pres. indic. 3 sg. of *mover*.

(3) *jauzén*. Pres. part. masc. obl. sg. of *jauzir*; modifies *chan*.

(3) *joyós*. Masc. obl. sg. modifying *rossinhol* or *chan*. Invariable; *-s* is part of the root.

(4) *remíra*. Pres. indic. 3 sg. of *remirar*.

(5) *ríeu ... cl[a]r*. Masc. nom. pl.

(5) *prat ... gen*. Masc. nom. pl.

(6) *rénha*. Pres. indic. 3 sg. of *renhar*.

(7) *ven*. Pres. indic. 3 sg. of *venir*.

(7) *grant joy*. Obl. sg., although the phrase is the subject of *ven*. 'Great joy comes to fall into my heart.'

II

D'un'amistat° soi° enveios°	for a friendship; I am; avid
car no sai° joia° tan valen°,	I don't know; a joy; so precious
10 *c'or° e dezir° que bona.m fos°*	I pray; I desire; she would be
si°.n fazia° d'amar parven°,	if; she made; appearance
que.l cors° a gran°, delgat°, e gen,	body (person); tall; slender
e sen° ren° que.l descovenha°:	without; anything; doesn't suit her
es s'amor° bon'° ab° bosaber°.	her love; good; with; pleasure

(8) *soi*. Pres. indic. 1 sg. of *éser*.

(9) *sai*. Pres. indic. 1 sg. of *saber*.

(10) *or*. Pres. indic. 1 sg. of *orar*.

(10) *dezir*. Pres. indic. 1 sg. of *dezirar*.

(10) *fos*. Past subj. 3 sg. of *éser*.

(11) *fazía*. Imperfect 3 sg. of *faire*.

(13) *descovenha*. Pres. subj. 3 sg. of *desconvenir*.

(14) *amor*. Fem. nom. sg.

(14) *bon'*. That is, *bona*. fem. nom. sg. of *bon*.

III

15 *D'est'amor° soi fort° cossiros°*	about this love; very; worried
velhan°, e pueys° son° ja° dormen°,	waking; then; I am; already; sleeping
car lay° ay° joy meravilhos°	there [in sleep]; I have; marvelous
per qu'°ieu la° jau° ab joy jauzen;	because; it (*amor*, v. 15); enjoy
mas sa beutatz° no°.m val° nïen,	beauty; no ... nïen, not at all; helps me
20 *c'amicx° mielhs° no sec° la senha°*	no lover; better; follows; track
de mi° ab° m[en]s° de bel plazer°.	than I; with; less; delightful pleasure

(16) *velhán*. Pres. part. of *velhar*.

(16) *son*. Pres. indic. 1 sg. of *éser*; alternative to *soi* (v. 15).

(16) *dormén*. Pres. part. of *dormir*.

(17) *ay*. Pres. indic. 1 sg. of *aver*.

(18) *la jau*. 'I enjoy it' ('this love,' v. 15) or 'I enjoy her.'

(18) *jáu*. Pres. indic. 1 sg. of *jauzir*.
(19) *beutatz*. Nom. sg. of *beutat*, fem.
(19) *val*. Pres. indic. 3 sg. of *valer*.
(20) *amicx*. Nom. sg. of *amic*.
(20) *sec*. Pres. indic. 3 sg. of *segre*. He follows the track of love, like a hunter.

IV

D'aquest'amor soi tant cochos°	eager
que cant yeu vau° vas luy° corren°	I go; toward her; running
vejaire m'es° qu'[a] ra[ü]zos°	it seems to me; backwards
25 *m'en torn°, e qu'ela m'an° fugen°,*	I turn; goes away; fleeing me
e sos chivaus° cor° aitan len°	her horse; runs; so slowly (far)
que greu er mays qui l'atenha°	catch
s'amors no la.m fay remaner°.	stop

(23) *vau*. Pres. indic. 1 sg. of *anar*.
(23) *luy*. Fem. (as here) or masc.
(25) *torn*. Pres. indic. 1 sg. of *tornar* (reflexive).
(25) *an*. Pres. subj. 3 sg. of *anar*.
(25) *fugén*. Pres. part. of *fugir*.
(26) *sos chiváus*. Masc. nom. sg.
(26) *cor*. Pres. indic. 3 sg. of *corre*.
(26) *len*. May mean 'slowly' or 'far' (*len* can be a form of *lonh*). "In this dream world, 'slowly' is not to be excluded" (Pickens, *Songs* 85).
(27–28) 'That it will be hard for anyone to catch her if love doesn't make her stop for me.'
(27) *aténha*. Pres. subj. 3 sg. of *aténher*.

V

Amors, alegre°.m part° de vos	happy; I part ways with
30 *per tal car° vau mo mielhs° queren°,*	because; my better; seeking
e soi de tan aventuros°	so fortunate
qu'en breu° n'auray° mon cor jauzen	soon; I will have
la merce de° mon bel guiren°,	thanks to; my fair protector
que.m vol e.m dezir e.m denha°	finds me worthy
35 *e m'a tornat° en bon esper°.*	brought back; to good hope

(29) *part*. Pres. indic. 1 sg. of *partir* (reflexive).
(29–30) Unexpectedly, the lover says he is leaving one lady for another. The song is a *chanson de change* (Fr.), a 'song of change (or exchange)': he has exchanged his earlier loves for this one.
(30) *querén*. Pres. part. of *querre*.
(32) *auráy*. Fut. 1 sg. of *aver*.
(33) *mon bel guirén*. May be taken simply or as a *senhal*, a secret name: *mon Bel Guiren*.
(34) *dénha*. Pres. indic. 3 sg. of *denhar*.
(35) *tornát*. Past part. of *tornar* (transitive).

Form

Five *coblas unissonans* of seven lines.

SCHEME

a   b   a   b   b   c   d

RHYMES

os   en   os   en   en   énha   er

METER

8   8   8   8   8   7'   8

Corrected Readings

(5) *cl[a]r. R: clier* (cf. OFr. *cler*).

(11) *si.n. R: si en* (+1).

(19) *sa. R: sas* (makes *beutatz* nom. pl. with sg. *val*).

(21) *ab m[en]s de. R: ab mays de.*

(22) *tant cochos. R: tant cossiros cochos* (*cossiros* expunctuated).

(24) *qu'[a] ra[ü]zos. R: que raizos.* "To my knowledge, *raïzos*, which I connect with *raïz*, 'root' [*razitz* PD], is not attested elsewhere" (Pickens, *Songs* 85). Not in *DOM*.

Uc Catola and Marcabru
Amics Marchabrun, car digam

Two manuscripts: *D* (attributed to Ugo Catola), *z* (attributed to Marcabru). *BEdT* 451.1 (under Uc) and 293.6 (under Marcabru). Major editions: Roncaglia; Gaunt et al. (98–106).

This *tensó*, or dialogue, is initiated by Uc Catola, whom Roncaglia (208) identified as a friend of the abbot of Cluny, Peter the Venerable, a learned knight who made a pilgrimage to Jerusalem (not necessarily an armed pilgrimage, or Crusade). Gaunt and his colleagues agree only that the poet "may be" Peter's friend (99). Uc invites the troubadour Marcabru to talk about love, which Uc sees in a positive light, Marcabru in a critical one (as he does in other poems). Gaunt and his colleagues find no persuasive evidence for the date except the period of Marcabru's poetic activity, circa 1130 to 1154.

D, fol. 208r, cols. 1–2.

Ugo Catola

I (Uc)

Amics Marchabrun, car° digam°	please (with subj.); let's say
un vers d'amor, que° per cor° am°,	for; sincerely; I love
q'° a l'hora° qe nos partiram°	so that; when; we will part
4 *en sia° loing° lo chanz° auziz°.*	will be; far away; our song; heard

(1) *digám.* Pres. subj. 1 pl. of *dire*, expressing a wish.

(2) *am.* Pres. indic. 1 sg. of *amar*.

(3) *q'.* That is, *que*.

(3) *partirám.* Fut. 1 pl. of *partir*, usually *partirém*. The fut. ending *-ám* is normal in Gascon (Rohlfs 219), and the *vida* says Marcabru was born in Gascony (no. 9). Nevertheless, this word is not a distinctive Gasconism since it also occurs in Oc. of Rouergue (Brunel, *Plus*

anciennes chartes 2: xxix) and other regions, as well as in Italian and Spanish (Grafström 104–05).

(4) *sía*. Pres. subj. 3 sg. of *éser*.

(4) *lo chanz*. Nom. sg. of masc. *chan*. The definite article *lo* can express possession.

(4) *auziz*. Past part. of *auzir*, masc. nom. sg.

II (Marcabru)

Ugo Catola, er° fazam°,	now; let's do [it]
mas de faus'amistat° me clam,°	false friendship (love); I complain
q'anc° pos° la serps° baissa lo ram	anc . . . no, never; since; serpent
8 *no foron° tant enganairiz°.*	have there been; deceiving women

(5) *fazám*. Pres. subj. 1 pl. of *faire*, expressing a wish.

(6) *faus'*. That is, *fausa*. Fem. obl. sg.

(6) *amistát*. The relationship with an *amic* 'friend' or 'lover.'

(6) *clam*. Pres. indic. 1 sg. of *clamar* (reflexive).

(7) 'Never, since the serpent lowered the branch.' "The serpent presumably lowered the branch so that Eve might pluck an apple" (Gaunt et al. 104).

(7) *serps*. Nom. sg. of fem. *serp*. The serpent in Eden, *serpen* (see no. 3, v. 9).

(7) *baissa*. The sense is preterit, but the form (if stressed *báissa*) is present. The "vicarious present" represents the preterit in narratives in medieval Occitan, French, and Spanish (*Old Occitan* 245 and 249–51). Another interpretation would stress the word *baissá*, like the simple past in Fr.

(8) *fóron*. Pret. 3 pl. of *éser*.

(8) *enganairíz*. Fem. nom. pl.

III (Uc)

Marcabrun, ço no m'es pas bon°	it doesn't please me
qe d'amar digaz° si ben non°;	you say; anything but good
per zo°.us en move° la tenzon°	per zo . . . qe, because; I propose; debate
12 *qe d'amor° fui° naz° e noiriz°.*	with love; I was; born; raised

(10) *digáz*. Pres. subj. 2 pl. of *dire*; subj. because subordinate to *no m'es pas bon*. Uc addresses Marcabru with respect (2 pl.).

(11) *.us*. Nonsyllabic form of *vos*.

(11) *móve*. Pres. indic. 1 sg. of *mover*; unusual to have *-e* for 1 sg.

(11) *tenzón*. Later became the name of the genre of debate poems.

(12) *fúi*. Pret. 1 sg. of *éser*.

(12) *naz*. Past part. of *náiser*.

(12) *noiríz*. Past part of *noirir*.

IV (Marcabru)

Catola, non entenz° razon;	you don't understand
non saps° d'amors° cum trais°	don't you know; love; how it betrayed
Samson?	
Vos cuidaz° e.ill autre bricon°	you think; the other fools
16 *qe tot° sia ver° quant vos diz°.*	tot . . . quant, whatever; is true; you say

(13) *entenz.* Pres. indic. 2 sg. of *entendre.* Marcabru addresses Uc familiarly (2 sg.); *vos cuidaz* (v. 15) and *vos diz* (v. 16) are plural for Uc and the other fools. Later he will speak more respectfully (see vv. 29–31 note).

(14) *saps.* Pres. indic. 2 sg. of *saber.*

(14) *amors.* Obl. sg. of *amor,* invariable (as here) when it means 'the force of love' personified (*Old Occitan* 360).

(14) *tráis.* Pret. 3 sg. of *traïr.* Counts as one syllable; *traïs* (two syllables) also occurs (Anglade 350–51).

(14) Samson loved Delilah, who betrayed him (Judg. 16.4–31).

(15) *cuidáz.* Pres. indic. 2 pl. of *cuidar.*

(16) *e.ill autre bricon.* Masc. nom. pl.

(16) *diz.* Pres. indic. 2 pl. of *dire.*

V (Uc)

Marcabrun, nos troba[m]° auctor°	we find; a witness
de Sanso.l fort e de s'uxor°	his wife
q'ela n'avi'estat° s'amor	had been
20 *a l'or[a] qu'e[l en] fo deliz°.*	destroyed

(17) *trobá[m].* Pres. indic. 1 pl. of *trobar.*

(17) *auctór.* Obl. sg. The biblical book of Judges.

(18) *uxor* (nom. *úxor* in Lat.), here adapted as obl. *uxór. Samson amavit mulierem,* loved a woman (Judg. 16.4). Lat. accusative *muliérem* gives Oc. obl. *molhér,* woman or wife. Uc adds that Delilah had been Samson's *amor* (v. 19). He says Samson and Delilah were married lovers.

(19–20) 'She had been his love when he was destroyed by her' (*en*).

(19) *aví'.* That is, *avia,* imperfect 3 sg. of *aver.*

(19) *estát.* Past part. of *estar* 'to be' (in a situation).

(20) *fo.* Pret. 3 sg. of *éser.*

(20) *delíz.* Past part. of *delir.*

VI (Marcabru)

Catola, qar a sordeior°	to a worse [man]
la det° e la tolc° al meillor,	she gave it (her love); she took it
lo dia° perdet° sa valor°	on that day; she lost; her worth
24 *qe.l seus fo per l'estraing traïz.*	

(21–22) 'Because Delilah gave her love' (*la,* v. 22 = *amor,* fem., v. 19) 'to a worse man and took it from the better one.' Delilah betrayed Samson at the urging of the Philistines (Judg. 16.5). Medieval Lat. *Philistinus* could mean 'secular person'; hence *sordeior* than Samson, who was dedicated to God from birth (Judg. 16.17).

(22) *det.* Pret. 3 sg. of *dar.*

(22) *tolc.* Pret. 3 sg. of *tolre; -c* for pret.

(23) *perdét.* Pret. 3 sg. of *perdre.*

(24) 'When her [man] was betrayed for the foreigner.'

(24) *séus.* Masc. nom. sg.

(24) *traïz.* Past part. masc. nom. sg. of *traïr.*

VII (Uc)

Marcabrun, si cum declinaz°	as you claim
qu'amors si' ab° engan° mesclaz°,	with; deceit; mixed
dunc° es lo almosna° pechaz°,	then; alms; sin
28 *la cima° devers° la raïz°.*	top; toward; root

(25–26) 'If [it is true], as you claim, that love is mixed with deceit.'

(25) *declinaz.* Pres. indic. 2 pl. of *declinar.*

(26) *si'.* That is, *sia,* pres. subj. 3 sg. of *éser.*

(26) *mesclaz.* Past part. masc. nom. sg. of *mesclar,* treating *amors* as masc., like Lat. *amor,* although Oc. *amor* is fem. elsewhere. Masc. *amors* is another Latinism, like *uxor* (see v. 18 note). The nom. *-s* is Oc., not Lat.

VIII (Marcabru)

Catola, l'amors dont parlaz°	of which you speak
camja° cubertament° los daz°;	loads; secretly; dice
aprop° lo bon lanz°, vos gardaz!°—	after; the good throw; look out!
32 *ço dis° Salomons e Daviz.*	said

(29–31) Now Marcabru uses the polite pl. in *parlaz* (v. 29) and in *vos gardaz* (v. 31); see also *seaz* (v. 48).

(29) *parlaz.* Pres. indic. 2 pl. of *parlar.*

(30) *camja.* Pres. indic. 3 sg. of *camjar,* 'to change,' here 'to load' (dice).

(30) *daz.* Obl. pl. of masc. *dat.*

(31) *lanz.* Obl. sg. The *-z* is part of the root; cf. *lansar* 'to throw.'

(31) *gardaz.* Imperative 2 pl. of *gardar* (reflexive).

(32) *dis.* Pret. 3 sg. of *dire.*

(32) Solomon was considered the author of biblical books including Proverbs, Ecclesiastes, the Song of Songs, and the Wisdom of Solomon. David is the author of the book of Psalms. Marcabru enlists Solomon and David as authorities against love.

IX (Uc)

Marcabrun, amistaz dechai°	declines
car a trobat° joven° sav[ai]°!	it has found; youth; wicked
Eu [n]'ai al cor ir'° ez esclai°,	dismay; distress
36 *qar l'en alevaz tan laiz criz*	

(33) *dechái.* Pres. indic. 3 sg. of *decazer.*

(34) *trobát.* Past part. of *trobar.*

(35) *ir'.* That is, *ira* 'anger and grief.'

(36) 'Because you raise such ugly cries to it.' Here *l'* = *li,* referring to *amistaz* (v. 33).

(36) *aleváz.* Pres. indic. 2 pl. of *alevar.*

(36) *laiz.* Masc. obl. pl. of *lait.*

(36) *criz.* Obl. pl. of masc. *crit.*

X (Marcabru)

Catol', Ovides mostra° chai°	shows; here (i.e., in this world)
e l'ambladura° o retrai°	experience; repeats it
que non soana° brun ni bai°,	[love] refuses; brown nor bay (i.e., any horse)
40 *anz se trai° plus aus achaïz°.*	but is more attracted to; the decadent ones

(37) *Ovides.* In the *Art of Love,* Ovid wrote, "Inde fit, ut quae se timuit committere honesto / vilis in amplexus inferioris est" 'So it happens that she who hesitated to commit herself to an honest man is in the embraces of a vile inferior' (1.769–70; my trans.). Ovid urges his mistress to be bold enough to accept him. For Marcabru, love refuses no man; love is a prostitute.

(37) *mostra.* Pres. indic. 3 sg. of *mostrar.*

(38) *retrai.* Pres. indic. 3 sg. of *retraire.*

(39) *soána.* Pres. indic. 3 sg. of *soanar.*

(40) *trai.* Pres. indic. 3 sg. of *traire* (reflexive).

(40) *achaïz.* Masc. obl. pl. of *acaït* 'fallen.'

XI (Uc)

Marchabrun, anc non° cuit° t'ames°	never; I think; loved you
l'amors ves cui° es tant engres°,	toward which; angry
ni no fo anc res° meinz° prezes°	anything; less; [love] esteemed
44 *d'aitals° joglars° esbaluïz.°*	than such; joglars; scatterbrained

(41–44) Uc addresses Marcabru familiarly: *te* (v. 41), *es* (v. 42), both 2 sg. He scorns him (v. 43) and insults him (v. 44). Earlier he had spoken to him as a friend (*Amics*, v. 1) and used respectful second person plural forms: *digaz* (v. 10), *.us* (v. 11), *declinaz* (v. 25), *alevaz* (v. 36). Uc expresses outrage at Marcabru's vehemence in stanza X. Stanza XI is the emotional high point of the exchange.

(41) 'I think love never loved you.'

(41) *cuit.* Pres. indic. 1 sg. of *cuidar.*

(41) *amés.* Past subj. 3 sg. of *amar.*

(43) 'There never was anything that it (love; I) respected less.'

(43) *prezés.* Past subj. 3 sg. or 1 sg. of *prezar.*

(44) *aitals joglars esbaluïz.* Masc. obl. pl.

XII (Marcabru)

Catol', anc de ren° non fo pres°	a creature; taken
un pas° que tost° no s'en loignes°,	step; soon; [love] took her distance
et enqer° s'en loingna° ades°	still; takes its distance; always
48 *e fera° tro° seaz° feniz°.*	will do; until; you are; finished

(45–48) 'Never has any creature taken a step but that soon it (love) took her distance, and still it always takes its distance and will do so until you are dead.' In the previous stanza Uc said love never loved Marcabru (vv. 41–42); here Marcabru responds that love never will love Uc.

(45) *pres.* Past part. of *prendre.*

(46) *loignés.* Past subj. 3 sg. of *lonhar.*

(47) *lóingna.* Pres. indic. 3 sg. of *lonhar.*

(48) *ferá.* Fut. 3 sg. of *faire,* vicarious.

(48) *seáz.* Pres. subj. 2 pl. of *éser.* Another "possible Gasconism" (Gaunt et al. 104) in comparison to usual *siátz;* but related *séa,* 3 sg., occurs in the Comtessa de Dia (no. 15, v. 6).

(48) *feníz.* Past part. masc. nom. sg. of *fenir.*

XIII (Uc)

Mar[ca]brun, quant sui las° e.m duoill°   when I am weary; I suffer
e ma bon'amia m'acuoill°   welcomes
ab° un baissar° quant me despuoill°,   with; a kiss; when I undress
52 *me.n vau sans e saus° e gariz°.*   I go away hale and hearty;
                     healed

(49) *duóill.* Pres. indic. 1 sg. of *dolér.*

(50) *acuóill.* Pres. indic. 3 sg. of *acolhir.*

(51) *despuóill.* Pres. indic. 1 sg. of *despolhar.*

(52) *vau.* Pres. indic. 1 sg. of *anar* (reflexive).

(52) *sans e saus.* Masc. nom. sg.

(52) *gariz.* Past part. masc. nom. sg. of *garir.*

XIV (Marcabru)

Catola, per amor deu truoill°   winepress
tressaill° l'avers al fol° lo suoill,°   leaps over; the fool's wealth; threshold
e puois mostra la vi'° a l'uoill°   road; clearly
56 *aprop° los autres escharniz°.*   after; the other scorned [ones]

(53–54) 'For love of the winepress, the fool's wealth leaps over the threshold' (escapes him). He drinks too much.

(53) *deu.* Equivalent to *de lo.*

(54) *tressáill.* Pres. indic. 3 sg. of *trasalhir.*

(54) *avers.* Masc. nom. sg.

(55–56) 'And then he (the fool) shows the way clearly, following the others who have been mocked.' Failed lovers drink.

(55) *vi'.* That is, *via.*

(55) *uóill.* Obl. sg. of *olh.*

(56) *escharníz.* Past part. masc. obl. pl. of *escarnir.*

Form

Fourteen *coblas doblas* of four lines. The **b**-rhyme is constant.

SCHEME

	a	a	a	b

RHYMES

	a	a	a	b
I–II	*am*	*am*	*am*	*iz*
III–IV	*on*	*on*	*on*	*iz*
V–VI	*or*	*or*	*or*	*iz*
VII–VIII	*az*	*az*	*az*	*iz*
IX–X	*ai*	*ai*	*ai*	*iz*
XI–XII	*es*	*es*	*es*	*iz*
XIII–XIV	*uóill*	*uóill*	*uóill*	*iz*

METER

	8	8	8	8

Corrected Readings

(17) *troba[m]*. D: *troban*.

(18) *s'uxor*. D: *sa uxor* (+1).

(19) *avi'estat*. D: *avia estat* (+1).

(20) *a l'or[a] qu'e[l en] fo deliz*. D: *alor que ce fo deliz*, as emended by Gaunt et al.

(34) *sav[ai]*. D: *savia*.

(35) *[n]'ai*. D: *vai*.

(35) *ir' ez*. D: *ira ez* (+1).

(37) *Catol', Ovides*. D: *Catola Ovides* (+1).

(44) *joglars*. So D (major editors read *ioglair*).

(45) *Catol', anc*. D: *Catola anc* (+1).

(49) *Mar[ca]brun*. D: *Marbrun*.

(49) *sui las*. D: *sui en las* (*en* expunctuated).

(50) *bon'amia*. D: *bona amia* (+1).

(55) *vi' a*. D: *via a* (+1).

Marcabru
Cortesamen vuoill comensar

Eight manuscripts: *A, C, G, K, N, R, a¹, d. BEdT* 293.15.
Major editions: Roncaglia; Gaunt et al. (200–07). *Vida* in *BT* (10–11); Gaunt
et al. (38).

Attributions of this poem are divided. Two manuscripts name Marcabru in
the rubrics (*R, d*), two place the poem immediately after his *vida* (*A, K*), two
credit the poem to minor troubadours (*C, a¹*), and two provide no attribution
(*G, N*). For Gaunt and his colleagues, "[t]here can be no serious doubt that this
song is the work of Marcabru, although the reasons for the misattributions are
obscure" (200).

The poem begins on a relatively idealistic tone, in contrast to Marcabru's
acerbity in the *tenso* with Uc Catola (no. 8). Here the poet purifies his song (v. 5),
and the high-mindedness seems to prompt clarity of vocabulary and expres-
sion. In stanzas V and VI, however, he reverts to his customary misogyny and
cynicism.

K, fols. 102r, col. 2–102v, col. 1. The section of poems by Marcabru begins with
his *vida*, written in red ink (it is a rubric). The following edition of the *vida* is
abbreviated by omitting a quotation from another poem. It is lineated according
to the metrical points (periods) in *K*. In the poems such points indicate the ends
of verse lines.

Marcabruns si fo de Gascoingna,°	Gascony
fils° d'una paubra° femna°....	son; poor; woman
Trobaire° fo dels premiers c'om° se recort.°	troubadour; one; remembers
De caitivetz° vers	wretched (nasty)
e de caitivetz serventes°	satires
fez° e dis° mal de las femnas° e d'amor.	he made; he spoke evil; women

Gascoingna. Gascony is a region from Bordeaux to the Pyrenees.

fils. Nom. sg. of *filh.*

Trobáire. Nom. sg. of *trobadór.* Shifting declension. 'He was a troubadour among the first that people remember.'

recort. Pres. subj. 3 sg. of *recordar*; subj. after *premier* (*Old Occitan* 261).

caitivétz. Masc. obl. pl. of *caitivet*; 'of poor quality' or 'of foul humor.'

vers. The term that early troubadours including Marcabru applied to their songs, without distinguishing genres.

serventés. The word was not used by Marcabru.

fez. Pret. 3 sg. of *faire.*

dis. Pret. 3 sg. of *dire.*

I

Cortesamen° vuoill° comensar°	courteously; I want; to begin
un vers, si es qi l'escoutar°;	will hear it
e pos° tant me.n sui entremes°,	since; I have taken so much trouble
veirai° si.l poirai° afinar°,	I will see; if I will be able; to refine it
5 *q'era° voill mon chan esmerar°;*	now; to purify
e dirai° vos de mantas° res°.	I will tell you; about many; things

(1) *Cortesamen.* As can be seen in the digital copy of the manuscript online, in *K* the poem begins with a historiated initial *C* of *Cortesamen* (see URL in MS list). The letter, in blue, is contained within a red frame and backed in gold. Inside the letter stands the troubadour, crowned in a garland or coronal such as people wore for festivals (Lightbown 122). He wears a bright orange cloak and crosses his arms, perhaps pensively.

(1) *vuóill.* Pres. indic. 1 sg. of *voler*, with diphthongization of short *ó* (> *uó*) and yod for 1 sg.

(2) 'If there is anyone who will hear it.'

(2) *escoutar.* Fut. subj. 3 sg. of *escoutar.* Subj. because of the indefinite antecedent (*si es qi*). On the future subjunctive, see *Old Occitan* (63–64).

(3) *entremés.* Past part. of *entremetre* (reflexive).

(4) *veirái.* Fut. 1 sg. of *véire.*

(4) *poirái.* Fut. 1 sg. of *poder.*

(6) *dirái:* Fut. 1 sg. of *dire.*

(6) *mantas.* Fem. obl. pl. of *mant.*

(6) *res.* Obl. pl. of fem. *ren.*

II

Assaz° pot hom vilaneiar°	a lot; act like a buffoon
qi cortesia vol blasmar,°	to criticize
qe.[l] plus savis° e.l meils° apres°	wisest; most; learned
10 *non sap° tantas° dire ni far*	know how; so many [things]
c'om non li puesca° enseignar°	could; teach
petit o pro, tals hora es.	

(9) *sávis.* Masc. nom. sg. of *sávi.*

(9) *aprés.* Past part. of *aprendre.*

(10) *sap.* Pres. indic. 3 sg. of *saber.*

(10) *tantas.* That is, *res* (v. 6).

(11) *puésca.* Pres. subj. 3 sg. of *poder*; subj. after *tantas* (v. 10).

(12) 'A little or a lot, depending on the moment.' It is foolish to criticize courtesy since there is so much to learn about it.

III

De cortesia.is pot vanar°	boast
qui ben sap mesura° esgardar,°	moderation; to observe
15 *e qui tot° vol auzir° cant es°*	*tot … cant,* all that; hear; there is
ni tot qant ve° cuid'° amassar°,	sees; intends; amass
lo tot l'es ops° a mesurar,°	he must; use with moderation
o ja no° sera trop cortes.°	never; very courteous

(13) *.is.* Equivalent to *.s,* reflexive pron.

(15) 'And if someone wants to hear all that there is' (to be taught, v. 11) 'and intends to amass all that he sees, he must use everything with moderation.'

(16) *ve.* Pres. indic. 3 sg. of *véire.*

(16) *cúid'.* That is, *cúida,* pres. indic. 3 sg. of *cuidar.*

(17) *ops.* 'Necessary'; *l'es ops,* 'it is necessary to him (her),' 'he (she) must.'

(18) *será.* Fut. 3 sg. of *éser.*

IV

Mesura es en gent parlar°	in noble speech
20 *e cortesia es d'amar°;*	in loving
et qui° no vol esser mespres,°	if someone; reproached
de tota vilania°.is gar°	rudeness; he must keep from
d'escarnir° e de foleiar°,	of being scornful; acting like a fool
puois° sera savis ab que.ill pes.	then

(21) *qui.* Without antecedent, as in v. 15.

(21) *mesprés.* Past part. of *mesprendre.*

(22) *gar.* Pres. subj. 3 sg. of *gardar.* Subj. expresses imperative.

(24) *ab que.ill pes.* 'Although it displeases him.' It is less congenial (for Marcabru) to be a sage than a critic.

(24) *pes.* Pres. subj. 3 sg. of *pezar.*

V

25 *C'aissi pot savis hom regnar°*	live
e bona dompna meillurar,°	better herself
mas cella q'en pren dos o tres	
e per un no si vol fiar°—	entrust
ben deu° sos prez° asordeiar°	must; her reputation; be sullied
30 *e sa valors° a chascu mes.*	her worth

(27–28) 'But one (a woman) who takes two or three and refuses to entrust herself to one (man),' i.e., a husband.

(28) *fiar.* Reflexive.

(29) *déu*. Pres. indic. 3 sg. of *dever*.
(29) *sos prez*. Masc. nom. sg.
(30) *sa valors*. Fem. nom. sg.
(30) *a chascu mes*. Literally, 'at each month,' i.e., 'with every month that passes' (Gaunt et al. 206).

VI

A[i]tals amors° fai° a prezar°	such love; deserves; to be esteemed
que si mezeissa° ten en car°,	itself (i.e., *amors*); shows respect for
e s'ieu en dic° nuill vilanes°	say; any rude remark
per lleis°, que m'o teingn'a amar;	for her (i.e., as she takes it)
35 be.ill lauzi° fassa°.m pro musar°,	I advise her; to make me; waste time
qu'eu n'aurai° so qe.m n'es promes°.	will get; promised

(31) *A[i]tals amors*. Fem. nom. sg.
(31–32) *A[i]tals ... que*. 'Such ... that.' *Faire a* + infinitive 'to deserve to.'
(32) *mezeissa*. Fem., referring to *amors* (v. 31).
(33) *dic*. Pres. indic. 1 sg. of *dire*.
(33) *núill vilanés*. Masc. obl. sg.
(34) 'May she take it as [an effect of my] love.'
(34) *téingn'*. That is, *teingna*, pres. subj. 3 sg. of *tener*.
(35) *láuzi*. Pres. indic. 1 sg. of *lauzar*, with unusual yod (*-i*) for 1 sg.
(35) *fassa*. Pres. subj. 3 sg. of *faire*.
(36) 'For I will get from her (n'_1) what is promised me by her (n'_2).' Perhaps they are betrothed; he tells her to punish his rudeness by delaying their marriage but insists that they will marry. Gaunt and his colleagues take the first *n'* as an abbreviated *non*: 'I shall not have....'
(36) *aurái*. Fut. 1 sg. of *aver*.
(36) *promés*. Past part. of *prometre*.

VII

Lo vers e.l son° voill enviar°	melody; send
a.n Jaufre Rudel oltra mar°;	across the sea
e voill que l'aion° li Frances	get
40 per lor coratges° alegrar°,	hearts; gladden
que° Dieus lor o pot perdonar°	for; pardon
o sia peccaz° o merces°.	sin; good deed

(37–38) Marcabru commissions a performer (a *joglar*) to sing the song for Jaufre Rudel.
(38–39) Evidence that the troubadour Jaufre Rudel went to the Holy Land, perhaps on the Second Crusade in 1148 (Gaunt et al. 201), with the French army led by Louis VII. See no. 6.
(39) *áion*. Pres. subj. 3 pl. of *aver*.
(42) If *o* (v. 41) refers to Crusade in general, v. 42 expresses uncertainty about its merit. In another poem by Marcabru, a girl curses Louis VII for taking her lover on Crusade (*BEdT* 293.1; Gaunt et al. 40–45). See also no. 22, v. 48 note. Gaunt and his colleagues take *o* (v. 41) as the crusaders' gladdening their hearts: "Whether listening to such a secular song is a sin for the crusaders for whom it is intended or not" (207).

Form

Seven *coblas unissonans* of six lines.

SCHEME

a　a　b　a　a　b

RHYMES

ar　ar　es　ar　ar　es

METER

8　8　8　8　8　8

Corrected Readings

(9) *qe.[l] plus. K: qe plus.*
(16) *cuid'. K: cuida* (+1).
(31) *A[i]tals. K: Aatals.*

Raimbaut d'Aurenga

Brails, cantz, qils, critz

Nine manuscripts: *A, D, Dc* (vv. 43–48), *E, I, K, M, N²*, *a*. BEdT 389.21.
Major editions: Pattison (93–96); Riquer, *Trovadores* (1: 439–41).

Raimbaut, lord of Aurenga, now Orange (Vaucluse), lived from about 1145 to 1173. His will, which survives, refers to two girls who may have been his daughters or nieces; it does not mention a wife (Pattison 218–19). He may have died in an epidemic of influenza (Pattison 25). He was mourned by the trobairitz Azalais de Porcairagues (no. 11). Several of his highly wrought songs concern married lovers.

M, fols. 140r, col. 2–140v, col. 2.

Raimbaud d'Orenja

The Gallicizing orthography of the attribution may reflect the Franco-Venetian literary language, which was used in the thirteenth and fourteenth centuries. *M* was executed in the fourteenth century, probably in Naples, from a Venetian exemplar (Camps 16).

I

Brails°, cantz°, qils°, critz°	harsh caws; songs; sharp calls; cries
aug° dels auzels° pels plaisaditz°,	I hear; birds; hedges
hoc°! Mas no los enten° ni deinh°,	yes; understand; approve
qar vius° m'esteinh°	ardent; kills me
5 le cors°, on dols° m'es pres asitz°,	my body (heart); grief; seated near
qar no.m sofer°.	I support myself

(1) Four masc. nouns, all obl. pl.
(2) *áug*. Pres. indic. 1 sg. of *auzir*.
(2) *auzéls*. Masc. obl. pl.
(2) *pels*. Equivalent to *per los*.

(2) *plaisadítz*. Masc. obl. pl.

(3) *entén*. Pres. indic. 1 sg. of *entendre*.

(3) *déinh*. Pres. indic. 1 sg. of *denhar*.

(4–6) 'My ardent body (heart) kills me, in which grief is seated near me, because I do not (cannot) bear myself.' His lover's anguish makes him unable to enjoy birdsong.

(4) *víus*. Masc. nom. sg. of *víu*. Modifies *le cors* (v. 5).

(4) *estéinh*. Pres. indic. 3 sg. of *esténher*.

(5) *dols*. Masc. nom. sg. of *dol*.

(5) *asítz*. Past part. masc. nom. sg. of *asir*.

(6) *sofér*. Pres. indic. 1 sg. of *soferre* (reflexive).

II

Si fos° grazitz°	it were; welcomed
mos chan[tars]°, ni ben acuilhitz°	my singing; or well received
per cella° qe m'a en desdeinh°,	by her; holds me in disdain
10 *d'aitan° me feinh°*	this much; I flatter myself
q'en maintz bos luecs° fora° auzitz°	many good places; it would be; heard
mas° qe non er°.	more; than it will be

(7) *fos*. Past subj. 3 sg. of *éser* for a condition contrary to fact.

(7) *grazítz*. Past part. masc. nom. sg. of *grazir*.

(8) *acuilhítz*. Past part. masc. nom. sg. of *acolhir*.

(10) *féinh*. Pres. indic. 1 sg. of *fénher* (reflexive).

(11) *fóra*. Second conditional 3 sg. of *éser*.

(11) *auzítz*. Past part. masc. nom. sg. of *auzir*.

(12) *non*. Pleonastic (does not negate) after a comparison (*mas qe*).

(12) *er*. Fut. 3 sg. of *éser*.

III

Tristz° e marritz°	sad; lost
er mos chantars aissi° fenitz°	now; finished
15 *per totz temps mais° tro q'° ela.m deinh°*	forevermore; until; takes me
pel sieu manteinh°;	as her support (lover)
era° mos bes°, er° es delitz°.	it was; my good; now; a crime
Mas no°.l sofer°!	no longer; she allows it

(13) Both words masc. nom. sg.

(14) *fenítz*. Past part. masc. nom. sg. of *fenir*.

(15) *déinh*. Pres. subj. 3 sg. of *denhar*; subj. after *tro que*.

(16) *pel*. Equivalent to *per lo*.

(17) *era*. Imperfect 3 sg. of *éser*. The subject is *chantars* (v. 14).

(17) *mos bes.* Nom. sg. *ben,* usually an adv., is here used as a masc. noun.

(17) *delítz.* Nom. sg. His song, which pleased her, now offends her.

(18) *sofér.* Pres. indic. 3 of *soferre.* She no longer allows him to sing.

IV

<table>
<tr><td> </td><td>*Jois me fon° gitz°*</td><td>was; my guide</td></tr>
<tr><td>20</td><td>*un pauc°—mas tost° me fon failhitz°!*</td><td>a little; soon; had failed me</td></tr>
<tr><td> </td><td>*S'anc° me volc°, ar° m'a en desdeinh.*</td><td>ever; wanted; now</td></tr>
<tr><td> </td><td>*Qom° non ateinh°*</td><td>how; I succeed</td></tr>
<tr><td> </td><td>*qan prec° merce° de mos destritz°?*</td><td>I beg; mercy; pains</td></tr>
<tr><td> </td><td>*Ren non° conqer°.*</td><td>nothing; I gain</td></tr>
</table>

(19) *fon.* Pret. 3 sg. of *éser.*

(19) *gitz.* Masc. nom. sg.

(20) *failhítz.* Past part. of *falhir;* masc. nom. sg. modifying *Jois* (v. 19).

(21) *volc.* Pret. 3 sg. of *voler;* *-c* marks pret.

(22–23) 'How do I not succeed when I beg for mercy for my pains?'

(22) *atéinh.* Pres. indic. 1 sg. of *aténher.*

(23) *prec.* Pres. indic. 1 sg. of *pregar.*

(23) *destrítz.* Masc. obl. pl. of *destric.*

(24) *conqér.* Pres. indic. 1 sg. of *conquerre.*

V

<table>
<tr><td>25</td><td>*Mos cors° me ditz,°*</td><td>my heart (body); says to me</td></tr>
<tr><td> </td><td>*"Per q'°eu sui° per leis° envelitz°?"*</td><td>why; am I; by her; made old</td></tr>
<tr><td> </td><td>*Qar sap° qe null'autra° no deinh°,*</td><td>she knows; no other [woman]; I take</td></tr>
<tr><td> </td><td>*per so° m'estreinh°.*</td><td>that's why; she belittles me</td></tr>
<tr><td> </td><td>*Morrai°, qe mos cors° enfolitz°*</td><td>I'll die; for my body (my heart;
i.e., I); driven mad</td></tr>
<tr><td>30</td><td>*ren no° li qer°.*</td><td>nothing; asks her for</td></tr>
</table>

(25) *ditz.* Pres. indic. 3 sg. of *dire.*

(26) *sui.* Pres. indic. 1 sg. of *éser.*

(26) *envelítz.* Past part. masc. nom. sg. of *envelhir.* Root *velh* 'old': 'Why does she make me [feel] old?'

(28) *estréinh.* Pres. indic. 3 sg. of *estrénher.*

(29) *Morrái.* Fut. 1 sg. of *morir.* Infinitives ending in *-ir* often reduce *-ir* to *-r* in fut.

(29) *mos cors.* Masc. nom. sg.

(29) *enfolítz.* Past part. masc. nom. sg. of *enfolir.* Root *fol* 'fool.'

(30) *qer.* Pres. indic. 3 sg. of *querre.*

VI

    [C]on° sui traïtz°!   how; I am betrayed

Bona donn'ab° talentz° voutitz°,   with; desires; fickle

ab cor dur, qar autra non deinh,

      mesclat° ab geinh°,   mixed; deceit

35 *volez° qe torn° flacs°, endormitz°?*   do you want; me to become; flaccid; sleepy

      En qe° demer°?   in what [way]; am I guilty

---

(31) *traïtz.* Past part. masc. nom. sg. of *traïr.*

(32–35) 'Good lady . . . , (you) with a hard heart mixed with deceit, because I do not take another (lover), do you want. . . ?' He pursues the idea (from stanza V) that his lady belittles him because he shows no interest in other women.

(32) *talentz.* Masc. obl. pl.

(32) *voutítz.* Masc. obl. pl.; invariable.

(34) *mesclát.* Past part. of *mesclar.* Modifies *cor dur* (v. 33).

(35) *voléz.* Pres. indic. 2 pl. of *voler.*

(35) *torn.* Pres. subj. 1 sg. of *tornar.*

(35) *flacs.* Masc. nom. sg.

(35) *endormítz.* Past part. masc. nom. sg. of *endormir* (reflexive), 'to go to sleep.'

(36) *demér.* Pres. indic. 1 sg. of *demerir.*

VII

    Trop sui arditz°!   bold

Donn[a], mos sens° e[i]saboisitz°   mind; made giddy

m'a fach dir° fols motz° q'ieu non deinh°:   made me say; foolish words; approve

40   *contra mi° reinh°.*   against myself; I act

Tan sui fors° de mon sen issitz°   out of; gone

     non sen° qi.m fer°.   [that] I don't feel; who strikes me

---

(37) *ardítz.* Masc. nom. sg.

(40) *réinh.* Pres. indic. 1 sg. of *renhar.*

(41) *issítz.* Past part. masc. nom. sg. of *eisir.*

(42) *sen.* Pres. indic. 1 sg. of *sentir.*

(42) *fer.* Pres. indic. 3 sg. of *ferir.*

(42) Proverbial: a fool cannot tell who beats him. Cf. "Fols no tem, tro que pren" 'A fool doesn't fear until he takes [a blow],' Bernart de Ventadorn (*BEdT* 70.30, v. 21; Appel, *Bernart von Ventadorn* 181; my trans.).

VIII

    Mout fon petitz°   small

Le tortz° e[n] q'ieu vos fui failhitz°,   wrong; I failed you

45 *e per qe m'aves° en desdeinh.*   you hold me

    Fatz° en deveinh°!   a fool; I am becoming

Pendutz° sia° per la cervitz°   hanged; may he be; by the neck

     qi° a moilher°!   anyone who; wife

(43) *petítz*. Masc. nom. sg.
(44) *tortz*. Masc. nom. sg.
(44) *fúi*. Pret. 1 sg. of *éser*, here auxiliary.
(45) *avés*. Pres. indic. 2 pl. of *aver*.
(46) *Fatz*. Masc. nom. sg.
(46) *devéinh*. Pres. indic. 1 sg. of *devenir*.
(47) *Pendútz*. Past part. masc. nom. sg. of *pendre*.
(47) *sía*. Pres. subj. 1 sg. of *éser*, expressing a wish.
(47–48) 'Anyone who has a wife should be hanged by the neck!' He curses himself.
(48) *moilhér*. Obl. sg. Rhyme assures the stress position, in contrast with nom. sg. *mólher*. Shifting declension.

IX

Humil°, ses° geinh,	humble; without
50 *donna, le vostre fals°, failhitz°,*	false; failed [man]
merce vos qer°.	begs

(49) *humil*. Possibly obl. expressing an adverbial sense (Jensen, *Syntax* 28–29), like the adverbial accusative in Lat. Otherwise, declension on the noun (*failhitz*) but not on the adj. (*humil*).
(51) *qer*. Pres. indic. 3 sg. of *querre*.

Form

Eight *coblas unissonans* of six lines and one *tornada* of three.

SCHEME

a   a   b   b   a   c

RHYMES

itz itz enh enh itz er

METER

4   8   8   4   8   4

Rhyme words often repeat: in the third line of the stanza, *deinh/desdeinh*; in the fifth, *failhitz*; in the sixth, *sofer/fer* and *conqer/qer*.

Corrected Readings

(8) *chan[tars]*. M: *chanz* (−1).
(31) *[C]on*. M: *eon*.
(38) *Donn[a]*. M: *donne*.
(38) *e[i]saboisitz*. M: *ensaboisitz*.
(44) *e[n] q'ieu vos fui failhitz*. M: *e q'ieu. fui g failhitz*.

Azalais de Porcairagues

Ar em al freg temps vengut

Six manuscripts of version 1: *C, D, H* (vv. 37–52), *I, K, d. BEdT* 43.1.
Major editions: Rieger (480–504); Bruckner et al. (34–37); Paden, "System"
  (44–52; version 1).

Azalais de Porcairagues, from the town now called Portiragnes (Hérault),
grieves for Raimbaut d'Aurenga (no. 10). She refers to him in stanza II (v. 14) and
mourns for him in stanza VI. These passages make the poem a *planh*, a funeral
lament. Surprisingly, in stanzas IV and V she declares that she has a happy love
for a living lover. Add that stanza V rhymes only with itself (see "Form," rhymes
a and **b**), whereas the first four stanzas rhyme in pairs, and the suspicion arises
that the text comprises fragments of two original songs, a *planh* (I–III, VI) and
a *cansó* or love song (IV–V).

The manuscripts present the poem as a single text, however. The system of
genres had not crystallized by this time, so love and mourning could be mixed.
The first stanza of happy love (IV) matches the rhymes of the preceding stanza
of mourning (III), so the two emotions are undeniably linked. Perhaps Azalais
still mourns for the loss of her first husband, whom she intended to marry for
life (v. 47), even though she has become betrothed to another. We know she has
not married again, since she must not make love with her new man (vv. 39–40).
Remarriage was a difficult option that confronted every widow.

D, fols. 190r, col. 2–190v, col. 1.

I

Ar° em° al freg° temps vengut	now; *em … vengut,* we have come; cold
que°.l gells° e.l neus° e la faingna°	when; the frost; snow; mud
e l'auçellet° estan° mut°,	little birds; are; mute

c'°us° de chantar non s'afraingna°;	so that; *us … non*, not one; breaks into
5 *e son sec° li ram° pels plais°,*	dry; branches; hedges
que flors° ni foilla° no.i nais°;	flower; leaf; appears
ni rrossignols° no i crida°,	a nightingale; cry
que l'am'° e mai° me rreissida°.	my soul; May; awakens

(1) *em.* Pres. indic. 1 pl. of *éser.*
(1) *vengút.* Past part. masc. nom. pl. of *venir.*
(2) *gells … neus.* Masc. nom. sg.
(3) *auçellét … mut.* Masc. nom. pl. Cf. no. 10, vv. 1–3.
(3) *están.* Pres. indic. 3 pl. of *estar* 'to be' (in a situation).
(4) *us.* Masc. nom. sg. of *un.*
(4) *afráingna.* Pres. subj. 3 sg. of *afránher* (reflexive); subj. for result of *estan mut* (v. 3).
(5) *sec li ram.* Masc. nom. pl.
(5) *pels.* Equivalent to *per los.*
(5) *pláis.* Obl. pl., invariable. Cf. obl. sg. *plais.*
(6) *flors.* Fem. nom. sg. of *flor.*
(6) *náis.* Pres. indic. 3 sg. of *náiser.*
(7) *rrossignóls.* Masc. nom. sg. of *rosinhol.*
(7) *crída.* Pres. indic. 3 sg. of *cridar.*
(8) *am'.* That is, *ama.* Fem. obl. sg.
(8) *e.* Followed by nasal (*mai*), *e* is equivalent to *en.*
(8) *rreissída.* Pres. indic. 3 sg. of *reisidar.*

II

Tant ai lo cors° deseubut°	my body (my self); distressed
10 *per qu'eu soi a toz estraigna°,*	estranged from everyone
e sai que l'om a perdut°	one has lost
molt plus tost° que non gasaingna°;	much sooner; one wins
e s'ieu faill° ab motz verais°,	I stumble; true words (lyrics)
d'Aurenga me moc° l'esglais°,	started; grief
15 *per qu'eu m'estauc° esbaïda°*	remain; astonished
e.n pert° solatz° en partida°.	I lose; comfort; part

(9) *deseubút.* Past part. of *decébre*: 'I am so distressed that. …'
(10) *estráigna.* Fem. of *estranh.*
(11–12) Proverbial: 'you can't win for losing.'
(11) *perdút.* Past part. of *perdre.*
(11) *gasáingna.* Pres. indic. 3 sg. of *gazanhar.*
(13) *fáill.* Pres. indic. 1 sg. of *falhir.*
(14) *moc.* Pret. 3 sg. of *mover*; *-c* marks pret.
(14) *esglais.* Masc. nom. sg. of *esglai.*
(15) *estauc.* Pres. indic. 1 sg. of *estar* (reflexive).
(15) *esbaïda.* Past part. fem. of *esbaïr.*
(16) *pert.* Pres. indic. 1 sg. of *perdre.*
(16) *partida.* She is in part bereaved and in part joyful (stanzas IV–V).

III

Dompna met° mot° mal s'amor	places; very
que ab° ric ome° pladeia°,	with; a powerful man; pleads
ab plus aut° de vavasor°,	higher; vavasor (lesser noble)
20 *e s'ill° o fai° il folleia°;*	she; does that; she commits folly
car so diz om en Veillai°	Velay
que ges° per ricor non vai,	*ges ... non,* not at all
e dompna que n'es chauzida°	distinguished
en renc° per envilanida°.	for this reason I rank; as debased

(17) *met.* Pres. indic. 3 sg. of *metre.*
(17) *mot.* Equivalent to *molt.*
(18) *pladéia.* Pres. indic. 3 sg. of *plaidejar.*
(20) *folléia.* Pres. indic. 3 sg. of *folejar.*
(21) *Veillai.* Velay is the region around Le Puy-en-Velay (Haute-Loire).
(22) 'It (love) scarcely goes by wealth.' Proverb; cf. "Ges amors segon ricor non vai" 'Love certainly does not go according to wealth,' Bernart de Ventadorn (*BEdT* 70.10, v. 35; Appel, *Bernart von Ventadorn* 63; my trans.).
(22) *vai.* Pres. indic. 3 sg. of *anar.*
(23) 'A lady who distinguishes herself by this' (i.e., by placing her love on a rich man).
(23) *chauzida.* Past part. fem. of *cauzir.*
(24) *renc.* Pres. indic. 1 sg. of *rengar.*
(24) *envilanida.* Past part. fem. of *envilanir* 'to become like a peasant' (*vilan*).

IV

25 *Amic° ai° de gran valor°*	friend (lover); I have; worth
que sobre toz° seignoreia°,	over all [others]; lords it
e non a cor trichador°	a deceitful heart
vas me°, que amor m'autreia°.	toward me; grants me
Eu dic° que m'amors l'eschai°,	I say; suits him
30 *e cel° que dis° que non fai°,*	[as for] one; who said; it doesn't
Dieus li don° mal'esgarida°,	give him; bad luck
qu'eu m'en teing fort per guerida.	

(26) *seignoréia.* Pres. indic. 3 sg. of *senhorejar.*
(27) *trichadór.* Masc. obl. sg., in contrast to nom. *tricháire.* Shifting declension.
(28) *autréia.* Pres. indic. 3 sg. of *autrejar.*
(29) *dic.* Pres. indic. 1 sg. of *dire.*
(29) *eschai.* Pres. indic 3 sg. of *escazer.*
(30) *dis.* Pret. 3 sg. of *dire; -s* marks pret.
(30) *fai.* Pres. indic. 3 sg. of *faire;* vicarious, represents repetition of *eschai.*
(31) *don.* Pres. subj. 3 sg. of *donar,* expressing a wish.
(32) 'I consider myself very much healed by it.'
(32) *téing.* Pres. indic. 1 sg. of *tener.*
(32) *guerída.* Past part. fem. of *garir.* She is healed of grief by her new love.

V

Bels amics, de bon talan°	gladly
son° ab° vos toz jorz° en guaje°,	I am; with; always; engaged
35 *corteza°, de bel semblan°,*	gracious; smiling
sol° no.m demandes° outraje°.	if only; you don't ask me; for an outrage
Tost° en veirem° a l'assai°,	soon; we will see; test
qu'en vostra merce°.m metrai°.	at your mercy; I will put myself
Vos m'aves° la fe° plevida°	have; your faith; sworn to me
40 *que no.m demandes° faillida°.*	that you will not ask; for an impropriety

(33) 'I am always glad to be engaged' (involved; perhaps betrothed) 'with you,' even when I mourn my loss.
(34) *son.* Pres. indic. 1 sg. of *éser.*
(35) *cortéza.* Fem. of *cortés.*
(35) *semblán.* 'Expression'; *bel semblan* 'smile.'
(36) *demandés.* Pres. subj. 2 pl. of *demandar*; subj. after *sol no.*
(37) *veirém.* Fut. 1 pl. of *vezer.*
(37–38) 'Soon we'll see in the test, for I shall put myself at your mercy.'
(38) *metrái.* Fut. 1 sg. of *métre.*
(39) *avés.* Pres. indic. 2 pl. of *aver.*
(39) *plevída.* Past part. fem. of *plevir.*
(40) *demandés.* Pres. subj. 2 pl. of *demandar.* The pres. subj. may refer to future time (*Old Occitan* 265).

VI

A Dieu coman° Belesgar	I commend
e plus° la siutat° d'Aurenga	also; city
e Gloriet' e.l caslar°	castle
e lo seignor° de Proenza,	lord
45 *e tot cant° vol mon ben° lai*	anyone who; wishes me well
e l'arc° on son fag° l'assai°.	arch; shown; the assaults
Cellui° perdiei° c'a ma vida,	him (the man); I lost
e.n serai° toz jorz marrida°.	I will always be; aggrieved for him

(41) *comán.* Pres. indic. 1 sg. of *comandar.*
(41) *Belesgar.* Beauregard, castle near Courthézon (Vaucluse), where Raimbaut wrote his will (Pattison 218).
(42) *Aurenga.* Orange (Vaucluse).
(43) *Gloriét'.* Glorieta, a palace of the princes of Orange mentioned in OFr. epic poetry.
(44) *seignór.* Masc. obl. sg., in contrast with nom. *sénher.* Shifting declension.
(44) *Proenza.* The lord of Provence in 1173 was either Raymond V of Toulouse, to whom Raimbaut d'Aurenga did homage in 1154, or Alfonso II of Aragon, marquis of Provence, whose court Raimbaut attended in 1162 and 1170 (Pattison 9 and 216).
(46) *fag.* Past part. of *faire.*
(46) *assái.* Masc. nom. pl. The first-century arch at Orange depicts a battle between Roman legionaries and Gauls. The reference to a building of archeological interest is very unusual in this poetry.

(47) *perdiéi*. Pret. 1 sg. of *pérdre*.
(48) *serái*. Fut. 1 sg. of *éser*.
(48) *marrída*. Past part. fem. of *marrir*.

VII

Joglar° que aves° cor gai,	[you] *joglars*; who have
50 *ves Narbona° portas° lai*	Narbonne (Aude); carry
ma chanson a la fenida°	with this *tornada*
lei° cui jois e jovenz° guida°.	to her; joy and youth; guide

(49) *Joglár*. Masc. nom. pl., here vocative.
(49) *avés*. Pres. indic. 2 pl. of *aver*.
(50) *portás*. Form of *portátz*. Imperative 2 pl. of *portar*.
(52) *lei*. Ermengarde, viscountess of Narbonne.
(52) *jois e jovenz*. Masc. nom. sg.
(52) *guida*. Pres. indic. 3 sg. of *guidar*, agreeing with the closer noun in the compound subject.

Form

Six stanzas of eight lines and one *tornada* of four. Both *coblas doblas* (I–IV) and *singulars* (V–VI).

SCHEME

a	b	a	b	c	c	d	d

RHYMES

	a	b	a	b	c	c	d	d
I–II	ut	anha	ut	anha	ais	ais	ida	ida
III–IV	or	éia	or	éia	ai	ai	ida	ida
V	an	aje	an	aje	ai	ai	ida	ida
VI	ar	enga	ar	enza	ai	ai	ida	ida
VII					ai	ai	ida	ida

Rhyme **c** is constant except for the *-s* in I–II; **d** is constant throughout.

METER

	a	b	a	b	c	c	d	d
I–VI	7	7'	7	7'	7	7	7'	7'
VII					7	7	7'	7'

Corrected Readings

(3) *e l'auçellet*. D: *e li auçellet* (+1).
(7) *ni rrossignols*. D: *nirrosignols*.
(8) *me rreissida*. D: *merreissida*.

Bernart de Ventadorn
Qan la freid' aura venta

Ten manuscripts: *A, C, D* (attributed to Peire Cardenal), *G, M, N, O* (anonymous), *R, V, a. BEdT* 70.37.
Major editions: Appel, *Bernart von Ventadorn* (212–18); Lazar (160–63).

Bernart de Ventadorn left more than forty love songs. His name refers to a castle that lies in ruins at Moustier-Ventadour (Corrèze). The *vida* says he was the son of a baker at the castle (*BT* 20). Although many say he was active between circa 1147 and circa 1172 (*DBT* 102), only the latter date, when he was mentioned by the troubadour Peire d'Alvenhe, is certain. A man with the same name was a son of Viscount Eble III of Ventadour; he became abbot of Tulle and died after 1234 (Paden, "Bernart de Ventadour"). Despite what the *vida* says, the viscount's son may have been the troubadour. The abbot of Tulle could have been a poet in his youth, like the troubadour Folquet de Marselha, who became a monk and died as bishop of Toulouse.

G, fols. 13r, col. 1–13v, col. 1; stanza I is entered below a blank staff. Reference to *A*, fol. 94v, cols. 1–2.

Idem
Idem. Lat. 'the same [man],' referring to an earlier attribution to *Bernard de Ventador* on fol. 9r, col. 1.

I

Qan° la freid' aura° venta°	when; cold breeze; blows
dever° vostre païs,°	from; your country
vejaire m'es° qe senta°	it seems to me; I feel
un vent° de paradis°	wind; from paradise
5 *per amor de la genta°*	noble (pretty) [one]
ves cui° [eu] sui aclis,°	toward whom; I am inclined

en cui ai mes° m'ententa°	on whom I have put; my affection
e mon corag'° assis,°	my heart; set
car de tutas° partis°	from all [other women]; I parted
10 *per lei°, tant m'atalenta.°*	for her; so much she attracts me

---

(1) *venta*. Pres. indic. 3 sg. of *ventar*; *-a* marks pres. indic. 3 sg. of *-ar* verbs.

(3) *vejáire*. Lat. *videatur* 'let it be seen' produced this noun meaning 'opinion.'

(3) *senta*. Pres. subj. 1 sg. of *sentir*; *-a* marks pres. subj. 3 sg. of non-*ar* verbs.

(6) *súi*. Pres. indic. 1 sg. of *éser*.

(6) *aclís*. Masc. nom. sg. Cf. obl. *aclin*.

(7) *mes*. Past part. of *metre*.

(8) *assís*. Past part. of *asire*.

(9) *tútas*. Fem. obl. pl. of *tot*/*tut*.

(9) *partís*. Pret. 1 sg. of *partir*. Root *part-* + pret. *-ís* + no ending for 1 sg. The speaker has left all other women for the sake of one. *Chanson de change.*

(10) *atalenta*. Pres. indic. 3 sg. of *atalentar*.

II

Sol° lo ben° qe.m presenta°	just; good [thing]; she offers me
(sei beil oil° e.l franc vis°—	her pretty eyes; her sweet face
qe° ja° plus° no.m consenta°!)	even if; *ja ... no*, never; more; grant
me deu° aver° conquis.°	must; have; conquered
15 *Non sai° per qe.us en menta,°*	I don't know; why I would lie
car de re° non sui fis;°	anything; sure
mas greu m'es° qe repenta,°	it is hard for me; to recant
q'una veç° me dis°	for once; she told me
qe pros hom° s'afortis°	a worthy man; persists
20 *e malva[t]z° s'espaventa.°*	a bad one; takes fright

---

(11) *ben*. Adv., used here as a noun, the subject of *deu* (v. 14). *Ben* must be understood as nom., although the form is obl. by attraction from the relative pronoun *qe*, which is obl. as the object of *presenta* in the subordinate clause (Appel, *Bernart von Ventadorn* 216). Cf. nom. *bes* (no. 13, v. 14).

(11) *presenta*. Pres. indic. 3 sg. of *prezentar*. The subject is the lady: *la genta* (v. 5), *léi* (v. 10).

(12) The line paraphrases the subject of *presenta* (v. 11).

(12) *béil óil*. Masc. nom. pl.; *-il* spells *-lh*. Cf. obl. sg. *belh olh*.

(12) *franc vis*. Nom. like *beil oil*, but the adjective is not declined (*francs*). *Vis* is invariable; the *-s* is part of the root.

(13) 'Even if she never grants me more.'

(13) *consenta*. Pres. subj. 3 sg. of *consentir*; *-a* marks pres. subj. 3 sg. of non-*ar* verbs.

(14) *déu*. Pres. indic. 3 sg. of *dever*. Root *dev-* > *deu*; no ending for pres. indic. 3 sg. of non-*ar* verb.

(14) *conquís*. Past part. of *conquerer*.

(15) *sai*. Pres. indic. 1 sg. of *saber*. Root *sa-* + yod for 1 sg. of non-*ar* verb.

(15) *menta*. Pres. subj. 1 sg. of *mentir*; *-a* for pres. subj. 1 sg. of non-*ar* verb. Subj. after *non sai*.

(16) *fis*. Masc. nom. sg. of *fin*.

(17) *repenta*. Pres. subj. 1 sg. of *repentir*; *-a* for pres. subj. 1 sg. of non-*ar* verb.

(18) *una veç.* Fem. obl. sg. in an adverbial phrase. *Veç/vetz* is invariable.

(18) *dis.* Pret. 3 sg. of *dire.* Root *di-* + *-s* for pret.

(19–20) Proverbial. Cf. "Mout fai gran vilanatge / qui trop leu s'espaventa, / qu'apres lo fer auratge / vei que.lh dous'aura venta" 'He acts like a peasant [*vilan*] / who becomes frightened too easily, / for after the rough wind / I see that the gentle breeze blows,' Raimbaut de Vaqueiras (?) (*BEdT* 392.27, vv. 33–36; Appel, *Bernart von Ventadorn* 288; my trans.).

(19) *pros hom.* Masc. nom. sg.; *pro-* + *-s*; *hom/om,* nom. sg. of *óme.*

(19) *afortís.* Pres. indic. 3 sg. of *afortir.* Root *afort-* + inchoative *-is* (*Old Occitan* 167); no personal ending for pres. indic. 3 sg. of non-*ar* verb.

(20) *malva[t]z.* Invariable (*-s/-z* part of root) for masc.; here nom. sg.

(20) *espaventa.* Pres. indic. 3 sg. of *espaventar; -a* marks pres. indic. 3 sg. of *-ar* verb.

III

De donas° m'es vejaire°	ladies; it seems to me
qe gran fallimen° fan°	a great error; they make
per cho car° non° s[o]n gaire	because; *non . . . gaire*, not at all
ama[t]° li fin aman.°	loved; the true lovers
25 *Eu non° dei° ges retraire°*	*non . . . ges*, not at all; must; say
mas cho q'°elas voldran,°	anything but what; they will want
mas° greu m'es c'uns trichaire°	but; a deceiver
a° d'amor ab engan°	gets; deceit
o plus° o atretan°	*o . . . o*, either . . . or; more; as much
30 *con cel q'es° fin amaire.°*	as the one who is; a true lover

(21) *dónas.* Fem. obl. pl. *-s.*

(22) *fallimén.* The *-ll-* spells *-lh-* (*falhimen*).

(22) *fan.* Pres. indic. 3 pl. of *faire.* Root *fa-* + *-n.*

(23) *s[o]n.* Pres. indic. 3 pl. of *éser.* Root *so-* + *-n.*

(24) *amá[t].* Past part. of *amar;* masc. nom. pl., no ending.

(24) *li fin amán.* Masc. nom. pl., no ending.

(25) *déi.* Pres. indic. 1 sg. of *dever.* Root *de-* + yod for pres. indic. 1 sg. of some non-*ar* verbs.

(26) *elas.* Fem. nom. pl. Root *ela* +*-s.*

(26) *voldrán.* Fut. 3 pl. of infinitive *volér; -ér* reduced, as often in fut., to *-r; l + r > ldr* (transitional *-d-*); fut. *-á;* + 3 pl. *-n.*

(27) *uns. Un* + masc. nom. sg. *-s.*

(27) *trichaíre.* Masc. nom. sg. in shifting declension. Cf. nom. pl. *trichadór* (no. 13, v. 35).

(28–30) 'Gets more of love, or as much, with deceit as [does] the one who is a true lover.'

(30) *fin amáire.* Declension on the noun but not the adj. *Amáire* is nom. sg., like *trichaire* (v. 27); cf. nom. pl. *amadór* (no. 13, v. 34).

IV

Domna, qe cuidaz° faire	what do you think
de mi qe vos am° tan,	who love you
c'aissi°.m veëz° maltraire°	this way; you see; suffer
e morir° de talan?°	die; desire
35 *Ha, francha° de bon aire,°*	sweet; family
faichaz° m'un bel semblan°	give; pretty look

tal don° mos cors° s'esclaire,°	such that; heart (body; self); will rejoice
qe molt trai° gran afan°	I suffer; very great grief
e no.i dei° aver dan°	should; loss
40 *car no me.n° puosc° estraire.*	*me.n . . . estraire*, give it up; I cannot

---

(31) *cuidáz*. Pres. indic. 2 pl. of *cuidar*. Root *cuid-* + 2 pl. *átz/áz* for *-ar* verb.

(31) *am*. Pres. indic. 1 sg. of *amar*. Root *am-* + no ending for pres. indic. 1 sg.

(33) *veëz*. Pres. indic. 2 pl. of *vezer/veër*. Root *ve-* + pres. indic. 2 pl. *-étz/éz* for non-*ar* verb.

(35) *francha*. Fem.

(36) *faicház*. Pres. subj. 2 pl. of *faire*; subj. expressing a wish. Root *fass-/faich-* + pres. subj. 2 pl. *-átz/-áz* for non-*ar* verb.

(37) *escláire*. Pres. subj. 3 sg. of *esclairar*. Root *esclair-* + *-e* (support vowel for *-ir*) + no ending for pres. subj. 3 sg. of *-ar* verb.

(38) *trái*. Pres. indic. 1 sg. of *traire*. Root *trai-* + no ending for pres. indic. 1 sg.

(40) *puosc*. Pres. indic. 1 sg. of *poder*. Root *posc-* (short *o* > *uó*) + no ending for 1 sg.

V

Si non fos° genz° vilana°	if there were no; people; boorish
e lausengier savai,°	nasty gossips
eu agr'° amor certana,°	would have; certain
mas aicho° m'en retrai.°	that; keeps me from it
45 *De solatz° m'es° humana°*	solace; [she] is; kind
qan luocs° es ni s'eschai,°	there is place [for it]; it is suitable
per q'eu sai q'a sosmana°	secretly
n'aurai° enqera mai;°	I will get; still more
c'austrux° sejorn'° e jai°	a lucky [one]; rests up; lies around
50 *e malastrux° s'afana.°*	an unlucky [one]; labors

---

(41) *fos*. Past subj. 3 sg. of *éser*. Root *fo-* + *-s* for past subj. + no ending for 3 sg.

(41) *genz*. Fem. nom. sg.; *gent* + nom. sg. *-z/s*.

(41) *vilana*. Fem. of *vilan*.

(42) *lausengier savai*. Masc. nom. pl.

(43) *agr'*. That is, *agra*. Second conditional 1 sg. of *aver*. Root *ag-* + *-ra* for second conditional + no ending for 1 sg.

(43) *certana*. Fem. of *certan*.

(44) *aicho*. Or *aiso*. Neuter pron. referring to a thought in context (*genz vilana . . . lausengier savai*, vv. 41–42).

(44) *retrái*. Pres. indic. 3 sg. of *retraire*. Root *retrai-* + no ending for pres. indic. 3 sg. of non-*ar* verb.

(45) *es*. Pres. indic. 3 sg. of *éser*. Root *es-* + -zero for pres. indic. 3 sg. non-*ar* verb.

(45) *humana*. Fem. of *uman*.

(46) *eschái*. Pres. indic. 3 sg. of *escazer*. Root *escai-* + no ending for pres. indic. 3 sg. of non-*ar* verb.

(47) *a sosmana*. Literally, 'underhandedly' (*sotz* 'under'; *man* 'hand').

(48) *aurái*. Fut. 1 sg. infinitive of *avér* with *-ér* reduced to *-r* (as in *voldrán*, v. 26) + fut. *-á* + yod for 1 sg.

(49–50) Proverbial. Cf. "Astruc ni malastruc non cal mati levar" 'A lucky man or an unlucky one doesn't want to get up in the morning,' identified as a *proverbi* by Guilhem de l'Olivier d'Arle (*BEdT* 246.19, vv. 11–12; Schultz-Gora 1: 39, no. 12; my trans.).

(49) *austrux*. Masc. nom. sg. Root *austruc* + nom. sg. *-s* (*-cs* spelled *-x*).

(49) *sejorn'*. That is, *sejorna*. Pres. indic. 3 sg. of *sejornar*. Root *sejorn-* + *-a* for 3 sg. of *-ar* verb.

(49) *jái*. Pres. indic. 3 sg. of *jazer*. Root *jai-* + no ending for pres. indic. 3 sg. of non-*ar* verb.

(50) *malastrux*. 'Ill-starred' (*astre* 'star'); cf. *austrux* (v. 49).

(50) *afana*. Pres. indic. 3 sg. of *afanar* (reflexive). Root *afan-* + *-a* pres. indic. 3 sg. for *-ar* verb.

VI

Cel sui qe° no soana°	I am one who; does not refuse
lo ben° qe Dex° li fai,°	the good; God; gives
q'en aqella° semana°	the same; week
qan eu partic° de lai°	when I left; from there (her)
55 *me dis° en raçon plana°*	she told me; plain words
qe mos chantars° li plai.°	my singing; pleases
Tot'arma° cristiana°	soul; Christian
volgr'° agues° aital jai°	I wish; could have; such joy
com eu agui° ez° ai°	had; and; have
60 *car° sol de tan° se vana.°*	because; only of this; [my song] boasts

(51) *soána*. Pres. indic. 3 sg. of *soanar*. Root + *-a* for 3 sg.

(52) *Dex*. Masc. nom. sg. *De-* + *-us* (spelled *-x*).

(52) *fái*. Pres. indic. 3 sg. of *faire*. Root *fai-* + no ending for non-*ar* verb.

(54) *partíc*. Pret. 1 sg. of *partir*. Root *part-* + *-í* for pret. + *-c* for 1 sg.

(55) *dis*. Pret. 3 sg. of *dire*. Root *di-* + *-s* for pret. + no ending for 3 sg.

(56) *mos chantars*. Masc. nom. sg. *-s*.

(56) *plái*. Pres. indic. 3 sg. of *plazer*. Root *plai-* + no ending for pres. indic. 3 sg. of a non-*ar* verb.

(58) *volgr'*. That is, *volgra*, second conditional 1 sg. of *voler*. Root *vol-*; *-k/g* for past group; *-ra* for second conditional; no ending for 1 sg.

(58) *agués*. Past subj. 3 sg. of *aver*. Root *a-* + *-k/g* for past group + *-és* for past subj. + no ending for 3 sg.

(59) *aguí*. Pret. 1 sg. of *aver*. Root *a-* + *-k/g* for past group + *-í* for pret. + no ending for 1 sg.

(59) *ái*. Pres. 1 sg. of *aver*. Root *a-* + yod for 1 sg. of non-*ar* verb.

(60) *vana*. Pres. 3 sg. of *vanar* (reflexive). Root *van-* + *-a* for 3 sg. of *-ar* verb.

VII

Si d'aicho m'es certan[a],	
d'altra veç° la crerai;°	another time; I'll believe her
o si [q]e non,° jamai°	if not; *jamai non*, never
64 *non crera[i] cristiana.*	

(61) 'If she is reliable about that,' when she says she likes my songs (vv. 55–56).

(62) *crerái*, (64) *crerá[i]*. Fut. 1 sg. of *créire*. Root *crer-* + *-á* for fut. + yod for 1 sg.

Grammar Review

Masculine nouns, adjectives
Nom. sg. -*s/x*: *aclis* (v. 6), *francs* (as *franc*, v. 12), *fis* (v. 16), *pros* (v. 19), *Dex* (v. 52), *mos chantars* (v. 56)
Obl. sg. -zero: *un vent* (v. 4)
Nom. pl. -zero: *beil oil* (v. 12), *fin aman* (v. 24), *lausengier savai* (v. 42)

Nouns of shifting declension (stress pattern shifts from nom. sg. to other forms)
Masc. nom. sg.: *hom/om* (v. 19) vs. *óme*, *tricháire* (v. 27) vs. *trichadór*, *amáire* (v. 30) vs. *amadór*

Infinitives in -*ar*

PRESENT INDICATIVE

1 sg. -zero: *am* (v. 32)
3 sg. -*a*: *venta* (v. 1), *atalenta* (v. 10), etc.
2 pl. -*átz/áz*: *cuidáz* (v. 31)

PRESENT SUBJUNCTIVE

3 sg. -zero: *escláire* (v. 37); -*e* is a support vowel

Infinitives in non-*ar*

PRESENT INDICATIVE

1 sg.
-zero: *trái* (v. 38); -*i* is part of the root
-yod: *súi* (v. 6), *déi* (v. 25), *ái* (v. 59)
3 sg. -zero: *déu* (v. 14); *es* (v. 45); *retrái* (v. 44), *eschái* (v. 46), *jái* (v. 49), *fái* (v. 52), *plái* (v. 56)
2 pl. -*étz/éz*: *veëz* (v. 33)
3 pl. -*n*: *fan* (v. 22), *son* (v. 23)

PRESENT SUBJUNCTIVE

1 sg. -*a*: *senta* (v. 3), *menta* (v. 15), *repenta* (v. 17)
3 sg. -*a*: *consenta* (v. 13)
2 pl. -*átz/-áz*: *faicház* (v. 36)

FUTURE (TENSE MARKED BY -Á)

1 sg. -*ái*: *aurái* (v. 48), *crerái* (vv. 62, 64)
3 pl. -*án*: *voldrán* (v. 26)

PRETERIT (TENSE MARKED VARIOUS WAYS)

1 sg.
  -i: aguí (v. 59)
  -k: partíc (v. 54)
  -s: partís (v. 9)
3 sg. *-s: dis* (v. 55)

PAST SUBJUNCTIVE (TENSE MARKED BY *-s*)

3 sg.
  -s: fos (v. 41)
  -és: agués (v. 58)

SECOND CONDITIONAL (TENSE MARKED BY *-RA*)

1 sg. *agr' (agra)* (v. 43), *volgr' (volgra)* (v. 58)

Form

Six *coblas doblas* of ten lines and one *tornada* of four.

SCHEME

a	b	a	b	a	b	a	b	b	a

RHYMES

I–II	*enta*	*is*	*enta*	*is*	*enta*	*is*	*enta*	*is*	*is*	*enta*
III–IV	*aire*	*an*	*aire*	*an*	*aire*	*an*	*aire*	*an*	*an*	*aire*
V–VI	*ana*	*ai*	*ana*	*ai*	*ana*	*ai*	*ana*	*ai*	*ai*	*ana*
VII							*ana*	*ai*	*ai*	*ana*

METER

6′	6	6′	6	6′	6	6′	6	6	6′

Corrected Readings

(1) *freid' aura.* G: *freida aura* (+1).
(6) *cui [eu] sui.* G: *cui sui* (−1); A: *cui ieu sui.*
(8) *corag' assis.* G: *corage assis* (+1); *assis* corrected above the line from *sis* (−1) in the line.
(12) The verse is written twice in *G*; the second time it is expunctuated.
(20) *malva[t]z.* G: *malvalz* ; A: *malvatz.*
(23) *non s[o]n gaire.* G: *non san gaire,* with *non* inserted above line; A: *no.is fant gaire.*

(24) *ama[t]*. G: *amar*; A: *amar a fin aman*.

(28) *a. So A.* G: *ait*.

(32) *qe vos*. G: *qe.us* (−1); A: *que vos*.

(36) *faichaz m'un*. G: *faichaz me un* (+1); A: *faitz me un*.

(42) *lausengier. So A.* G: *lausengiers*.

(43) *agr' amor*. G: *agra amor* (+1).

(44) *aicho*. G: *chom*, with *ai* entered above line and *-m* expunctuated; A: *so*.

(55) *raçon*. G: *traçon*, form of *traïcion* (DOM) 'treachery'; A: *razon*.

(57) *Tot'arma*. G: *toto arma* (+1); A: *tot'arma*.

(58) *volgr' agues*. G: *volgra agues* (+1).

(61) *certan[a]. So A.* G: *certan*.

(63) *[q]e*. G: *ce*; A: *que*.

(64) *crera[i]*. G: *crera*; A: *creirai*.

Bernart de Ventadorn
Non es meraveilla s'eu chan

Twenty-two manuscripts: *A, C, D, F, G, I, K, Ka, L* versions 1 and 2 (anonymous), *M, N, O* (anonymous), *P, Q, R, S, U, V, W* (anonymous), *a, g. BEdT* 70.31. *G* and *W* have music.

Major editions: Appel, *Bernart von Ventadorn* (186–93); Lazar (60–63). Music: van der Werf and Bond (51*–54*).

This edition respects departures from standard declension (vv. 14, 15, 16), like other editions from manuscripts with music (nos. 6 and 7).

G, fols. 9r, col. 1–9v, col. 1.

Bernard de Ventador
Written twice: with black ink in the left margin and with red above the incipit.

I

Non es meraveilla° s'eu chan°	marvel; sing
meilz° de nul° autre chantador°,	better; any; singer
qe plu°.m tira°.l cors° vers amor	more; draws me; my body (heart)
e meillç sui faiç° al seu coman°.	I am made more; to [love's] command
5 *Cor° e cors° e saber° e sen°*	heart; body; knowledge; wit
e forç'°e poder° i a[i] mes°;	strength; power; spent on it (love)
si°.m tira vas° amors lo fres°	si . . . que, so much . . . that; toward; rein
q'enver altra part° no m'aten°.	in another direction; pay attention

(1) *chan.* Pres. indic. 1 sg. of *cantar.*
(2) *méilz.* Equivalent to *meillç* (v. 4), normalized *melhs*; *-il* spells *-lh.*
(2) *chantadór.* Obl. sg. Cf. nom. sg. *cantáire.* Shifting declension.
(3) *plu.* Usually *plus.*
(3) *tira.* Pres. indic. 3 sg. of *tirar.*

(4) *faiç.* Past part. of *faire.*

(6) *mes.* Past part. of *metre.*

(7) *amors.* Obl. sg. (object of *vas*), so the *-s* shows that the word is here obl. (invariable), meaning 'the force of love' personified (see no. 8, v. 14, note).

(7) *fres.* Nom. sg. of *fren.*

(8) 'I think of no other woman.'

(8) *atén.* Pres. indic. 1 sg. of *atendre* (reflexive).

II

Aqest'° amor mi fer° tan gen°	this; strikes; gently
10 *al cor d'una dolça° sabor°,*	sweet; savor
cen veç° mor° lo jorn° de dolor°	times; I die; each day; grief
e reviu° de cor° altras cen°.	I revive; gladly; another hundred [times]
Tant° es mos mals° de dolç scemblan°	*Tant . . . qe,* so much . . . that; my bad; appearance
qe mais val° mos mal° c'autre bes°,	is worth more; my bad; good
15 *e pois° mon mal aitan bon° m'es,*	since; so good for me
molt val° tal ben° apres l'afan°.	is worth; such good; after my grief

---

(9–11) *tan gen . . . mor.* 'So sweetly . . . [that] I die.'

(9) *Aqest'.* That is, *aqesta,* fem. of *aquest.*

(9) *fer.* Pres. indic. 3 sg. of *ferir.*

(10) *dolça.* Fem. of *dolç* (v. 13).

(11) *veç.* Equivalent to *vetz.*

(11) *mor.* Pres. indic. 1 sg. of *morir.*

(12) *revíu.* Pres. indic. 1 sg. of *revíure.*

(12) *altras cen. Altras,* fem., modifies the implied repetition of *veç* (v. 11).

(14) *val.* Pres. indic. 3 sg. of *valer.*

(14) *mos mal. Mos* is nom. sg., although *mal* is obl. sg.; the phrase is the subject of *val.*

(15) *mon mal.* Obl. sg. for subject of *es.*

(15) *bon.* Masc. obl. sg. modifying *mon mal.*

(16) *ben.* Used as noun in obl. sg.; subject of *val.*

III

Per bona fe° e sens enjan°	in good faith; without deceit
am° la plus bell'°e la meillor°.	I love; the prettiest [woman]; the best
Del cor suspir° e dels oillç plor°	I sigh; I weep
20 *qe trop l'amai°, per q'eu n'ai dan;*	I loved
e qe.n posc° al°, q'amors mi pren°,	what can I [do]; else; captures
e la carcer° on° [i]l° m'a mes	prison; where; it (*amor*)
no pot° claus° obrir° mais merces°,	can; key; open; but mercy
e d'aqella° non tro[p]° nïen°.	of that (*merces,* v. 24); I find; nothing

---

(18) *am.* Pres. indic. 1 sg. of *amar.*

(19) 'From my heart I sigh and from my eyes I weep.'

(19) *suspir.* Pres. indic. 1 sg. of *sospirar.*

(19) *óillç*. Obl. pl. of *ólh*.
(19) *plor*. Pres. indic. 1 sg. of *plorar*.
(20) 'Because I loved her too much, which is why I get grief from it.'
(20) *amái*. Pret. 1 sg. of *amar*.
(21) *posc*. Pres. indic. 1 sg. of *poder*.
(21) *pren*. Pres. indic. 3 sg. of *prendre*.
(22) *cárcer*. Fem. obl. sg., object of *obrir* (v. 23).
(22) *[i]l*. Fem. (refers to *amors*, v. 21).
(23) *pot*. Pres. indic. 3 sg. of *poder*.
(23) *claus*. Masc. nom. sg. of *clau*.
(24) *aqella*. Fem. of *aquel*. Fem. because it refers to fem. *merces* (v. 23).
(24) *tro[p]*. Pres. indic. 1 sg. of *trobar*.

IV

25 Qan eu la ve°, be m'es parven°   I see her; apparent
  als oillç, al vis°, a la color,   in my face
  q'aissamenç trem[ble]° de paor°   I tremble; fear
  con fai° la foilla° contra.l ven°.   does; leaf; wind
  Non ai de sen plus° d'un enfan°,   more wit; child
30 aisi° sui d'amor entrepres°,   so; seized
  e d'ome° q'es aissi conqes°   a man; so conquered
  pot don'°aver almosna° gran.   a lady; pity

(25) 'When I see her, it (my love) is quite apparent in me.'
(25) *ve*. Pres. indic. 1 sg. of *véire*.
(27–28) *aissamenç ... con fai*. 'Just as [the leaf] does.'
(27) *trém[ble]*. Pres. indic. 1 sg. of *tremblar*.
(28) 'As does (trembles) a leaf in the wind.'
(28) *Fai*. Vicarious; represents repetition of *trem[ble]* (v. 27).
(29) 'I don't have more wit than a child.'
(30) *entreprés*. Past part. of *entreprendre*.
(31) *óme*. Masc. obl. sg. Cf. nom. sg. *om*.
(31) *conqés*. Past part. of *conquerer*.
(32) *don'*. That is, *dona*, fem. nom. sg.

V

  Ben volgra° qe fosson° trian°   I would like; they were; recognizable
  entre.ls fals° li fin amador°,   among false [ones]; true lovers
35 e.ill lausenger°, cil trichador°,   gossips; those deceivers
  portesson° corn° e.l fron° denan°.   wore; a horn; on their forehead; in front
  Tot l'aur° del mon° e tut l'argen°   gold; world; silver
  i volgr'aver dat°, s'eu l'agues°,   to have given; if I had had it
  sol qe° ma donna conegues°   if only; knew
40 aissi com eu l'am finamen.

(33) *vólgra*. Past conditional 1 sg. of *voler*.
(33) *fósson*. Past subj. 3 pl. of *éser*.

(33) *trián.* Pres. part. masc. nom. pl. of *triar*, to choose (passive sense).

(33) *fósson*, (36) *portésson*, (38) *agués*, (39) *conogués.* These past subjunctives express wishes unlikely to be fulfilled (*Old Occitan* 267), in contrast to pres. indic. *am* (v. 40) 'I love.'

(34) *fin amadór.* Masc. nom. pl., subject of *fosson* (v. 33).

(35) *e.ill lausengér, cil trichadór.* Masc. nom. pl.; subjects of *portésson* (v. 36).

(38) *dat.* Past part. of *dar*.

(38) *agués.* Past subj. 1 sg. of *aver*.

(39) *conegués.* Past subj. 3 sg. of *conóiser*.

(39–40) 'If only my lady knew how truly I love her.'

VI

Bona domna, plus no.s deman°	ask you no more
mas qe°.m prendaç° per servidor°,	but that; you take; servant
qe.us servirai° com bon segnor°	I will serve you; as a good lord
coman qe° del guiderdon° m'an°.	however; reward; it goes for me
45 *Ve.us mi° al vestre mandamen°,*	here I am; your command
bel cors gentil°, francs° e cortes°;	charming; sincere; courteous
ors° ne lions° non° es vos ges,	bear; lion; *non … ges*, not at all
qe m'auciaç° s'a vos mi ren°.	so that you would kill me; surrender

(41) *demán.* Pres. indic. 1 sg. of *demandar*.

(42) *prendáç.* Form of *prendatz.* Pres. subj. 2 pl. of *prendre*.

(43) *servirái.* Fut. 1 sg. of *servir*.

(43) *com bon segnór.* In the simile, who is the lord? Is she? (Yes.) Is he?

(44) *an.* Pres. subj. 3 sg. of *anar*.

(45) *Ve.us mi.* Fr. *me voici*.

(45) *vestre.* Usually *vostre*.

(46) *gentíl.* Obl., modifying *cors* (masc., invariable), so *bel cors gentil* seems to describe *mi* (the speaker; v. 45). *Francs* is masc. nom. (or vocative) sg., however, and *cortes* is invariable, so *francs e cortes* addresses the lady. But the line seems to describe one person as masc. *cors.* Which one? Both? Emending *gentil* to *gentils* would make the whole line nom., describing the lady.

(47) *es.* Or *etz.* Pres. indic. 2 pl. of *éser*.

(48) *auciáç.* Pres. subj. 2 pl. of *aucire*.

(48) *mi ren.* Pres. indic. 1 sg. of *rendre* (reflexive).

VII

A ma tortre°, lai on° il° es,	°turtledove; where; she
50 *tramet° lo vers°, e [ja] no.il pes*	°I send; song
qar eu no la vei° plus soven°.	°I don't see her; more often

(49) *ma tórtre.* A simple endearment or a *senhal* (secret name).

(50) *tramét.* Pres. indic. 1 sg. of *trametre*.

(50) *ja no.il pes.* 'May it never distress her.'

(50) *pes.* Pres. subj. 3 sg. of *pezar*; subj. expressing a wish.

(51) *véi.* Pres. indic. 1 sg. of *véire*.

Form

Seven *coblas singulars* of eight lines and one *tornada* of three.

SCHEME

a b b a c d d c

RHYMES

	a	b	b	a	c	d	d	c
I	an	or	or	an	en	es	es	en
II	en	or	or	en	an	es	es	an
III	an	or	or	an	en	es	es	an
IV	en	or	or	en	an	es	es	an
V	an	or	or	an	en	es	es	en
VI	en	or	or	en	an	es	es	an
VII	an	or	or	an	en	es	es	en
VIII						es	es	en

Rhymes **b** and **d** are constant. Rhyme **a** alternates between *an* and *en*. Rhyme **c** alternates between *en* and *an*.

METER

8 8 8 8 8 8 8 8

Corrected Readings

(6) *i a[i] mes. G: ia mes.*
(18) *bell'. G: belle e* (OFr. *belle*; cf. Oc. *bella*).
(22) *[i]l. G: el*; cf. *il* (v. 49).
(24) *tro[p]. G: trou.*
(27) *trem[ble] de. G: trem plu de.*
(32) *don'aver. G: dona aver* (+1).
(49–50) G divides the lines: *A ma tortre, lai on il es tramet lo / vers....*
(50) *e [ja] no.il pes. G: e no.il qi.l pes.*

La Comtessa de Dia
Fin joi me don' alegranssa

One manuscript: *D. BEdT* 46.5.
Major editions: Rieger (605–08); Bruckner et al. (12).

The trobairitz called the Comtessa de Dia was apparently a countess of Die (Drôme) in the southern French Alps, but scholars have not identified her with a historical woman. Intertextual relations of her four songs suggest she was a contemporary of Bernart de Ventadorn (active around 1170), Raimbaut d'Aurenga (who died in 1173), and Azalais de Porcairagues, who grieved for Raimbaut (Rieger 614–19). She could, however, have been earlier or later. Bernart de Ventadorn may have been active as early as the 1140s. He came to be treated as a classic, remembered long after he composed.

D, fol. 85v, col. 2.

La Comtessa de Dia

I

Fin joi° me don'° alegranssa°	true joy; gives me; happiness
per qu'° eu chan° plus gaiamen,°	so that; I sing; more merrily
e no m'o teing° a pensanssa°	I don't consider it; a burden
ni a negun° penssamen,°	any; grief
5 *car sai° que son° a mon dan°*	I know; they seek; my harm
[li] fals° lausengier° truan;°	false; gossips; vile
e lor mals diz° non [m]'esglaia,°	evil speech; frighten me
anz° en son° dos tanz° plus gaia.°	rather; I am; two times; merrier

---

(1) *Fin joi.* Obl. sg.; direct object of *don'* (*dona*). Cf. nom. *fins jois.*
(1) *don'.* That is, *dona.* Pres. indic. 3 sg. of *donar;* -*a* (elided) marks pres. indic. 3 sg. of -*ar* verbs.

(1) *alegranssa.* Subject of *don'*.

(2) *chan.* Pres. indic. 1 sg. of *chantar*. No ending for pres. indic. 1 sg. of *-ar* verbs.

(3) *o.* Neuter pron. 'it' (referring to a preceding or following thought). Anticipates *car* (v. 5).

(3) *téing.* Pres. indic. 1 sg. of *tener*. Root *ten-* + yod; *n-* + yod > *nh* (Sp. *ñ*), spelled *-ing*. Yod marks 1 sg. of some pres. indic. non-*ar* verbs.

(3) *pensánssa,* (4) *penssamén.* Derived rhymes, as throughout no. 15.

(5) *sai.* Pres. indic. 1 sg. of *saber*. Root *sa-* + yod, as in *teing* (v. 3).

(5) *son.* Pres. indic. 3 pl. of *éser*. Root *so-* + 3 pl. *-n*. *Éser* + *a*, 'to be occupied with.'

(6) The four words are masc. nom. pl.; *fals* is invariable (*-s* is part of the root).

(7) *mals diz.* Masc. nom. sg. *-s/-z*.

(7) *esgláia.* Pres. indic. 3 sg. *-a* on an *-ar* verb.

(8) *son.* Pres. indic. 1 sg. of *éser*. Classical Lat. *sum* escapes normal conjugation within Oc.

(8) *gáia.* Fem. of *gai*.

II

En mi non° a[n]° ges fianssa°	*non ... ges,* not at all; have; ally
10 *li lausengier maldizen,°*	evil-speaking
c'om non pot° aver° honranssa°	cannot; have; respect
qu'a° ab els° acordamen,°	who has; with them; an agreement
qu'ist° son d'altrestal° semblan°	they; of the same; appearance
com la nivol° que s'espan°	as the cloud; that spreads
15 *qe°.l sole[l]s° en pert° sa raia,°*	until; the sun; loses; its light
per qu'°eu non am° gent° savaia.°	so; I don't like; people; wicked

(9) *a[n].* Pres. indic. 3 pl. of *aver*. Root *a-* + 3 pl. *-n*.

(11) *pot.* Pres. indic. 3 sg. of *poder*. No ending for pres. indic. 3 sg. of non-*ar* verb. Made final, *-d* > *-t*.

(13–14) *altrestal ... com.* 'The same ... as.'

(13) *ist.* Masc. nom. pl.

(14) *espán.* Pres. indic. 3 sg. of *espandre*. No ending for pres. indic. 3 sg. of non-*ar* verbs.

(15) *solé[l]s.* Masc. nom. sg. *-s*.

(15) *pert.* Pres. indic. 3 sg. of *perdre*. No ending, as for *espan* (v. 14). Made final, *-d* > *-t*.

(16) *am.* Pres. indic. 1 sg. of *amar*. No ending for pres. indic. 1 sg.

(16) *saváia.* Fem. of *savai*.

III

E vos,° gelos° malparlan,°	you (pl.); jealous ones; evil-saying
no.s cuges° qu'eu m'[a]n tarçan°	don't think; I wait
que jois e jovenz° no.m plaia°—	youth; to please me
20 *per tal que° dols° vos deschaia!°*	provided that; grief; befall you

(17) *gelós.* Invariable for masc. because the *-s* is part of the stem, not a declensional ending. Here masc. nom. pl. (see next).

(17) *malparlán.* Masc. nom. pl. because there is no ending.

(18) 'Don't think I wait for joy and youth to please me.'

(18) *cugés.* Pres. subj. 2 pl. of *cuidar/cujar*, here imperative. Root *cuj-* + 2 pl. *-étz/és*.

(18) *[a]n*. Pres. subj. 1 sg. of *anar*, 'to go.' No ending for pres. subj. 1 sg. of *ar*-verbs. When used as an auxiliary verb with a pres. part. (here *tarçan*, from *tarzar*, to wait), *anar* loses its primary meaning.

(19) *jovénz*. Masc. nom. sg. *-s* (spelled *-z*).

(19) *no*. Redundant (does not negate) because subordinate to negative *no.s cuges* (v. 18).

(19) *pláia*. Pres. subj. 3 sg. of *plazer*. Root *plai-*; *-a* marks pres. subj. 3 sg. of non-*ar* verbs.

(20) *dols*. Masc. nom. sg. *-s*.

(20) *descháia*. Pres. subj. 3 sg. of *descazer*. Root *descai-*; pres. subj. 3 sg. *-a* for non-*ar* verb.

Grammar Review

Masculine nouns, adjectives, pronouns
>   Nom. sg. *-s/z*: *mals diz* (v. 7), *sole[l]s* (v. 15), *jois* (v. 19), *jovenz* (v. 19), *dols* (v. 20)
>   Obl. sg. –zero: *Fin joi* (v. 1), *altrestal semblan* (v. 13)
>   Nom. pl. -zero: *lausengier truan* (v. 6), *lausengier maldizen* (v. 10), *ist* (v. 13)
>   Obl. pl. *-s*: *els* (v. 12)

Infinitives in *-ar*

PRESENT INDICATIVE
1 sg. -zero: *chan* (v. 2), *am* (v. 16)
3 sg. *-a*: *don'* (*dona*) (v. 1), *esglaia* (v. 7)

PRESENT SUBJUNCTIVE
1 sg. -zero: *[a]n* (v. 18)
2 pl. *-étz/és*: *cuges* (v. 18)

Infinitives in non-*ar*

PRESENT INDICATIVE
1 sg. -yod: *teing* (v. 3), *sai* (v. 5)
3 sg. -zero: *pot* (v. 11), *espan* (v. 14), *pert* (v. 15)
3 pl. *-n*: *son* (v. 5), *a[n]* (v. 9)

PRESENT SUBJUNCTIVE
3 sg. *-a*: *plaia* (v. 19), *deschaia* (v. 20)

Form

Two *coblas unissonans* of eight lines and one *tornada* of four.

SCHEME

a   b   a   b   c   c   d   d

RHYMES

ánsa en ánsa en an an áia áia

METER

7'   7   7'   7   7   7   7'   7'

Corrected Readings

(1) *don'*. D: *dona* (+1).
(6) *[li]*. D: *li* omitted (−1).
(7) *non [m]'esglaia*. D: *non esglaia*.
(9) *non a[n]*. D: *non a*. Here *a*, pres. indic. 3 sg. of *aver*, must agree with nom. pl. *lausengier* (v. 10).
(12) *qu'a ab*. D: *qui ab*.
(15) *sole[l]s*. D: *soles*.
(18) *m'[a]n tarçan*. D: *mon tarçan*.

La Comtessa de Dia

Ab joi e ab joven m'apais

Eight manuscripts: *A, B, D, H, I, K, T, a. BEdT* 46.1.
Major editions: Rieger (585–91); Bruckner et al. (2–5).

D, fol. 85v, col. 1, with reference to A, fols. 167v, col. 2–168v, col. 1.

La Comtessa de Dia

I

Ab joi° e ab joven° m'apais°	with joy; youth; I nourish myself
e jois e jovenz m'apaia,°	please me
car° mos amics° es lo plus gais,°	for; my friend (lover); merriest
per qu'°eu soi° coindet'° e gaia;	which is why; I am; charming
5 *e pois° eu li soi veraia,°*	since; true to him (*li*)
ben taing° q'il° me sea° verais;	it befits; he; be true to me
c'anc° de lui amar° no m'estrais,°	anc ... no, never; loving him; I ceased
ni ai en cor° que.m n'estraia°.	I have in [my] heart; to cease

---

(1) *jovén*. Masc. obl. sg. Cf. *jovénz* (v. 2), with nom. sg. *-s/-z*.

(1) *apáis*. Pres. indic. 1 sg. of *apaisar*. Root *apais*; no ending for pres. indic. 1 sg.

(2) *apáia*. Pres. indic. 3 sg. of *apaiar*. Root *apai* + *-a* for 3 sg. of *-ar* verb. Singular verb matches the nearer of two nouns in the compound subject (nom. sg. *jovenz*).

(3) *amícs*. Nom. sg. *-s*. Cf. obl. sg. *amic*.

(3) *gáis*. Masc. nom. sg. *-s*; cf. fem. nom. sg. *gaia* (v. 4).

(4) *sói*. Pres. indic. of *éser*. Root *so-* + yod for pres. indic. 1 sg. of some non-*ar* verbs.

(6) *táing*. Pres. indic. 3 sg. of *tánher*; *-ing* spells *-nh*.

(6) *il*. Masc. as in Fr.; usually *el* in Oc. as in Sp.

(6) *séa*. Variant of *sia*, pres. subj. 3 sg. from *éser*; *-a* marks pres. subj. 3 sg. in non-*ar* verbs.

(7) *estráis*. Pret. 1 sg. of *estraire* (reflexive); *-s* marks pret. of some non-*ar* verbs.

(8) *estráia*. Pres. subj. 1 sg. of *estraire*; *-a* marks pres. subj. 1 sg. of non-*ar* verbs.

II

Mot° me plaz° car sap que val mais	much; pleases
10 cel qu'eu plus desir° que m'aia,°	I desire; to have me
e cel qu'en primer° lo m'atrais°	as for him who first; attracted him to me
Deu prec° que gran joi l'atraia;°	I pray God; to bring him
e qui que° mal l'en retraia,°	whoever; may tell him
no creza° for cho° que.ill retrais;°	let him not believe; except what; I told him
15 c'om coill° maintas vez° los b[al]ais°	gathers; many times (often); switches
ab q'°el mezeis° se balaia.°	with which; he himself; beats himself

---

(9) *plaz.* Pres. indic. 3 sg. of *plazer.* Root *plaz-;* no ending for pres. indic. 3 sg. of non-*ar* verbs.

(9–10) *sap que val mais / cel.* . . . 'I know that he is worth more whom. . . .'

(9) *sap.* Pres. indic. 1 sg. of *saber;* no ending for 1 sg.; made final, *-b > -p.*

(9) *val.* Pres. indic. 3 sg. of *valer;* no ending for pres. indic. 3 sg. of non-*ar* verbs.

(10) *desír.* Pres. indic. 1 sg. of *dezirar.* No ending for 1 sg. of pres. indic. *-ar* verbs.

(10) *áia.* Pres. subj. 3 sg. of *aver.* Root *ai-;* *-a* for pres. subj. 3 sg. of non-*ar* verbs.

(11) *atráis.* Pret. 3 sg. of *atraire;* *-s* marks pret. of some non-*ar* verbs.

(12) *prec.* Pres. indic. 1 sg. of *pregar.* No ending for 1 sg. of pres. indic. *-ar* verbs. Made final, *-g > -k* (spelled *-c*).

(12) *l'.* Equivalent to *li.*

(12) *atráia.* Pres. subj. 3 sg. of *atraire;* *-a* marks pres. subj. 3 sg. of non-*ar* verbs.

(13) *qui que.* Takes subj.

(13) *retráia.* Pres. subj. 3 sg. of *retraire.*

(14) *créza.* Pres. subj. 3 sg. of *creire,* expressing a wish. Root *crez-* + *-a* for pres. subj. of non-*ar* verb.

(14) *retráis.* Pret. 1 sg. of *retraire;* *-s* marks preterit of some non-*ar* verbs.

(15) *cóill.* Pres. indic. 3 sg. of *cólher;* *-ill* spells *-lh.*

(16) *baláia.* Pres. indic. 3 sg. of *balaiar;* *-a* marks pres. indic. 3 sg. of *-ar* verbs. The proverb warns the lover not to hurt himself by believing nasty gossip.

III

Donna° qu[e] en bon prez° s'enten°	a lady; good reputation; cares about
deu° ben paussar° s'entenden[ss]a°	should; place; her thought
en un [pro]° cavaler° valen°	worthy; knight; valiant
20 pos° [qu'ill]° conois° la valenssa;°	once; she; recognizes; his worth
qe l'aus° amar° a presenssa,°	may she dare; love him; openly
e donna, pois° am'° a presen,°	once; she loves; publicly
ja pois° li pro ni ll'avenen°	ja pois . . . non, never again; attractive
non dira[n]° mais° avenenssa.°	will say; anything but; praise

(17) *entén.* Pres. indic. 3 sg. of *entendre.* No ending.

(18) *déu.* Pres. indic. 3 sg. of *dever.* Root *dev-*; no ending for 3 sg. Made final, *-v* > *-u.*

(20) *conóis.* Pres. indic. 3 sg. of *conóiser.* No ending.

(21) *l'aus.* The pronoun *l'* (him) is the object of *amar* but precedes the independent verb (*aus*).

(21) *áus.* Pres. subj. 3 sg. of *auzar*, introduced by *que*, expresses a wish. No ending in pres. subj. 3 sg. of *-ar* verbs.

(23) *li pro ni ll'avenén.* Masc. nom. pl., hence no ending.

(24) *dirá[n].* Fut. 3 pl. of *dire.* Root *dir-* + fut. *-á* + *-n* for 3 pl.

IV

25 Qu'eu n'ai chausit° un pro e gen°	I have chosen one; noble
per cui° prez meillor'° e genssa,°	by whom; improves; becomes nobler
larc° [e] adrez° e conoissen,°	generous; clever; knowing
on° es sen[s]° e conoissenssa.°	in whom; wit; knowledge
Prec li° que n'aia crezenssa,°	I beg him; to have trust in me
30 ni hom no.l posca° far cre[z]en°	[and that] no one can; make him believe
qu'eu fassa° vas lui° faillimen°—	that I commit; toward him; disloyalty
sol non trop° en lui faillenssa.°	provided that I not find; a failing

(25) *chausít.* Past part. of *cauzir.*

(26) *meillór'.* Equivalent to *melhóra*, pres. indic. 3 sg. of *melhorar*; *-ill-* spells *-lh-*; *-a* marks pres. indic. 3 sg. of *-ar* verbs.

(26) *genssa.* Pres. indic. 3 sg. of *gensar.*

(27) The three glossed words are obl.

(28) *sen[s].* Masc. nom. sg. *-s.* Cf. obl. *sen.*

(29) *Prec.* As in v. 12.

(29) *n'.* Also spelled *en, ne.* Equivalent to *de* + pronoun. Context indicates 'in me.'

(29) *áia.* As in v. 10.

(30) *hom.* Masc. nom. sg. Cf. obl. *óme.*

(30) *posca.* Pres. subj. 3 sg. of *poder.* Root *posc-* + *-a* for pres. subj. 3 sg. of non-*ar* verbs.

(30) *cre[z]én.* Pres. part. of *créire/crezér.*

(31) *fassa.* Pres. subj. 1 sg. of *faire.* Root *faz-*; *-a* for pres. subj. 1 sg. of non-*ar* verbs.

(31) *faillimén.* Equivalent to *falhimen*; *-ill-* spells *-lh-.*

(32) *trop.* Pres. subj. 1 sg. of *trobar*; subj. after *sol.* No ending for pres. subj. 1 sg. of *-ar* verbs. Made final, *-b* > *-p.*

V

Floris, la vostra valenssa°	your worth
sabon° li pro e li valen,	they know
35 per q'°eu vos qer° de mantenen,°	so; I ask of you; urgently
si.os plaz°, vostra mantenenssa.°	if you please; your support

(33) *Florís*. Hero of *Floire et Blanchefleur*, a French romance written circa 1150 by Robert d'Orbigny (edited by Leclanche). Floris and Blanchefleur love one another from their early childhood. Separated by dramatic events, they strive to reunite and finally marry.

(34) *sábon*. Pres. indic. 3 pl. of *saber*. Root *sab-* + *-on* for pres. indic. 3 pl. of non-*ar* verbs.

(35) *qer*. Pres. indic. 1 sg. of *querre*. Root *quer-* + no ending for pres. indic. 1 sg.

Grammar Review

Masculine nouns, adjectives, pronouns
  Nom. sg. *-s/z*: *jois e jovenz* (v. 2), *mos amics* (v. 3)
  Obl. sg. *-zero*: *larc* (v. 27)
  Nom. pl. *-zero*: *pro . . . valen* (v. 34)

Nouns in shifting declension, in which stress or syllabic pattern shifts for case (*Old Occitan* 69 and 213–18)
  Nom. sg. *hom* (v. 30) vs. obl. *óme* (no. 11, v. 18, etc.)

Infinitives in *-ar*

PRESENT INDICATIVE
1 sg. *-zero*: *apais* (v. 1), *desir* (v. 10), *prec* (vv. 12, 29), *trop* (v. 32)
3 sg. *-a*: *apaia* (v. 2), *balaia* (v. 16), *am'* (*ama*) (v. 22)

PRESENT SUBJUNCTIVE
3 sg. *-zero*: *aus* (v. 21)

Infinitives in non-*ar*

PRESENT INDICATIVE
1 sg.
  -zero: *sap* (v. 9), *qer* (v. 35)
  -yod: *soi* (v. 5), *ai* (v. 25)
3 sg. *-zero*: *plaz* (vv. 9, 36), *val* (v. 9), *coill* (v. 15)
3 pl. *-on*: *sabon* (v. 34)

PRESENT SUBJUNCTIVE
1 sg. *-a*: *estraia* (v. 8)
3 sg. *-a*: *sea* (v. 6), *aia* (vv. 10, 29), *posca* (v. 30), *fassa* (v. 31)

PRETERIT (TENSE MARKED IN THESE VERBS BY *-S*)
1 sg. *-s*: *estrais* (v. 7), *retrais* (v. 14)
3 sg. *-s*: *atrais* (v. 11)

FUTURE (TENSE MARKED BY *-Á*)
3 pl. *-án*: *dira[n]* (v. 24)

Form

Four *coblas doblas* of eight lines and one *tornada* of four.

SCHEME

a	b	a	b	b	a	a	b

RHYMES

I–II	ais	aia	ais	aia	aia	ais	ais	aia
III–IV	en	ensa	en	ens	ensa	en	en	ensa
V					ensa	en	en	ensa

METER

8	7'	8	7'	7'	8	8	7'

The rhymes are "derived" (Kay): paired lines have differing rhyme sounds but the same lexical root, as in *gais* and *gaia* (vv. 3–4). Exceptionally, *apais* and *apaia* (vv. 1–2) represent different verbs (*apaisar* 'to nourish'; *apaiar* 'to please'); *mais* and *m'aia* (vv. 9–10), too, are related by sound but not by meaning.

Corrected Readings

(4) *coindet' e.* D, A: *coindeta e* (+1).

(5) *veraia.* So A; D: the final *a* is small, perhaps a correction.

(15) *b[al]ais.* D: *biais* 'faults'; the derived rhyme *balaia* (v. 16) prompts the correction; A: *balais.*

(17) *qu[e] en.* D, A: *quen* (−1).

(17) *s'enten.* So A; D: *s'enten* above the line (correction).

(18) *s'entenden[ss]a.* D: *sor entendencha* (?) (+1); A: *s'entendenssa.*

(19) *un [pro] cavaler.* D: *un cavaler* (−1); A: *un pro cavallier.*

(20) *pos [qu'ill] conois.* D: *pos conois* (−1); A: *pois qu'ill conois.*

(21) *qe l'aus amar.* D: *qels aus amar* 'May she dare love them'; A: *que l'aus amar.*

(22) *am' a.* D, A: *ama a* (+1).

(24) *dira[n].* D: *dirai,* fut. 1 sg., but the subject (v. 23) is plural; A: *dirant.*

(26) *meillor' e.* D, A: *meillora e* (+1).

(27) *larc [e] adrez.* D: *larc adrez* (−1); *larc e adreig* A.

(28) *sen[s].* D: *sen*; A: *sens.*

(30) *cre[z]en.* D: *creien*; A: *crezen.* Derived rhyme with *crezenssa* (v. 29).

(31) *qu'eu.* D: *qu'eu* or *qu'en* (?); A: *q'ieu.*

(32) *trop en.* D: *trop eu en* (+1); A: *trob en.*

Bertran de Born
Belh m'es quan vey camjar lo senhoratge

Two manuscripts: *C, M. BEdT* 80.7.
Major editions: Gouiran (2: 751–64); Paden et al., *Poems of the Troubadour* (294–99).

Bertran de Born was lord of the castle of Autafort ('High-strong'), now Hautefort (Dordogne). His forty-odd poems express zest for change, often to the point of violence. In this song he reflects on age and youth in women, then youth and age in men. The succession from old to young brings renewal.

C, fols. 139v, col. 2–140r, col. 1, with reference to *M*, fol. 228v, cols. 1–2.

Bertran de Born

I

Belh m'es quan vey° camjar° lo senhoratge°,	I see; change hands; lordship
e.l viel[h]° laixan° als joves° lurs maizos°;	old; leave; young; their houses
e quascus° pot giquir° a son linhatge°	each [man]; bequeath; lineage
aitans d'efans que l'us puesc'° esser pros°.	can; worthy
5 *Ladoncs° m'es belh, que.l segle° renovelh°*	then; world; is renewed
mielhs° que per flor° ni per chantar d'auzelh°;	better; flower; bird
e qui dona° ni senhor° pot camjar°,	a lady; a lord; change
vielh per jove ben deu renovelar°.	exchange

(1) *Belh m'es.* 'It is beautiful to me.' The blend of aesthetic, ethical, and social nuances echoes in *m'es belh* (v. 5), *belh* (v. 21), *belh* (v. 24).

(1) *vey.* Pres. indic. 1 sg. of *véire.*

(2) *viél[h]*. Masc. nom. pl. of *velh* with diphthongization (open *e* > *ié*).

(2) *láixan*. Pres. indic. 3 pl. of *laisar*.

(2) *jóves*. Masc. obl. pl. of *jóven*.

(2) *maizós*. Fem. obl. pl. of *maizon*. From 'homes,' 'buildings' to 'households,' 'dynasties.'

(3) *quascús*. Masc. nom. sg. of *cascun*.

(4) *aitans d'efans que l'us*. 'So many children that [at least] one.' Sardonic again in v. 18.

(4) *aitáns*. Masc. obl. pl. of *aitan*.

(4) *efáns*. Masc. obl. pl. of *enfan*.

(4) *puésc'*. That is, *puesca*, pres. subj. 3 sg. of *poder*. Root *posc-* with diphthongization (open *o* > *ué*) + -*a* for pres. subj. 3 sg. of a non-*ar* verb. Subj. of purpose.

(5) *ségle*. Nom. sg. without masc. -*s*. Lat. neuter nouns such as *saeculum* become masc. in Oc. but may lack nom. -*s* (*Old Occitan* 208).

(5) *renovélh*. Pres. subj. 3 sg. of *renovelar*; subj. after *m'es belh*.

(7) *qui*. When lacking an antecedent, *qui* means 'anyone who,' 'if someone.'

(7) *dona ni senhor*. Objects of *camjar*. The words imply relations with a lord (female or male) or a spouse (wife or husband).

(8) 'Should indeed exchange old for young.'

(8) *viélh*. Masc., like the nearer noun in the compound phrase (*senhor*, v. 7). Object of *renovelar*.

II

Vielha la tenc°, dona, pus c'°a pel° [l]aya°, I consider; if; skin; ugly
10 et es vielha quan cavalier° non a; knight (lover)
vielha la tenc si de dos° drutz° s'apaya°, two; lovers; satisfies herself
e es vielha si avols° hom lo[.il] fa°; base; does it to her
vielha la tenc s'ama° dins° son castelh°, she loves; within; her castle
[ez es vieilha qan lh'a ops° de fachell°. she needs; magic
15 Vielha la tenc pos l'enuejon° juglar°,] annoy; joglars
et es vielha que° trop vuelha parlar°. que … vuelha, who wants;
                                            to talk too much

(9) *Viélha*. Fem. of *velh*.

(9) *tenc*. Pres. indic. 1 sg. of *tener*; -*c* for 1 sg.

(9) *[l]aya*. Fem. of *lag*.

(11) *drutz*. Obl. pl. of *drut*.

(11) *apáya*. Pres. indic. 3 sg. of *apagar* (reflexive).

(12) *ávols*. Masc. nom. sg of *ávol*.

(13) *ama*. Pres. indic. 3 sg. of *amar*.

(14) *ops*. 'Needful'; *lh'a ops de* 'it is needful to her,' 'she needs.'

(15) *enuéjon*. Pres. indic. 3 pl. of *enojar*.

(15) *juglar*. Nom. pl.

(16) *vuélha*. Pres. subj. 3 sg. of *voler*; subj. after indefinite *que*.

III

Jov'es dona que sap° honrar° paratge,°	knows how; to respect; nobility
e es joves per bos fagz°, quan los fa°;	deeds; she does
joves se te° quan a adreg° coratge,°	keeps herself; forthright; mind
20 *e vas° bon pretz° avol mestier° non a;*	for; reputation; way of acting
jove se te quan guarda° son cors belh,	she keeps
e es joves dona quan° be.s capdel°;	provided that; she behaves well
jove se te quan no.y cal° devinar°,	she doesn't care; to gossip
qu'°ab belh jovent° se guart de mal estar.	so that; with beautiful youth

(17) *Jóv'*. That is, *jóven*, fem. of *jóven*. The adj. does not change for gender, like Lat. *iuvenis* (third declension).

(17) *sap*. Pres. indic. 3 sg. of *saber*.

(18) *fagz*. Masc. obl. pl. of *fach*.

(18) *fa*. Pres. indic. 3 sg. of *faire*.

(20) 'And she does not have a base way of acting for the sake of good reputation.'

(21) *guárda*. Pres. indic. 3 sg. of *gardar*.

(22) *capdél*. Pres. subj. 3 sg. of *capdelar*; subj. after *quan* 'provided that.'

(23) *cal*. Pres. indic. 3 sg. of *caler* (impersonal) 'to matter'; *no.y cal* 'it doesn't matter to her' (*y*), 'she doesn't care.'

(24) *se guart de mal estar*. 'She keeps from being irritable.'

(24) *guart*. Pres. subj. 3 sg. of *gardar*; subj. after *qu'* (*que*) for purpose. Young lovers felt that gossips (*lausengier*) were hostile.

IV

25 *Joves es hom que lo sieu ben° enguatge°,*	his goods; risks
e es joves quan es ben sofraitos°;	needy
joves se te quan pro°.l costa° ostatge°,	a lot; costs him; hospitality
e es joves quan fa estraguat° dos°.	extravagant; gifts
Joves se te quant art° l'arqu'°e.l vaixelh°	he burns; chest; coffer
30 *e fai estorn° e vouta° e sembelh°;*	combat; tourney; ambush
jove se te quan li plai° domnejar,	pleases him
e es joves quan ben l'aman° juglar°.	love him; joglars

(25) *Jóves*. Masc. nom. sg. of *jóven*.

(25) *enguátge*. Pres. subj. 3 sg. of *engatjar*; subj. after indefinite *hom*.

(27) *costa*. Pres. indic. 3 sg. of *costar*.

(28) *estraguát dos*. Declension on the noun (*dos*, obl. pl.) but not on the modifier (*estraguat*).

(29) *art*. Pres. indic. 3 sg. of *ardre*.

(30) *fai*. Pres. indic. 3 sg. of *faire*; 'he plans.'

(31) *jóve se*. Equivalent to *joves se* (vv. 27, 29).

(31) *plai*. Pres. indic. 3 sg. of *plazer*.

(31) *domnejar*. To pursue ladies (*domnas*).

(32) *áman*. Pres. indic. 3 pl. of *amar*.

(32) *juglar*. Masc. nom. pl.

V

Vielhs es ricx hom° quan re no met° en gatge°,	a rich man; puts nothing; at risk
e li sobra blat[z]° e vis° e bacos°;	wheat; wine; bacon
35 *per vielh lo tenc quan liur'° huous° e fromatge°*	gives; eggs; cheese
a jorn carnal si° e sos companhos°,	to himself; companions
per vielh quan ve[s]t° capa° sobre mantelh°	he wears; cape; cloak
e vielh si a caval° qu'om sieu apelh°,	a horse; calls
per vielh quan [vol un jor en paz° estar]	peace
40 *e vielh si pot guandir° ses baratar°.*	escape; bargaining

(33) *viélhs.* Masc. nom. sg. of *velh* 'old.'

(33) *re no.* 'Nothing.'

(33) *met.* Pres. indic. 3 sg. of *metre.*

(34) *sóbra.* Pres. indic. 3 sg. of *sobrar,* 'to abound'; *li sobra* 'he has . . . to spare.'

(34) *blat[z], vis, bacós.* Masc. nom. sg. -*s/z.*

(35) *líur'.* That is, *líura,* pres. indic. 3 sg. of *liurar* (like Eng. 'deliver').

(35) *huóus.* Masc. obl. pl. of *óu,* with orthographic *h-*; *ó > uó.*

(36) *a jorn carnál.* That is, on a day when meat is permitted.

(36) *companhós.* Obl. pl. of *companhón.*

(37) *ve[s]t.* Pres. indic. 3 sg. of *vestir.* He dresses warmly.

(38) *apélh.* Pres. subj. 3 sg. of *apelar*; subj. after hypothetical *caval*: 'If he has a horse that people call his own.' The poet dislikes the security of wealth.

(40) 'And old if he can escape without bargaining' over a ransom, because he has the means to pay whatever is asked. Knights captured in a tournament were customarily held for ransom, as Richard Lionheart was on his return from the Third Crusade (see no. 21).

VI

Mon sirventesc° port'° e vielh e novelh°,	satire; carry; new
Arnaut juglar, a Richart, que.l capdelh°;	to guide him
e ja° thezaur° vielh no vuelh' amassar°,	*ja . . . no,* never; treasure; pile up
44 *qu'ab° thezaur jove pot pretz°*	with; merit; win
guazanhar°.	

(41) *sirventésc. Sirventes* with variant suffix.

(41) *port'.* That is, *porta,* imperative 2 sg. of *portar.*

(42) *Arnaut juglar.* Arnaut Daniel, troubadour and *joglar,* born in Ribérac (Dordogne), eighty kilometers west of Hautefort; author of nos. 18 and 19.

(42) *Richart.* Richard Lionheart, count of Poitou, duke of Aquitaine, king of England; author of no. 21.

(42) *capdélh.* Pres. subj. 3 sg. of *capdelar*; subj. of purpose.

(43) *vuélh'.* That is, *vuélha,* pres. subj. 3 sg. of *voler,* expressing a wish.

Form

Five *coblas unissonans* of eight lines and one *tornada* of four.

SCHEME

| a | b | a | b | c | c | d | d |

RHYMES

I	atge	os	atge	os	elh	elh	ar	ar
II	aya	a	aya	a	elh	elh	ar	ar
III	atge	a	atge	a	elh	el	ar	ar
IV	atge	os	atge	os	elh	elh	ar	ar
V	atge	os	atge	os	elh	elh	ar	ar
VI					elh	elh	ar	ar

METER

| 10' | 10 | 10' | 10 | 10 | 10 | 10 | 10 |

Corrected Readings

(2) *e.l viel[h].* C: *e.ls viels* (obl. for nom.); M: *e.l vieilh.*

(9) *pus c'a pel [l]aya.* C: *pus ca pel / aya*; M: *ma capell / aia.*

(12) *lo[.il].* C: *lo*; M: *lo.il.*

(13) *s'ama.* C: *si ama* (+1); M: *mas am.*

(14–15) Missing in C; supplied from M, fol. 228v, cols. 1–2.

(14) *qan lh'a ops.* M: *mal hi ops.*

(28) *estraguat.* So C; M: *estragatz.*

(29) *arqu'e.l vaixelh.* C: *arqæl vaixelh*; M: *archa ni son vaissell.*

(34) *blat[z].* C: *blat*; M: *blatz.*

(35) *quan liur' huous.* C: *quan liura huous* (+1); M: *pos liures.*

(37) *ve[s]t.* C: *vieit*; M: *vest.*

(39) *[vol un jor en paz estar].* C: *no.l plai domneyar* (−2; cf. v. 31); M: *vol un jor en paz estar.*

Bertran de Born

Miez sirventes vueilh far dels reis amdos

One manuscript: *M. BEdT* 80.25.
Major editions: Gouiran (2: 649–55); Paden et al., *Poems of the Troubadour* (396–401).

In June 1190 Richard Lionheart conferred Gascony upon Berengaria of Navarre as a betrothal gift. He defied his engagement to marry Alice, the sister of Philippe Auguste of France, and neglected the fact that his father, Henry II, had given Gascony to Eleanor, his daughter and Richard's sister, when she married Alfonso VIII of Castile. Richard had confirmed that gift. Now he gave Gascony to his fiancée.

The resulting strain in relations between Richard and Alfonso led Bertran de Born to hope that war was imminent. For him armed conflict, the preoccupation of aristocratic men, was a crucible of meaning. His exhortations to violence would be condemned by Dante (*Inferno* 28.118–42). The battle that Bertran eagerly imagined in this poem did not come to pass.

M, fol. 233r.

Senher Bertran del Bord
Sénher. Nom. sg. of *senhór* 'lord.'
Bord. Variant spelling of the place-name Born.

I

Miez° sirventes° vueilh far dels reis amdos°,	half; a satire; both kings
q'en brieu° veirem° q'aura mais cavailhiers°	soon; we'll see; more knights
del valen° rei de Castella, n'Anfos,	valiant

c'aug dir qe ven° e volra° sodadiers°;	comes; will want; mercenaries
5 *Richarz metra° a mueis° e a sestiers°*	will spend; hogsheads; bushels
aur° e argen°, e ten° s'a benanansa°	gold; silver; he thinks it; happiness
metr'° e donar°, e non vol sa	to spend; give; treaty
fianza°—	
anz° vol gerra° mais qe qaill'	rather; war
esparviers!	

(1) *Miéz sirventés*. Many *sirventes* have twice as many stanzas as this one.

(1) *vuéilh*. Pres. indic. 1 sg. of *voler*.

(2) *veirém*. Fut. 1 pl. of *véire*.

(2) *aurá*. Fut. 3 sg. of *aver* (impersonal) 'there will be' (Fr. *il y aura*).

(3) *Anfos*. Oc. *Anfos* = Sp. *Alfonso*.

(4) *aug dir*. 'I hear tell.'

(4) *áug*. Pronounced like Eng. *ouch!* Pres. indic. 1 sg. of *auzir*.

(4) *ven*. Pres. indic. 3 sg. of *venir*.

(4) *volrá*. Fut. 3 sg. of *voler*.

(5–6) 'Richard will spend gold and silver by hogsheads and bushels.'

(5) *metrá*. Fut. 3 sg. of *metre*.

(5) *muéis*. Obl. pl. of *muéi* 'a hogshead,' originally 'a wagonload.'

(6) *ten*. Pres. indic. 3 sg. of *tener*.

(7) *non vol*. '[Richard] doesn't want [Alfonso's] treaty.'

(7) *vol*. Pres. indic. 3 sg. of *voler*.

(8) 'More than a sparrowhawk [wants] quail.' Cf. no. 2, v. 1.

(8) *esparviérs*. Masc. nom. sg.

II

S'amdui° li rei son prou° ni corajos°	both; valiant; courageous
10 *en brieu veirem camps° joncatz° de*	fields; strewn; pieces
qartiers°	
d'elms° e d'escutz° e de branz° e d'arços°	helmets; shields; swords; saddlebows
e de fendutz° per bustz° tro als braiers°,	[men] split; torsos; to breeches
es arage° veirem anar° destriers°,	aimlessly; walking; warhorses
e per costatz° e per peichz° mainta lanza°,	through ribs; chests; many a lance
15 *e gaug° e plor° e dol° e alegrança°.*	joy; weeping; grief; rejoicing
Le perdr'° er granz° e.l gasainhz° er sobriers°.	loss; great; gain; greater

(9) *amdúi*. Masc. nom. pl.; cf. obl. pl. *amdos* (v. 1).

(10) *joncátz*. Past part. masc. obl. pl. of *jonchar* 'to strew' (as with *jonc* 'reeds').

(10) *qartiérs*. Masc. obl. pl. of *cartier* 'quarter.'

(12) *fendútz*. Past part. masc. obl. pl. of *fendre*.

(16) *perdr'*. That is, *perdre*, infinitive used as noun without nom. sg. *-s*.

(16) *perdr', granz, gasainhz, sobriers*. Masc. nom. sg.

III

Trompas°, tabors°, seinheras° e	trumpets; drums; banners;
penos°	pennons
e entreseinhs° e cavals° blancs e niers°	flags; horses; white and black
ve[i]rem en brieu, qe.l segles° sera bos°,	for the world; good
20 *qes° hom tolra° l'aver° als usuriers°,*	for; will take; wealth; usurers
e per camis° non anara° saumiers°	by roads; will never go;
	a packhorse
jorn afiçatz° ni borjes° ses duptansa°,	in safety; or a townsman; without
	fear
ni mercadiers° qi venga° dever°	or a merchant; comes; from
França;	
anz sera rics qi tolra volentiers.	

(19) *será.* Fut. 3 sg. of *éser.*

(20–24) Bertran threatens to violate the custom of the safe-conduct, by which nobles provided protection to traveling merchants for a fee.

(20) *qes.* Form of *que* before a vowel.

(20) *tolrá.* Fut. 3 sg. of *tolre.*

(21–22) *non ... jorn.* 'Not a day,' 'never.'

(21) *camis.* Masc. obl. pl. of *camin.*

(21) *anará.* Fut. 3 sg. of *anar.*

(21) *saumiers.* Masc. nom. sg. of *saumier.*

(22) *afiçatz.* Past part. masc. nom. sg. of *afizar* 'to provide with security.'

(23) *mercadiers.* Masc. nom. sg.

(23) *venga.* Pres. subj. 3 sg. of *venir*; subj. after indefinite antecedent.

(23) *França.* The kingdom ruled from Paris, not Aquitaine.

(24) 'Rather he will be rich who takes gladly.'

(24) *rics.* Masc. nom. sg. of *ric.*

IV

25 *Mas se.l reis° ven, ieu ai en Dieu fiansa°*	the king (Alfonso); faith
q'ieu sera[i]° vius° o serai per qartiers°;	I will be; alive; or in pieces
e si sui vius, er° mi gran benanansa°,	it will be; great happiness for me
e se ieu mueir°, er mi grans deliuriers°.	I die; deliverance

(25) *réis.* Alfonso, as in v. 4 (*ven*). Richard is in Aquitaine already.

(26) *será[i].* Fut. 1 sg. of *éser.*

(26) *víus.* Masc. nom. sg. of *víu.*

(27) *er.* Fut. 3 sg. of *éser.*

(27) *gran benanansa.* Declension on the noun, not the adj. (normal *grans*).

(28) *muéir.* Pres. indic. 1 sg. of *morir.*

(28) *deliuriérs.* Nom. sg. of *deliurier.*

Form

Three *coblas unissonans* of eight lines with one *tornada* of four.

SCHEME

a	b	a	b	b	c	c	b

RHYMES

ó(n)s   iers   ó(n)s   iers   iers   ansa   ansa   iers

METER

10   10   10   10   10   10′   10′   10

TORNADA

		c	b	c	b
		ansa	iers	ansa	iers
		10′	10	10′	10

M sets the last four lines as one *tornada*. Major editors have set two *tornadas* of two lines apiece, since most *tornadas* repeat the last rhymes from the preceding stanza, here *-ansa, -iers* (twice). This pattern was not always observed, however. This edition respects the format of the only manuscript.

A caesura falls after the fourth syllable in every line, as in the Oxford *Song of Roland*, which begins: "Carles li reis, / nostre emperere magnes . . ." (Segre 93). The meter carries warlike overtones.

Corrected Readings

(8) *qaill' esparviers*. M: *qaillæ / sparviers*.
(19) *ve[i]rem*. M: *verrem*.
(26) *sera[i] vius*. M: *sera vius*.
(27) *vius, er mi*. M: *vius o serai er mi* (*o* expunctuated).

Arnaut Daniel
En cest sonet coind' e leri

Fourteen manuscripts: *A, B, C, D, H, I, K, N, N²*, *R, Sg, U, V, a. BEdT* 29.10.
Major editions: Toja (271–83); Wilhelm (40–43 and 99–100); Eusebi (66–73); Riquer, *Arnaut Daniel* (141–47); Perugi (139–58).

Arnaut Daniel says he attended the coronation of Philip I of France (*BEdT* 29.8, vv. 57–58; Toja 302), which occurred at Reims in 1180. He sent a song to Anfos (Alfonso) II of Aragon (*BEdT* 29.13, v. 100; Toja 258). He remained active until about 1195. According to his *vida*, he was from the castle of Ribérac (Dordogne), a *gentils hom* (a 'wellborn man') who studied letters (Latin) but gave them up to become a *joglar* (*BT* 59), as Bertran de Born called him (no. 16, v. 42 note on *Arnaut juglar*). His poems represent the pinnacle of *trobar clus*, the art of 'closed composition.'

For Dante's encounter with the shade of Arnaut Daniel in *Purgatorio*, which refers to this poem, see no. 28. Petrarch echoed the *tornada* (see below vv. 43–44 note).

A, fols. 41r, col. 2–41v, col. 1.

Arnautz Daniels

En cest sonet° coind'° e leri°	little song; pleasant; *léri*, joyful
fauc° motz° e capuig° e doli°,	I make; words; I trim; plane [them]
que serant° verai° e cert°	they will be; true; plumb
qan n'aurai° passat° la lima°;	I will have; applied; [carpenter's] file
5 *qu'amors m'a de plan°, e daura°*	*de plan*, certainly; it gilds
mon chantar, qe de liei° mou°	from her; begins
qe° pretz manten° e governa°.	who; maintains; governs

---

(1) *coind'*. Equivalent to *cóinde*.

(2) *fáuc.* Pres. indic. 1 sg. of *faire.*

(2) *capúig.* The *-ig* spells Eng. *-tch*; pres. indic. 1 sg. of *capuzar.*

(2) *dóli.* Pres. indic. 1 sg. of *dolar.*

(3) *seránt.* Fut. 3 pl. of *éser.*

(3) *verái e cert.* Masc. nom. pl.

(4) *aurái.* Fut. 1 sg. of *aver.*

(4) *passát.* Past part. of *pasar.*

(5) 'For love certainly holds me.'

(5) *dáura.* Pres. indic. 3 sg. of *daurar.*

(6) *móu.* Pres. indic. 3 sg. of *movér.*

(7) *mantén.* Pres. indic. 3 sg. of *mantener.*

(7) *govérna.* Pres. indic. 3 sg. of *governar.*

II

Mil messas° n'aug° e'n proferi°	a thousand Masses; I hear; offer
e n'art° lum° de cera° e d'oli°,	I burn; a candle; wax; oil
10 *qe Dieus m'en don° bon issert°*	[praying] that God will give; result
de lieis on no.m val escrima;	
e qand remir° sa crin° saura°	I see; hair; blond
e.l cors° q'a graile° e nou°,	her body; slender; young
mais l'am qe qi°.m des° Luserna.	[someone] who; gave me

(8) *áug.* The *-g* spells Eng. *-tch*; pres. indic. 1 sg. of *auzir.*

(8) *proféri.* Pres. indic. 1 sg. of *proferre.*

(9) *art.* Pres. indic. 1 sg. of *ardre.*

(10) *don.* Pres. subj. 3 sg. of *donar.*

(11) 'From her with whom parrying (fencing) doesn't help me.'

(12) *remir.* Pres. indic. 1 sg. of *remirar.*

(13) 'And her body, that is' (literally, 'the body that she has') 'slender and young.'

(13) *graile e.* Without elision. The line counts seven syllables.

(14) *am.* Pres. indic. 1 sg. of *amar.*

(14) *des.* Past subj. 3 sg. of *dar.*

(14) *Luserna.* Legendary Spanish city in epic poems.

III

15 *Tant l'am de cor° e la queri°*	so sincerely; seek
c'ab trop voler cuig la.m toli,	
s'om ren° per ben amar pert°.	anything; loses
Lo sieus cors° sobretracima°	her body (heart; self); soars above mine
lo mieu tot, e non s'isaura°;	[mine] does not catch a breeze
20 *tant ai de ver° fait renou°*	in truth; interest
c'obrador° n'ai e taverna°.	workman; tavern

(15) *quéri.* Pres. indic. 1 sg. of *querre.*

(16) 'That by wanting [her] too much, I fear I take her from myself.'

(16) *cúig.* Pres. indic. 1 sg. of *cujar.*

(16) *tóli.* Pres. indic. 1 sg. of *tolre.*

(17) 'If one loses anything by loving [it] well.'

(17) *pert.* Pres. indic. 3 sg. of *perdre.*

(18–19) She outdoes him as a better hawk surpasses an inferior one (Riquer, *Arnaut Daniel* 144; Perugi 145 and 153).

(18) *sobretracíma.* Pres. indic. 3 sg. of *sobretracimar = sobre- + trans-/tras- + cima* 'summit' + *-ar*; cf. *encimar* 'to raise.'

(19) *isáura.* Pres. indic. 3 sg. of *eisaurar* (reflexive) = *ex-/eis- + aura* 'breeze' + *-ar.*

(20–21) 'I have in truth made so much interest that I have a workman and a tavern.' Her love has made him prosper in unexpected ways.

IV

Tot jorn° meillur° e esmeri°	all day; I improve; become pure
car la gensor° serv° e coli°	the noblest [lady]; I serve; adore
del mon°, so.us dic° en apert°.	in the world; I tell you; openly
25 *Sieus sui° del pe° tro en cima°,*	I am hers; from my foot; to [my] top
e si tot° venta°.ill freid'[a]ura°,	si tot, although; blows; the cold wind
l'amors q'inz° del cor me mou	inz de, within
mi ten° chaut° on plus iverna°.	keeps me; warm; when most it is wintry

(22) *meillúr.* Pres. indic. 1 sg. of *melhurar.*

(22) *esméri.* Pres. indic. 1 sg. of *esmerar.*

(23) *serv.* Pres. indic. 1 sg. of *servir.*

(23) *cóli.* Pres. indic. 1 sg. of *colre.*

(24) *dic.* Pres. indic. 1 sg. of *dire.*

(25) *súi.* Pres. indic. 1 sg. of *éser.*

(26) *vénta.* Pres. indic. 3 sg. of *ventar.*

(26) *fréid'.* That is, *freida.* Fem. of *freg/freit.*

(27) 'The love that moves within my heart.'

(27) *móu.* Pres. indic. 3 sg. of *mover.*

(28) *ten.* Pres. indic. 3 sg. of *tener.*

(28) *ivérna.* Pres. indic. 3 sg. of *ivernar.*

V

Ges° pel maltraich° q'ieu soferi°	Ges … no, not at all; pain; suffer
30 *de ben amar no.m destoli°*	do I take myself from
liei°; anz dic en descobert°	her; openly
car° si°.m fatz° los motz en rima°,	that; even though; I make; in rhyme
pieitz° trac° aman° c'om que laura°,	worse; I bear; in loving; labors
c'anc plus non amet° un ou°	never loved more; [by] an egg (the least bit)
35 *cel de Moncli n'Audierna*	

(29) *pel.* Equivalent to *per lo.*

(29) *soféri.* Pres. indic. 1 sg. of *soferre.*

(30) *destóli.* Pres. indic. 1 sg. of *destólre.*

(31) *liéi*. Object of *amar* (v. 30).

(32) *fatz*. Pres. indic. 1 sg. of *faire*.

(33) *trac*. Pres. indic. 1 sg. of *traire*.

(33) *amán*. Pres. part. of *amar*.

(33) *láura*. Pres. indic. 3 sg. of *laurar*.

(34) *amét*. Pret. 3 sg. of *amar*.

(34) *un ou*. By a trivial amount.

(35) *Cel de Moncli*. 'The man from Moncli' and his lady Audierna must have been protagonists in a lost romance.

(35) *cel*. Masc. nom. sg.

(35) *n'*. That is, *na*. Reduced form of *domna* 'lady'; title introducing a woman's name.

VI

Non vuoill° de Roma l'emperi°	I don't want; empire
ni c'om mi fassa° apostoli°,	make me; pope
q'en lieis non aia° revert°	if in her I would not have; shelter
per cui m'art lo cors e.m rima;	
40 *e si.l maltraich no.m restaura°*	she does not reward
ab un baisar° anz° d'annou°,	with a kiss; *anz de*, before; New Year's
mi auci° e si enferna°.	she kills me; sends herself to hell

(36) *vuóill*. Pres. indic. 1 sg. of *voler*.

(36–37) The Roman Empire and the papacy were both vacant in 1191. Arnaut may have composed the song in that year.

(37) *fássa*. Pres. subj. 3 sg. of *faire*.

(38) *áia*. Pres. subj. 1 sg. of *aver*.

(39) 'For whom my body (heart; self) burns (*art*) and cracks (*rima*).'

(39) *art*. Pres. indic. 3 sg. of *ardre*.

(39) *ríma*. Pres. indic. 3 sg. of *rimar*.

(40) *restáura*. Pres. indic. 3 sg. of *restaurar*.

(42) *aucí*. Pres. indic. 3 sg. of *aucire*.

(42) *enférna*. Pres. indic. 3 sg. of *enfernar* (reflexive).

VII

Ieu sui Arnautz, q'amas° l'aura°	who amass; the breeze
e chatz° la lebre° ab lo bou°	hunt; hare; with the ox
45 *e nadi° contra° suberna°.*	swim; against; the tide

(43) *amas*. Pres. indic. 1 sg. of *amasar*.

(43–44) Cf. Petrarch's *Canzoniere* 239, v. 36: "Et col bue zoppo andrem cacciando l'aura" 'And with the lame ox we shall go hunting the wind,' punning on *l'aura* and *Laura* (Durling 403; my trans.).

(43–45) The rhetorical figure called *adynaton* extends exaggeration to impossibility (Perugi 157–58).

(44) *chatz*. Pres. indic. 1 sg. of *casar*.

(45) *nadi*. Pres. indic. 1 sg. of *nadar*.

Form

Six *coblas unissonans* of seven lines and one *tornada* of three. Each line in the stanza has a different rhyme; the rhymes repeat only from one stanza to another.

SCHEME

a	b	c	d	e	f	g

RHYMES

éri	óli	ert	íma	áura	ou	érna

METER

I–VI	7′	7′	7	7′	7′	7	7′
VII				7′	7	7′	

Corrected Readings

(26) *freid'[a]ura.* A: *freidura* (violates rhyme).
(41) *baisar.* A: *baissar* 'to lower'; as noun, 'a lowering.'

Arnaut Daniel
Lo ferm voler q'el cor m'intra

Twenty manuscripts: *A, B, C, D, E, G, H, I, K, M, N²*, *Q, R, S, Sg, U, V* (anonymous), *VeAg, a, c.* BEdT 29.14.
Major editions: Toja (373–85); Wilhelm (2–5 and 84–85); Eusebi (128–36); Riquer, *Arnaut Daniel* (91–97); Perugi (329–52).

With this poem Arnaut Daniel invented the sestina, which Ezra Pound called "a form like a thin sheet of flame, folding and infolding upon itself" (*Spirit* 27). Arnaut chose rhyme words that fill the mouth with consonants. Each rhyme occurs only once in the stanza (as in no. 18). The rhymes fold and infold in an intricate pattern:

The sixth (and last) rhyme in stanza I becomes the first in stanza II.
The first rhyme in I becomes the second in II.
The fifth rhyme in I becomes the third in II.
The second rhyme in I becomes the fourth in II.
The fourth rhyme in I becomes the fifth in II.

The pattern repeats until each word has appeared in every position, and the dance is done. The *tornada* repeats them all, one in the next to last position of the line and another at the end.

After Arnaut, other troubadours cultivated the sestina. Dante and Petrarch transferred the form to Italian, followed by later poets in Italy, France, Portugal, and England. The sestina lost favor among the Romantics but was revived in the twentieth century by Pound ("Sestina: Altaforte"), W. H. Auden ("Paysage Moralisé"), Elizabeth Bishop ("Sestina"), John Ashbery ("Farm Implements and Rutabagas in a Landscape"), and Raych Jackson ("A Sestina for a Black Girl Who Does Not Know How to Braid Hair").[iii]

---

iii. For discussions of the sestina form, see Chambers (121–23); Preminger et al.

A, fol. 39v, cols. 1–2, with reference to *a*, p. 106.

Arnautz Daniels

I

Lo ferm° voler° q'el cor m'intra°   constant; wish; enters
no.m pot becs° jes esco[ise]ndre° ni ongla°   beak; scratch out; or nail
de lausengier qui pert° per mal dir° s'arma°,   loses; speaking evil; his soul
e car no l'aus batr'am ram ni ab verga,
5 sivals a frau, lai on non aurai oncle,
jauzirai joi en vergier° o dinz cambra°.   orchard; bedroom

(1–3) 'A beak or fingernail of a gossip cannot scratch out the constant wish that enters my heart.' The poet's love is impervious to hostile rumors.
(1) *intra*. Pres. indic. 3 sg. of *intrar*.
(3) *pert*. Pres. indic. 3 sg. of *perdre*.
(4–6) 'And since I don't dare to beat him with a branch (*ram*) or stick (*verga*), at least by stealth, where I will have no uncle' (no rival), 'I will enjoy joy.'
(4) *aus*. Pres. indic. 1 sg. of *auzar*.
(4) *am . . . ab*. 'With . . . with.'
(5) *aurái*. Fut. 1 sg. of *aver*.
(6) *jauzirái*. Fut. 1 sg. of *jauzir*.

II

Can mi soven° de la cambra   I remember
o a mon dan° sai que nuils hom° non intra,   where to my harm; no man
anz me son tuich° plus que fraire° ni oncle,   all [men]; brothers
10 non ai membre° no.m fremisca° ni ongla   limb; tremble
aissi cum fai° l'enfas° denant° la verga,   does; child; before
tal paor° ai que.il sia trop de l'arma.   fear

(7) *soven*. Pres. indic. 3 sg. of *sovenir* (impersonal).
(8) *núils hom non*. Masc. nom. sg. No man (including himself) enters his lady's bedroom.
(9) 'Rather they all are more than brothers or uncles to me.' They are just like him.
(9) *túich*. Masc. nom. pl. of *tot*.
(10) *fremísca*. Pres. subj. 3 sg. of *fremir*; subj. after negative antecedent.
(11) *fai*. Pres. indic. 3 sg. of *faire*; vicarious verb representing repetition of *fremisca*.
(11) *énfas*. Masc. nom. sg. of *enfán*. Shifting declension.
(12) 'I have such fear that I will be too much for her with my soul': that my desire will drive her away. Cf. *arma* in v. 13.
(12) *ai*. Pres. indic. 1 sg. of *aver*.

III

Del cors li fos°, non de l'arma,   [I wish] I were
mas cossentis° m'a celat° dinz sa cambra,   she had consented; secretly
15 que plus mi nafra°.l cor que colps° de verga   wounds; blow

car lo sieus sers° lai on ill° es non intra; her servant; she
totz temps° serai ab lieis° cum carns e ongla, always; with her
e non creirai° chastic° d'amic° ni d'oncle. obey; rebuke; friend

---

(13) 'I wish I were hers in body, not in soul.'
(13) *fos*. Past subj. 1 sg. of *éser* expressing an unlikely wish.
(14) *cossentís*. Past subj. 3 sg. of *consentir*.
(15) *nafra*. Pres. indic. 3 sg. of *nafrar*.
(15) *colps*. Masc. nom. sg.
(15–16) 'For it wounds my heart more than a blow with a stick that her servant' (himself)
    'does not enter where she is.'
(16) *lo siéus sers*. Masc. nom. sg.
(17) *serái*. Fut. 1 sg. of *éser*.
(17) *cum carns e ongla*. 'Like flesh and nail': as close as a finger and its fingernail.
(18) *creirái*. Fut. 1 sg. of *créire*.

IV

    Anc° la seror° de mon oncle anc ... non, never; sister
20 *non amei° tant ni plus per aqest'arma°,* I loved; by this (my) soul
c'aitant vezis° cum es lo detz° de l'ongla as close; finger
s'a leis plagues°, volgr'°esser de sa cambra: if it pleased her; I'd like
de mi pot far l'amors q'inz el cor m'intra
mieills a son vol c'om fortz de frevol verga.

---

(19) *serór*. Fem. obl. sg. His aunt or mother; a female relative.
(20) *améi*. Pret. 1 sg. of *amar*.
(21) *vezís*. Masc. nom. sg., modifying *detz*.
(21) *detz*. Masc. nom. sg.
(22) *plagués*. Past subj. 3 sg. of *plazer*.
(22) *volgr'*. That is, *volgra*, past conditional 1 sg. of *voler*.
(23–24) 'The love that enters my heart can do with me more as it wishes than a strong man
    with a weak stick.' My love overwhelms me.

V

25   *Pois flori° la seca° verga* flowered; dry
ni d'en° Adam mogron° nebot° ni oncle, sir; descended; nephews
tant fin'amors° cum cella q'el cor m'intra so true a love
non cuig° q'anc fos° en cors ni es en arma; I don't think; ever was
[on q'eu estei,] fors° en plaz'°o dinz chambra, outside; plaza
30 *mos cors no.is part de lieis tant cum ten° l'ongla.* as the fingernail fills

---

(25–28) His love is the truest since Christ (v. 25) and Adam (v. 26).
(25) 'Since the dry stick flowered.' The 'dry stick' (*sicca virga* in Lat. hymns) that blossomed is
    a symbol of the Virgin.
(25) *florí*. Pret. 3 sg. of *florir*.
(26) *mógron*. Pret. 3 pl. of *mover*.
(26) *nebot ni oncle*. Masc. nom. pl. Male relatives.

(27) *fin'amors.* The expression has been used to describe troubadour love in general, but they call it simply *amor* more often.

(27) *cella q'el cor m'intra.* 'The one (love) that enters my heart.' *Cella* is fem., like *amors.*

(28) *cúig.* Pres. indic. 1 sg. of *cujar.*

(28) 'I don't think ever was in a body or is in a soul.'

(28) *fos.* Past subj. 3 sg. of *éser.*

(29) *on q'eu estei.* 'Wherever I may be.'

(29) *estéi.* Pres. subj. 1 sg. of *estar.*

(29) *en plaza.* Suggests visual perception of a town square, unusual in troubadour poetry.

(30) 'My heart does not part from her.'

(30) *part.* Pres. indic. 3 sg. of *partir* (reflexive).

(30) *ten.* Pres. indic. 3 sg. of *tener.*

VI

C'aissi s'enpren° e s'enongla°	takes root; digs in
mos cors el sieu cum l'escorss'en la verga,	
q'ill° m'es de joi tors° e palaitz° e chambra;	she; tower; palace
e non am° tant fraire, paren°, ni oncle,	I love; relative
35 *q'en paradis n'aura° doble° joi m'arma*	will have; double
si ja° nuills hom° per ben amar [lai intra].	ever; any man

(31) *aissi ... cum.* 'Just like.' The initial *C'* (*que*) serves as a weak link ('for') to the preceding stanza; it may be ignored in translation.

(31) *enpren.* Pres. indic. 3 sg. of *emprendre* (reflexive).

(31) *enongla.* Pres. indic. 3 sg. of *enonglar* (reflexive), to dig in by the fingernails.

(32) 'My body (heart; self) in hers, just like bark on a branch.'

(34) *am.* Pres. indic. 1 sg. of *amar.*

(35) *paradís.* Dante put Arnaut's soul in *Purgatorio* (see no. 28), not *Paradiso,* as this line suggests.

(35) *aurá.* Fut. 3 sg. of *aver.*

(36) *núills hom.* Masc. nom. sg.

VII

Arnautz tramet° sa chansson d'oncle e d'ongla	sends
a grat° de lieis que de sa verg'a l'arma,	with consent
39 *son desirar, cui pretz en chambra intra*	

(37) *Arnautz.* Masc. nom. sg.

(37) *tramet.* Pres. indic. 3 sg. of *trametre.*

(38) *a.* Equivalent to *ab* 'with.'

(38) *grat.* Cf. *cossentis* (v. 14).

(38) 'Of her (*liéis*) who has the soul of his stick (branch; rod).'

(39) 'To [the object of] his desire, whom merit in chamber enters.'

(39) *desirar.* Verb ('to desire'), used here as a noun. Other MSS read *son desirat,* 'his desired one,' which MS *H* (fol. 12r margin) glosses as a reference to Arnaut's friend Bertran de Born (cf. no. 16, v. 42 note on *Arnaut juglar*).

Form

Six *coblas singulars* of six lines and one *tornada* of three. All the rhymes are words.

SCHEME

	a	b	c	d	e	f

RHYMES

	a	b	c	d	e	f
I	*intra*	*ongla*	*arma*	*verga*	*oncle*	*cambra*
II	*cambra*	*intra*	*oncle*	*ongla*	*verga*	*arma*
III	*arma*	*cambra*	*verga*	*intra*	*ongla*	*oncle*
IV	*oncle*	*arma*	*ongla*	*cambra*	*intra*	*verga*
V	*verga*	*oncle*	*intra*	*arma*	*chambra*	*ongla*
VI	*ongla*	*verga*	*chambra*	*oncle*	*arma*	*entra*
VII				*ongla*	*arma*	*intra*

METER

	a	b	c	d	e	f
I–VI	7′	10′	10′	10′	10′	10′
VII				10′	10′	10′

Corrected Readings

(2) *pot becs jes esco[ise]ndre*. A: *pot mais becs jes escondre*, but *escondre* ('to hide') makes no sense with *becs* and *ongla*; a: *escoisendre* (cf. Perugi 330; *DOM*).

(4) *no l'*. A: *no.ls*, but there is no plural noun; *l'* refers to *lausengier* (v. 3).

(27) *fin'amors*. A: *fina amors* (+1).

(29) *on q'eu estei*. A: *cal estet*; I, K, M: *on quieu estei*.

(29) *plaz'o*. A: *plaza o* (+1).

(32) *escorss'en*. A: *escorssa en* (+1).

(36) *lai intra*. A: *pert s'arma*; a: *lai intra*.

Raimon Jordan (?)
No puesc mudar no digua mon vejaire

One manuscript: *C. BEdT* 404.5.
Major editions: Riquer, *Trovadores* (1: 576); Rieger (704–13); Bruckner et al. (98–101).

Although the only manuscript attributes this song to Raimon Jordan, a minor troubadour active around 1178 to 1192, the general tone and especially the defense of women in the last stanza have persuaded many readers that the author must have been a trobairitz. Whether a female persona or a real woman, the speaker delivers a persuasive retort to Marcabru (see v. 25 note) and others who contributed to the misogynous tradition.

The speaker commits several irregularities that may indicate an inexperienced poet, fictional or real, if not a befuddled scribe (see the section on meter).

C, fol. 154r, cols. 1–2.

R. Jorda
Jordá. That is, *Jordán.*

I

No puesc mudar° no digua° mon vejaire°	avoid; saying; opinion
d'aisso don ay al cor molt gran error°,	bewilderment
ez er me molt mal e greu° a retraire°	difficult; tell
quar aquist antic trobador°	these ancient troubadours
5 *que.n son passat° dic° que son fort peccaire°,*	passed; I say; great sinners
qu'ilh° an mes lo segl'°en error	they; world
que an dig° mal de domnas a prezen°;	have spoken; in public
e trastug silh que auzon° crezo°.ls en,	those who hear [them]; believe

ez autreyon° tug° que ben es semblansa°,   agree; all; likelihood
10 ez aissi° an mes lo segl'en erransa°.   thus; in distress

---

(1) *no digua*. Pres. subj. 1 sg. of *dire*. *No* is redundant (it does not negate) after *No puesc*.
(1–2) 'My opinion about that (*aisso*) about which (*don*) I am bewildered.'
(4) *antíc trobadór*. Masc. nom. pl. *Antic* refers to the preceding century.
(5) *que.n*. The *.n* (*en* 'of them') may be omitted in translation.
(5) *passat*. Past part. of *pasar*.
(5) *dic*. Pres. indic. 1 sg. of *dire*.
(5) *fort peccáire*. Masc. nom. pl.
(6) *ilh*. Masc. nom. pl.
(7) *an dig*. *An*, pres. indic. 3 pl. of *aver*; *dig*, past part. of *dire*.
(8) *trastúg*. Equivalent to *trans* 'over' + *tot*; 'one and all.'
(8) *silh*. Equivalent to *cilh*, masc. nom. pl.
(8) *áuzon*. Pres. indic. 3 pl. of *auzir*.
(8) *crézo*. Pres. indic. 3 pl. of *créire*.
(9) 'And everyone agrees that it seems likely.'
(9) *autréyon*. Pres. indic. 3 pl. of *autrejar*.
(9) *tug*. Masc. nom. pl. (cf. *trastug*).
(10) *ez*. Form of *e* before a vowel.
(10) *an mes lo segl'*. 'They have put the world.'
(10) *segl'*. That is, *segle*.

II

E tug aquist° que eron° bon trobaire°   those; were; good
                                                  troubadours

tug se fenhon° per lial amador°,   claim to be; loyal lovers
mas ieu sai° be que non es fis amaire°   I know; a true lover
            nuls hom° que digua° mal   any man; speaks
            d'amor;
15 enans° vos dic qu'es ves° amor bauzaire° rather; toward; deceiver
            e fai l'uzatg'°al traïtor°,   behavior; traitor
            que de so on° plus fort s'aten° that from which; hopes for
            ditz° mal aissi° tot a prezen,   speaks; this way
    quar neguns° hom, s'avia° tota Fransa,   neguns . . . no, no; even if he
                                                  had
20 no pot ses don'°aver gran benestansa°.   without a lady; happiness

---

(11) *tug aquíst*. Masc. nom. pl.
(11) *éron*. Imperfect 3 pl. of *éser*.
(11) *bon trobáire*. Masc. nom. pl.
(12) *fénhon*. Pres. indic. 3 pl. of *fénher*.
(12) *liál amadór*. Masc. nom. pl.
(13) *sai*. Pres. indic. 1 sg. of *saber*.
(13) *fis amáire*. Masc. nom. sg.
(14) *digua*. Pres. subj. 3 sg. of *dire*; subj. because of the negative (*non . . . nuls*, vv. 13–14).
(17–18) 'Because about what he hopes for the most from' (ladies), 'he speaks badly in public.'

(17) *atén*. Pres. indic. 3 sg. of *atendre*.
(18) *ditz*. Pres. indic. 3 sg. of *dire*.
(19) *avía*. Imperfect 3 sg. of *aver*.
(20) *don'*. That is, *dona* 'lady'.

III

E ja° nulhs° hom que sia° de bon aire°
no sufrira° qu'om en digua folhor°,

mas silh que son ves amor tric e vaire°
ho tuzonon° e s'en tenon ab lor;
25 qu'en Marcabrus, a ley° de predicaire°
quant es en gleiz'°ho denant° orador°
que di° gran mal de la gen mescrezen°,
ez° el ditz mal de donas eyssamen°;
e dic° vos be que non l'es grans honransa°
30 selh° que ditz mal d'aisso° don nays enfansa.

ja ... no, never; any; is; family
will allow; folly about them (ladies, *en*)

tricky and fickle
stir up [as a fire]
manner; preacher
a church; before; a chapel
says; unbelieving people
too; in the same way
I tell you; no great honor to him

the one; that

---

(21) *sía*. Pres. subj. 3 sg. of *éser*.
(22) *sufrirá*. Fut. 3 sg. of *sofrir*.
(23–24) 'Those who are fickle toward love stir things up and take sides with them'; that is, with the *antic trobador* (v. 4), who speak badly of love.
(23) *tric e vaire*. Masc. nom. pl.
(24) *tuzónon*. Pres. indic. 3 pl. of *tuzonar/tizonar* (*DOM*).
(24) *ténon*. Pres. indic. 3 pl. of *tener*.
(25–28) 'Sir Marcabru, like a preacher ..., he too speaks badly of women in the same way.' On Marcabru's misogyny, see nos. 8 and 9.
(27) *di*. Pres. indic. 3 sg. of *dire*.
(29) *dic*. Pres. indic. 1 sg. of *dire*.
(29) *l'*. That is, *li* 'to him'.
(29) 'There is no great honor for him who speaks badly of that' (women) 'from whom children are born.'
(30) *aisso*. Neuter pron.
(30) *náys*. Pres. indic. 3 sg. of *náiser*.

IV

Ja no sia negus meravellaire°
s'ieu aisso dic ni vuelh° mostrar° alhor°,
que quascus hom° deu° razonar° son fraire°
             e queia donna° sa seror°,
35 quar Adams fo° lo nostre premier paire°
           ez avem° Damidieu° ad auctor°;

no one should be amazed
want; tell; elswhere (to others)
each man; should; defend; brother
each woman; sister
was; our first father
we have Lord God as [our] creator

e s'ieu per so vuelh far razonamen°   defense
a las donnas, no° m'o reptes° nïen,   *no ... nïen*, not at all; accuse
quar° dona deu az autra far   for; should make defense for
    razonansa°;   another
40 *e per aisso ai n'ieu dig ma semblansa°.*   opinion

---

(31) *meravelláire.* Masc. nom. sg. of *meravelhadór* 'one who marvels.'
(32) *vuélh.* Pres. indic. 1 sg. of *voler.*
(33) *quascús.* Masc. nom. sg. of *cascun.*
(33) *déu.* Pres. indic. 3 sg. of *dever.*
(34) *quéia.* Fem. of *quec.*
(35) *fo.* Pret. 3 sg. of *éser.*
(35) *premiér.* Masc. obl. sg. modifying nom. sg. *paire.* Cf. nom. sg. *premiers.* Declension on
    the noun but not the adjective.
(36) *avém.* Pres. indic. 1 pl. of *aver.*
(38) *reptés.* Form of *reptétz.* Pres. subj. 2 pl. (imperative) of *reptar.*
(39) *az.* Form of *a* 'to' (Classical Lat. *ad*) before a vowel.

Form

Four *coblas unissonans* of ten lines.

SCHEME

a	b	a	b	a	b	c	c	d	d

RHYMES

áire	*or*	*áire*	*or*	*áire*	*or*	*en*	*en*	*ansa*	*ansa*

METER

10′	10	10′	8/10	10′	8/10/9	10/8	10/8	10′	10′

Although the meter is irregular in lines that rhyme on **b** and **c** in all four stanzas, the irregular lines all make sense.

Corrected Readings

(16) *uzatg'al.* C: *uzatge al* (+1).
(26) *gleiz'ho.* C: *gleiza ho* (+1).

Richard Lionheart
Ja nus hom pris non dira sa raison

Three Occitan manuscripts: *P, S, f.* Also transmitted in eight French manuscripts. *BEdT* 420.2.

Major editions: Riquer, *Trovadores* (2: 752–54); Spetia edited all the manuscripts (108–11) and, separately, the Occitan ones (118–20).

In 1192, as he returned from the Third Crusade to France, Richard Lionheart was taken captive by Duke Leopold of Austria. Leopold sold him to Emperor Henry VI, who held him for ransom. Richard's mother, Eleanor of Aquitaine, acting as regent of England, raised an immense sum, and he was set free in 1194. During his imprisonment Richard wrote this song, complaining that his vassals were not doing enough to secure his release.

The text mixes elements of Occitan with French or Poitevin, the regional speech that echoes in the Harley lyric (no. 2) and Guilhem IX (no. 5).[iv] It was treated as Occitan by compilers who wrote it in Occitan manuscripts and as French by those who wrote it in French ones. The traces of Poitevin could be taken summarily as either.[v]

---

iv. In stanzas V to VIII, manuscripts *PS* rhyme Oc. *am* and *clam* with Fr. *-ain* and its variant *-aim*, as could be done in Poitevin (see notes to vv. 25 *am* and 38 *clam*). In nonrhyming positions, many forms may be Fr. or Poitevin (see notes). Some words are French (*guerroient*, v. 29) or Italian (*unca*, v. 28), like the scribe.

v. Poitevin has certain features in common with French, others in common with Occitan, and yet others that distinguish it from both (Pignon 1: 511–28). Several scholars have claimed that Richard's song was composed in French and acquired its Occitan traces in transmission; see Spetia (117–27); Lepage; and Lee, "Canzoni." The argument requires confidence in the editor's ability to reconstruct the process of transmission. Whether we share that confidence or not, the mixed traces remain in the MSS.

P, fol. 22r, cols. 1–2, with reference to *S*, fol. 1; and *f*, fol. 43v.

Reis Rizard

Rizard. Italian form (*Rizzardo*). *P* was copied by Petrus Berzoli de Gubbio, from Gubbio in Umbria (Brunel, *Bibliographie* 84, no. 290).

I

Ja° nus hom pris° non dira sa raison°	*Ja . . . non,* never; captured; story
adreitamen° se com hom dolent° non,	truly; grieving
mas per conort° pot il faire chanson.	comfort
Pro° a° d'amis, mas povre° son li don;°	plenty; there are; poor; gifts
5 *onta° i auron° se por ma reëzon°*	shame; they will have; ransom
soi° sai° dos yver[s]° pris.	I am; here; two winters

(1) *nus hom pris.* Masc. nom. sg. *Nus = nul* + *-s. Hom:* nom.; cf. obl. *óme. Pris:* past part. of *prendre.*

(1) *dirá.* Fut. 3 sg. of *dire* 'tell.'

(2) *se com . . . non.* 'Unless as.'

(4) *povre.* OFr. and Poitevin (Boucherie 50). Oc. *paubre.*

(4) *don.* Masc. nom. pl.

(5, 17) *aurón.* Fut. 3 pl. of *aver;* merges OFr. and Poitevin *aurónt* (Boucherie 254) with Oc. *aurán.*

(6) *soi.* Pres. indic. 1 sg. of *éser.*

II

Or sachon° ben mi hom'° e mi baron,°	know; my vassals; my great lords
Engles, Norman, Pettavin e Guascon,	
qe ge n'avoie si povre compagnon	
10 *q'eu laissasse por aver en preison.*	
Ge no.l di pas por nulla retraison,°	any reproach
mas anqar° soi ge pris.	still

(7) *sachon.* Pres. subj. 3 pl. of *saber.* Oc. *sach-* + *-on* (Appel, *Provenzalische Chrestomathie* xxxiii–xxxiv); OFr. and Poitevin *sachent* (Boucherie 13). Cf. *sachent* (v. 31 note).

(7) *mi hom', mi baron.* Masc. nom. pl.; *hom'* = *home.*

(8) All four nouns, masc. nom. pl. Richard's subjects as king of England, duke of Normandy, count of Poitiers, and duke of Aquitaine (including Gascony).

(9–10) 'I have not had so poor a companion' (fellow soldier) 'that I would have left [him] in prison for money.'

(9) *ge.* OFr. and Poitevin (Boucherie 8). Oc. *eu, ieu.*

(9) *n'.* Elided form of *non* (Levy and Appel 5: 413–14).

(9) *avóie.* OFr. and Poitevin imperfect 1 sg. of *aver.* Poitevin 1 sg. *aveie,* 3 sg. *aveies/avoies* (Boucherie 254). Oc. *avía.*

(10) *laissásse.* OFr. and Poitevin past subj. 1 sg. of OFr. *laissier* or Poitevin *laisser; lais-* + *-asse* (Boucherie 256). Oc. *laisés.*

III

Tan sai eu [ben] de ver° certanament°	in truth; certainly
c'om mort° ne pris n'a amic ne parent°;	dead; relative
15 *qant il me laissent° per or° ni per argent°*	leave; gold; silver
mal m'es de mi, mas peiz° m'es por ma gent,°	worse; followers
q'apres ma mort° n'auron reprozhament,°	death; reproach
tan longamen° soi pris.	for so long

(14) *om mort.* Declension on the noun: *om,* masc. nom. sg.; *mort,* obl. sg.

(15) *laissent.* Pres. indic. 3 pl. of OFr. *laissier,* Poitevin *laisser,* or Oc. *laisar.* The ending *-ent* is normal in OFr. and Poitevin (Boucherie 256) but infrequent in Oc. (Appel, *Provenzalische Chrestomathie* xxiii).

(15) *or.* OFr. and Poitevin (Boucherie 64). Oc. *aur.*

(16) *mal m'es de mi.* 'I feel bad for myself.'

(16) *mi.* Oc. (Appel, *Provenzalische Chrestomathie* xiii; *Old Occitan* 437), not OFr. or Poitevin *mei* (Boucherie 245).

IV

No.m merveill° s'eu ai lo cor dolent	I am not amazed
20 *qe mes senher° met° ma terr'°en torment;*	my lord; puts; land
no li menbra° del nostre segrament°,	he does not remember; oath
qe nos fimes° andos° comunelment.°	made; both; together
Be.m sai de ver qe gaire longament	
non serai° eu sa° pris.	I will be; here

(19) *mervéill.* Pres. indic. 1 sg. of *mervelhar/meravelhar.*

(20) Richard's lord for his Continental holdings was Philip II of France. They exchanged oaths of loyalty while on Crusade before Philip returned to France in late 1191. By early 1192, however, Philip laid claim to the Norman Vexin, which was Richard's fief, and sought to undermine his control of Aquitaine (Gillingham 223 and 229–30).

(20) *mes.* OFr. masc. nom. sg. of *mon;* cf. Poitevin *mis* (Boucherie 246), Oc. *mos.*

(20) *sénher.* Oc. masc. nom. sg.; obl. *senhór.* Shifting declension.

(20) *met.* Pres. indic. 3 sg. of *metre.*

(21) *ménbra.* Pres. indic. 3 sg. of *membrar* (impersonal).

(22) *fímes.* OFr. pret. 1 pl. of *faire.* I do not find pret. 1 pl. in Poitevin, but cf. 2 pl. *feistes* (Boucherie 264), which may imply 1 pl. *feïmes, fimes* (?). Cf. Oc. *fezém.*

(24) *serái.* Fut. 1 sg. of *éser.*

V

25 *Mi° conpagnon cui° j'amoi'°e cui j'am,°*	my; whom; I loved; I love
cil° de Chai[u] e cil de Persarain,	those (i.e., the men)
de lor chanzon q'il non sont pas°	*non ... pas,* not
certain.	
Unca° vers els° non oi cor fals ni vain;	*Unca ... non,* never; toward them
s'il me guerroient°, il feron qe vilain°	make war on; will act like oafs
30 *tan com° ge soie° pris.*	as long as; I am

(25–27) 'My companions, whom I loved and whom I love, those of Cayeux-sur-Mer (Somme) and those of Perche (a county in northwestern France), are not reliable about their song'; they change their tune. Guillaume III of Cayeux and Geoffroy III of Perche had been Richard's allies on Crusade but joined Philip in spring 1193 (Lee, "Nota" 147).

(25) *Mi.* OFr. and Poitevin masc. nom. pl. of *mon* (Boucherie 246). Oc. *mei.*

(25) *amói'.* That is, *amóie,* OFr. and Poitevin imperfect 1 sg. of *amer* (cf. *avoie,* v. 9 note). Oc. *amava.*

(25) *am.* Both *am* and *clam* (v. 38) are likely Oc. but could be Poitevin, which has -*a*- in *plan, publicán, remánent,* etc., although the more general reflex was *ai* (Pignon 1: 178). OFr. *aim, claim.*

(26) *cil.* Masc. nom. pl. of *cel.*

(27) *q'.* That is, *que.* May introduce an independent verb (*Old Occitan* 464).

(27) *pas.* Negates in Oc. (*DOM, pas₂*), OFr., and Poitevin (Boucherie 112).

(28) 'Never toward them did I have a treacherous or fickle heart.'

(28) *Unca.* It. (*FEW* 14: 26; Battaglia 21: 557). Oc. *oncas.*

(28) *oi.* OFr. and Poitevin (?) pret. 1 sg. of *aver.* Poitevin 1 sg. is usually *ogui,* but cf. 3 sg. *oi* (Boucherie 254). Oc. *aic/agui.*

(29) *guerróient.* Pres. indic. 3 pl. of OFr. *guerroiier.* Oc. *guerréjan.*

(29) *ferón.* Fut. 3 pl. of *faire;* merges OFr. and Poitevin *fer-* + -*ont* (Boucherie 260 and 264) with Oc. *farán* (cf. *aurón,* v. 5 note). *Faire que* 'to act like.'

(30) *sóie.* OFr. pres. subj. 1 sg. of *estre;* Poitevin *seie,* but -*ei*- alternates with -*oi*- (Boucherie 226 and 255). Oc. *sía.*

VI

Or sachent° ben Enjevin e Torain,   know
cil bachalier° qi son legier° e sain,°   upstart; agile; healthy
q'engombré° soi e pris en autrui° main.° caught; someone else's; power
Il m'ajuvassen, mas il no veün grain;° no … grain, not a bit
35 *de belles armes sont era voit° li plain°* empty; fields
  per zo qe° ge soi pris.   because

(31) *sachent.* Pres. subj. 3 pl. of *saber* in OFr., Poitevin, and Oc. Cf. *sachon* (v. 7 note).

(31) *Enjevin e Torain.* Men of Anjou and Touraine. Richard was count of Anjou and Tours.

(32) *bachalier.* Nom. pl. of *bachelier, bacalar,* term of contempt (*PD, DOM*).

(32) *sain.* OFr. and Poitevin (Boucherie 190). Oc. *san.*

(33) *engombré.* OFr. and Poitevin *encombré* (Boucherie 150), past part. of *encombrer.* Oc. *encombrat.*

(33) *main.* OFr. and Poitevin (Boucherie 28). Oc. *man.*

(34–35) 'They would help me, but they don't see a bit [of it]' (they do not see the possibility of helping), because 'now the fields are empty of bright weapons.' Richard, in captivity, is not making war.

(34) *ajuvássen.* Past subj. 3 pl. of hypothetical OFr. and Poitevin *ajuver* + past subj. 3 pl. -*ássent* (Boucherie 256). The corresponding form of rare Oc. *ajuvar* (*DOM*) would end in -*éssen,* -*ésson* (Appel, *Provenzalische Chrestomathie* xviii). OFr. *adjuver* since the fifteenth century (*FEW* 24: 165).

(34) *veün.* Pres. indic. 3 pl. of Oc. *vezer/veire.*

(34) *grain.* OFr. and Poitevin (Boucherie 212). Oc. *gran.*

(35) *voit li plain.* Masc. nom. pl.

VII

Contessa° soir,° vostre prez sob[ei]raim°	countess; sister; sovereign
sal° Deus e garde°, cel per cui me clam°	save; keep; I appeal
39 *et per cui ge soi pris.*	

(37–38) 'Countess, sister, may God, to whom I appeal, save and keep your sovereign merit.'
Marie, countess of Champagne, elder daughter of Louis VII and Eleanor of Aquitaine;
Richard's half sister.

(37) *soir.* So PS; *f: suer.* Oc. nom. *sor/sorre*, obl. *seror*. In Poitevin, "*Oir* alterne avec *orr*"
(Boucherie 226), which implies a possible *soir*. OFr. nom. *suer*, obl. *seror*.

(38) *sal.* Pres. subj. 3 sg. of *salvar*.

(38) *garde.* Pres. subj. 3 sg. of Poitevin *garder* with subj. *-e* (Boucherie 256). OFr. and Oc. *gart*.

(38) *clam.* Pres. indic. 1 sg. of *clamar*. See v. 25 note on *am*.

(39) 'And for whose sake I am captured.' Richard became a crusader for love of God. *Per* 'for
the sake of' (*Old Occitan* 455).

VIII

40 *Ge no.l di pas por cela de Certrain,°*	Chartrain (region around Chartres)
la mere [de] Loÿs	

(40–41) Alice, countess of Blois, Châteaudun, and Chartres, Richard's other half sister.
Alice's son Louis had earlier recognized Richard as his lord (Spetia 116n27). In January
1194, however, Louis opposed Richard before supporting him again in 1198 (Lee, "Nota"
150n30). Richard expresses affection for Marie but distrust of Alice and Louis.

(40) *cela.* Fem. of *cel* 'the one.'

Form

Six *coblas doblas* of six lines and two *tornadas*, the first of three lines, the second
of two.

SCHEME

a	a	a	a	a	b

RHYMES

I–II	*on*	*on*	*on*	*on*	*on*	*is*
III–IV	*ent*	*ent*	*ent*	*ent*	*ent*	*is*
V–VI	*am/ain*	*ein/ain*	*ain*	*ain*	*ain*	*is*
VII				*aim*	*am*	*is*
VIII					*ain*	*ys*

The **b**-rhyme *pris* 'captured' is used as a refrain until v. 41.

METER

I–VI	10	10	10	10	10	6
VII				10	10	6
VIII					10	6

Epic caesuras $(4' + 6 = 10)$ at vv. 15, 29, 34, and 35 create a warlike effect, as in no. 17. The unstressed fifth syllable in the line (') does not count. No such caesura at v. 38.

Corrected Readings

(6) *dos yver[s].* P: *dos yver;* f: *.ii. uverns;* S omits.

(13) *Tan sai eu [ben] de.* P, S: *Tan sai eu de* (-1); f: *C'or sapchon bien en.*

(20) *terr'en.* P, S: *terra en* $(+1)$; f omits.

(22) *fimes.* P, S: *feimes* (or *feïmes?* $+1$); f: *fezemis* $(+1)$.

(26) *Chai[u].* P, S: *Chaill* (-1); f omits. In French MSS: *Chaieu Za, Chaeu O, Cahiul U.* Editors read *Caheu* (Spetia 110); *Cahen,* i.e., Caen (Rosenberg and Tischler 382).

(32) *bachalier.* P, S: *bachaliers;* f omits.

(37) *sob[ei]raim.* P, S: *sobraim* (-1); f: *sobeiran.*

(41) *mere [de] Loÿs.* P: *mere Loys* (-1); f: *maire de Loys;* S omits.

The Monk of Montaudon
L'autrier fu en paradis

Eight manuscripts: *C, D, E, I, K, N* (anonymous), *R, d. BEdT* 305.12.
Major editions: Klein (30); Riquer, *Trovadores* (2: 1036–38); Routledge, *Poésies*
(105–12); Jensen, *Troubadour Lyrics* (344–47 and 556–57).

The Monk of Montaudon wrote from about 1192 to 1210. The *vida* says he
was born in Auvergne and became prior of Montaudon, perhaps referring to
Montaut (Lot-et-Garonne), with its church of Saint Peter (*BT* 307–10; *DBT*
361). In this *tensó*, or debate poem, he chats with God, reproaching him for the
capture and imprisonment of Richard Lionheart (see v. 41 note on *vis*).

I, fol. 137r, col. 1.

Lo Monges de Montaudon
Monges. Nom. sg. of masc. *monge/morgue* 'monk.'

I

L'autrier° fu° en paradis	the other day; I was
per qu'°eu fui° gais e joios°	so; I was; merry and joyous
car me fez° tant amoros°	he made me; loving
Deus°, a cui° totz° obezis°—	God; whom; everyone; obeys
5 *terra°, mars°, vals°, e montaingna°.*	land; sea; valley; mountain
E.m dis°, "Morgues, car° venguis°?	he said to me; why; did you come
Ni con° estai° Montaldos,	and how; is
lai on° as° major° compaingna°?"	where; you have; more; company

(1) *fu.* Pret. 1 sg. of *éser*.
(2) *fúi.* Pret. 1 sg. of *éser* with optional yod; alternative to *fu* (v. 1).
(2) *gais e joiós.* Masc. nom. sg.

(3–4) 'Because God made me so loving.' God, who loves song and laughter (v. 22), wanted the Monk to be merry and joyous.

(3) *fez*. Pret. 3 sg. of *faire*.

(4) *totz*. Masc. nom. sg.

(4) *obezís*. Pres. indic. 3 sg. of *obezir*. Root + inchoative *-is* (*Old Occitan* 167), as in pres. indic. 1 sg. *servís* (v. 12), *grazís* (v. 17).

(5) *mars, vals*. Masc. nom. sg.

(6) *dis*. Pret. 3 sg. of *dire*.

(6) *venguís*. Pret. 2 sg. of *venir*.

(7) *estái*. Pres. indic. 3 sg. of *estar* 'to be' (in a situation).

(7) *Montaldós*. Nom. sg. of *Montaudon* (rubric) or *Montaldon* (v. 24).

(8) *as*. Pres. indic. 2 sg. of *aver*.

(8) God implies that there are not many monks in paradise.

II (The Monk)

"*Seingner°, estat ai° aclis°*	Lord; I have been; submissive
10 *en claustra° un an° o dos,*	in a cloister; for a year
per qu'° ai perdut° los baros°;	which is why; I have lost; barons
sol car° vos am° e.us servís°,	just because; I love you; I serve you
me fan° lor amor estraingna°;	they make; distant from me
en° Randos, cui es° Paris,	sir; to whom belongs
15 *non° fo° anc fals ni gignos°;*	*non ... anc*, never; was; deceptive
el e mos cors crei° que.m plaingna°."	I believe; feel sorry for

(9) *séingner*. Form of *sénher*, nom. (vocative) sg. of *senhór*. Shifting declension.

(9) *estát*. Past part. of *estar*.

(11) *perdút*. Past part. of *perdre*.

(11) *barós*. Obl. pl. of *baron* 'great lord.'

(12) *am*. Pres. indic. 1 sg. of *amar*.

(12) *servís*. Pres. indic. 1 sg. of *servir*.

(13) *fan*. Pres. indic. 3 pl. of *faire*.

(13) *estráingna*. Fem. of *estranh*.

(14) *Randos, cui es Paris*. Randon de Castelnou, now Châteauneuf-de-Randon (Lozère); lord of a castle named Paris (not the capital of France).

(15) *fo*. Pret. 3 sg. of *éser*.

(16) 'He and I myself, I believe, feel sorry for me' (because I have lost the other great lords). *Mos cors*, literally 'my body,' is a paraphrase for 'myself,' 'I.'

(16) *créi*. Pres. indic. 1 sg. of *créire*.

(16) *pláingna*. Pres. subj. 3 sg. of *plánher*. Singular agrees with the closer of two compound subjects (*mos cors*).

III (God)

"*Morgues, ges° eu non grazis°*	*ges ... non*, scarcely; I am grateful
si'stas° en claustra rescos°	if you are; hidden
ni° vols° guerras° ni tenzos°	and; you want; wars; disputes
20 *ni peleg'° ab° tos vezis°*	conflict; with; your neighbors
per que° baillia°.t remaingna°.	so that; jurisdiction; remain yours

Anz° am° eu lo chant° e.l ris°   rather; I love; song; laughter
e.l segle° en es plus pros°   world; more worthy for it
e Montaldon i gazaingna°."   gains by it

---

(17) *grazís.* Pres. indic. 1 sg. of *grazir.*

(18) *'stas.* That is, *estás,* pres. indic. 2 sg. of *estar.*

(18) *rescós.* Past part. of *rescondre.*

(19–21) God sees through the Monk's complaint that the lords have abandoned him because of his piety. Rather, he has argued with them over property. Such quarrels arose between monasteries and neighboring lords.

(19) *vols.* Pres. indic. 2 sg. of *voler.*

(19) *tenzós.* Obl. pl. of *tenson;* also the name of the genre of the debate, as here.

(20) *pelég'.* That is, *peléga,* fem. obl. sg.

(20) *vezís.* Obl. pl. of *vezin.*

(21) *remáingna.* Pres. subj. 3 sg. of *remaner.*

(22) *am.* Pres. indic. 1 sg. of *amar.*

(23) *ségle.* Nom. sg. of *segle.* Oc. masculine nouns that had had no nominative *-s* in Lat., such as *saeculum* (neuter in Lat., masc. in Oc.), could take nom. sg. *-s* or not.

(24) *Montaldón.* Obl. sg. for subject of *gazaingna.* Proper nouns often defy declension (*Old Occitan* 287).

(24) *gazáingna.* Pres. indic. 3 sg. of *gazanhar.* The monastery is merrier.

IV (The Monk)

25 *"Seingner, eu tem° que faillis°*   I fear; I may go wrong
s'eu fatz° coblas° e chanzos°,   I make; couplets; songs
qu'om pert° vostr'amor e vos   a man (one) loses
qui son escïent° mentis°—   knowingly; lies
per que°.m part° de la bargaingna°.   which is why; I leave; this business
30 *Pe[.l] segle que° no.m n'aïs°,*   so that; I would not hate myself
me tornei° a las leizos°,   I returned; [monastic] lessons
e.m laissiei° l'anar° d'Espaingna."   I gave up; journey

---

(25) *tem.* Pres. indic. 1 sg. of *temer.*

(25) *faillís.* Past subj. 1 sg. of *falhir.*

(26) *fatz.* Pres. indic. 1 sg. of *faire.*

(26) *coblas.* Obl. pl. of *cobla* 'couplet,' 'stanza.' The genre of the freestanding *cobla* arose in the late twelfth century.

(27) *pert.* Pres. indic. 3 sg. of *perdre.*

(28) *son escïent.* 'To one's knowledge' (Lat. *se sciente* 'oneself knowing').

(28) *mentís.* Past subj. 3 sg. of *mentir.* Secular songs are false in the monastic opinion.

(29) *part.* Pres. indic. 1 sg. of *partir* (reflexive).

(30) 'So that I would not hate myself because of the world.'

(30) *aïs.* Past subj. 1 sg. of *aïr* (*DOM*).

(31) *tornéi.* Pret. 1 sg. of *tornar.*

(31) *leizós.* Obl. pl. of fem. *leison.*

(32) *laissiéi.* Pret. 1 sg. of *laissar* (reflexive).

(32) *anar.* Obl. sg. of noun from verb *anar,* to go. The Monk says he gave up a journey to Spain, perhaps a pilgrimage to Compostela, because he chose to remain cloistered.

V (God)

"Morgues, ben mal o fezis°	you acted
que tost° non anes° coichos°	at once; you did not go; in haste
35 *al rei° cui° es° Olairos*	king; to whom; belongs
qui tant era° tos amis,	used to be
per que° lau° que t'o afraingna°.	so; I advise; he break it off
Ha°, quanz° bos marcs° d'esterlis°	Ah!; how many; good marks; sterling coins
aura° perdutz e.ls teus dos°,	he will have; in your gifts (gifts to you)
40 *qu'el te levet° de la faingna°!"*	raised; mire

(33) *fezís*. Pret. 2 sg. of *faire*.

(34) *anés*. Past subj. 2 sg. of *anar*.

(35) *cúi*. 'To whom' (Lat. *cui*).

(35) *Olairós*. Oléron (Charente-Maritime), an island in the Bay of Biscay offshore from La Rochelle, which belonged at this time to the king of England, Richard, who was also duke of Aquitaine (including Montaut).

(36) *era*. Imperfect 3 sg. of *éser*.

(37) 'So I advise [Richard] to cease being your patron.'

(37) *láu*. Pres. indic. 1 sg. of *lauzar*.

(37) *afráingna*. Pres. subj. 3 sg. of *afránher*.

(38) *marcs*. Obl. pl. of *marc* 'mark,' a coin worth half a pound.

(38) *esterlís*. Obl. pl. of *esterlin* 'sterling,' an English silver coin.

(39) *aurá*. Fut. 3 sg. of *aver*.

(40) *levét*. Pret. 3 sg. of *levar*.

VI (The Monk)

"Seingner, eu l'agra ben vis°	I would have been happy to see him
si per mal de vos no.i fos°,	but for your fault
can anc° sofris° sas preisos°;	ever; you permitted; imprisonment
mas° la nau° dels Sarrazis°	but; ship; Saracens
45 *no.us membra° ges cosi°.s baingna°,*	you scarcely remember; how; it sails
car se dinz° Acra.s [culhis]°,	into; it had been welcomed
pro°.i agra enquer Turcs felos°.	plenty; treacherous Turks
Fols° es qui.us sec° en mesclaingna°!"	fool; follows you; into battle

(41) *ágra*. Second conditional 1 sg. of *aver*.

(41) *vis*. Past part. of *véire*. Returning from Crusade, Richard was taken prisoner and held for ransom from 1192 to 1194 (see no. 21). The song must have been written during this time. The Monk reproaches God for the capture of Richard.

(42) *fos*. Past subj. 3 sg. of *éser*.

(43) *sofrís*. Normally ending in *-ítz*; pret. 2 pl. of *sofrir*.

(45) *mémbra*. Pres. indic. 3 sg. of *membrar* (impersonal).

(45) *báingna*. Pres. indic. 3 sg. of *banhar* (reflexive).

(46) *Acra*. Fortress in Jerusalem that Richard conquered in 1191.

(46) *[culhís]*. Pret. 3 sg. of *colhir*.

(47) 'There would still be plenty of treacherous Turks there.'

(47) *ágra*. Second conditional 3 sg. of *aver* (impersonal).

(48) The Monk gives God no credit for the failure of the Muslims to reinforce Acra. For criticism of Crusade, see also no. 9, v. 42 note; Throop.

(48) *Fols*. Masc. nom. sg. 'He is a fool who. . . .'

(48) *sec*. Pres. indic. 3 sg. of *segre*.

Form

Six *coblas unissonans* of eight lines.

SCHEME

a b b a c a b c

RHYMES

is os os is ánha is os ánha

METER

7 7 7 7 7' 7 7 7'

Corrected Readings

(20) *peleg' ab*. I: *pelega ab* (+1).

(30) *Pe[.l]*. I: *per*.

(33) *ben mal o*. I: *ben o mal* (*mal* expunctuated).

(46) *[culhis]*. I: *quils*.

Castelloza
Ja de chantar non degr'aver tal[a]n

Five manuscripts: *A, I, K, N, d. BEdT* 109.2.

Major editions: Riquer, *Trovadores* (3: 1328); Paden et al., "Poems of the Trobairitz" (173–77); Rieger (529–38); Bruckner et al. (14–17).

With three songs and a possible fourth, Castelloza is the most prolific trobairitz after the Comtessa de Dia. She strikes a bleak tone, insisting on her unrelieved suffering. Her outlook is darker than that of the Comtessa or Bernart de Ventadorn, who found both grief and joy in love. She seems to have been active around the beginning of the thirteenth century; her *vida* says she came from Auvergne (*BT* 333–34).

A, fol. 169r, cols. 1–2, with reference to *I*, fol. 125r, col. 2; *K*, fol. 111r, col. 1; and *d*, fol. 311v, col. 1.

Na Castelloza
Na. Fem. noun: 'Lady' (title of respect).

I

Ja° de chantar non degr'°aver tal[a]n°,	Ja ... non, never; I should; desire
car on mais° chant°	the more; I sing
e pieitz° me vai° d'amor,	the worse; it goes for me
que plaing° e plor°	plaints; tears
5 *fant° en mi lor estatge°,*	make; home
car en mala merce°	disfavor
ai mes° mon cor° e me°,	put; heart; myself

e si.n breu° no.m rete°	if soon; [he] doesn't accept me
trop° ai° faich° long badatge°.	very; I have; made; waste of time

(1) *dégr'.* That is, *degra,* second conditional 1 sg. of *dever.*

(2) *chant.* Pres. indic. 1 sg. of *cantar.*

(3) *vai.* Pres. indic. of *anar.*

(4) *plaing, plor.* Masc. nom. pl.

(5) *fant.* Pres. indic. 3 pl. of *faire.*

(7) *mes.* Past part. of *metre.*

(8) *reté.* Pres. indic. 3 sg. of *retener.* The implicit subject is the man she loves (v. 10, etc.).

(9) *ai.* Pres. indic. 1 sg. of *aver.*

(9) *faich.* Past part. of *faire.*

(9) *badátge.* The action of *badar* 'to gape.'

II

10	*Ai° bels amics, sivals° un bel semblan°*	Oh!; at least; smile
	mi faitz° enan°	give me; *enan que,* before
	q'ieu muoira° de dolor°,	I die; grief
	qe.il amador°	lovers
	vos tenon° per salvatge°,	consider you; cruel
15	*car joia° no m'ave°*	joy; come my way
	de vos, don° no.m recre°	whom; I do not cease
	d'amar per bona fe°	in good faith
	totz temps° ses° cor volatge°.	always; without; fickle

(11) *faitz.* Imperative 2 pl. of *faire.*

(12) *muóira.* Pres. subj. 1 sg. of *morir;* subj. after *enan que.*

(13) *amadór.* Masc. nom. pl.; nom. sg. *amáire.* Shifting declension.

(14) *ténon.* Pres. indic. 3 pl. of *tener.*

(15) *avé.* Pres. indic. 3 sg. of *avenir.*

(16) *recré.* Pres. indic. 1 sg. of *recréire.*

III

	Mas ja vas° vos non aurai° cor truan°	toward you; will I have; false
20	*ni plen° d'engan°,*	full; deceit
	sitot° vos n'ai° peior°,	even though; I have; worse
	c'a grand honor	
	m'o teing° e mon coratge°;	I consider it; in my heart
	anz° pens°, qan mi sove°	rather; I think; I remember
25	*del ric pretz qe.us mante°,*	maintains you
	e sai° ben qe.us cove°	I know; befits
	dompna° d'aussor° paratge°.	a lady; higher; nobility

(19) *aurái.* Fut. 1 sg. of *aver.*

(21) *vos n'ai peiór.* 'I have you worse for it'; you treat me worse.

(23) *o.* Neuter pron., 'it' (an idea in context): to be loved by him.

(23) *téing.* Pres. indic. 1 sg. of *tener.*

(23) *e.* 'In'; *e* (+ *m-*) = *en.*

(24) *pens.* Pres. indic. 1 sg. of *pensar.*

(24) *sové.* Pres. indic. 3 sg. of *sovenir* (impersonal).

(25) *manté.* Pres. indic. 3 sg. of *mantener.*

(26) *sai.* Pres. indic. 1 sg. of *saber.*

(26) *cové.* Pres. indic. 3 sg. of *convenir.*

IV

Despois° vos vi°, fui° al vostre coman°,	ever since; I saw; I was; command
et anc° per tant°,	*anc . . . no,* never; because of that
30 *amics, no.us n'aic° meillor°,*	I had; better
qe preiador°	a messenger
no.m mandetz°, ni messatge°	you have not sent; message
que ja°.m viretz° lo fre°.	ever; you would turn; rein
Amics, non° fassatz° re!	*non . . . re,* nothing; do
35 *Car jois° no mi soste°,*	joy; sustain
a pauc° de dol° non ratge°.	*a pauc . . . non,* nearly; grief; I go mad

---

(28) *vi.* Pret. 1 sg. of *véire.*

(28) *fúi.* Pret. 1 sg. of *éser.*

(30) *aic.* Pret. 1 sg. of *aver.*

(30) *.us n'aic meillór.* 'I had you better for it'; you treated me better.

(31) *preiadór.* A messenger who acts as a proxy, courting a lady for the man who sends him. Root *pregar* 'to court.'

(32) *mandétz.* Pret. 2 pl. of *mandar.*

(33) *virétz.* Pres. subj. 2 pl. of *virar*; subj. after *messatge que* 'a message [saying] that' (vv. 32–33).

(34) *fassátz.* Imperative 2 pl. of *faire.*

(35) *jois.* Masc. nom. sg.

(35) *sosté.* Pres. indic. 3 sg. of *sostener.*

(36) *non.* Redundant after *a pauc.*

(36) *rátge.* Pres. indic. 1 sg. of *ratjar*; *-e* is a support vowel.

V

Si pro°.i agues°, be.us membri° en chantan	use; there were; I remind
q'aic° vostre gan°,	I got; glove
q'enbliei° ab gran temor°;	I stole; fear
40 *puois° aic paor°*	then; a fright
qe.i aguessetz° dampnatge°	you might have; damage
d'aicella° qe.us rete,	the one [woman]
amics, per q'ieu desse°	at once

l'i tornei°, car ben cre°   returned it to her; I believe
45 *q'eu no n'ai° poderatge°.*   do not have; rightful ownership

---

(37) 'If there were any use in it.'

(37) *agués.* Past subj. 3 sg. of *aver* (impersonal).

(37) *mémbri.* Pres. indic. 1 sg. of *membrar; -i* is a support vowel like *-e* in *ratge,* v. 36 (Appel, *Provenzalische Chrestomathie* xxii).

(38) *aic.* Pret. 1 sg. of *aver.*

(39) *enbliéi.* Pret. 1 sg. of *emblar.*

(41) *aguessétz.* Past subj. 2 pl. of *aver.*

(42) *aicella.* 'She'; fem. of *aicel* 'the one,' 'he.'

(42) *reté.* Pres. indic. 3 sg. of *retenir* 'to appoint' (as a vassal) or 'to take' (as a lover).

(44) *tornéi.* Pret. 1 sg. of *tornar.*

(44) *cre.* Pres. indic. 1 sg. of *créire.*

VI

Dels cavalliers° conosc° que fant   some knights (lovers); I know
   [lor dan]
            car ja° prei[a]n°   ever; court
   dompnas plus q'ellas lor,
         c'autra ricor°   wealth
50 *no.i ant° ni seignoratge°;*   they do not have; lordship
   qe pois° dompna s'ave   if
   d'amar, preiar deu be
   cavallier, s'en lui ve°   she sees in him
   proez'° e vassalatge°.   prowess; qualities befitting a vassal

---

(46) 'I know some knights (lovers) who cause their [own] loss.'

(46) *Dels.* Equivalent to *de + los; de* is partitive.

(46) *conósc.* Pres. indic. 1 sg. of *conóiser.*

(46) *fant.* Pres. indic. 3 pl. of *faire.*

(47) *préi[a]n.* Pres. indic. 3 pl. of *pregar.* Eye rhyme with *dan* (v. 46).

(48) 'More than they' (*ellas,* fem. = the ladies) '[do] them' (the knights).

(49–50) Some poor knights court ladies in hope of gaining a dowry.

(50) *ant.* Pres. indic. 3 pl. of *aver.*

(51) *avé.* Pres. indic. 3 sg. of *avenir* (impersonal) 'to befall.'

(51–52) 'Whereas if it befalls a lady to love, she should indeed court a knight.'

(53) *ve.* Pres. indic. 3 sg. of *véire.*

VII

55 *Bels Noms, ges no°.m recre°*   not at all; do I recant
   de vos amar jasse°,   forever
   car viu° en bona fe°,   I live; good faith
   bontatz°, e ferm coratge°.   kindnesses; steady heart

---

(55) *Bels Noms.* Masc. nom. (vocative) sg. 'Pretty Name,' an endearing *senhal,* or secret name, for her lover.

(55) *recré.* Pres. indic. 1 sg. of *recréire* (reflexive).
(57) *víu.* Pres. indic. 1 sg. of *víure.*
(58) *bontátz.* Obl. pl. of *bontat.*

Form

Six *coblas unissonans* of nine lines and one *tornada* of four.

SCHEME

a	a	b	b	c	d	d	d	c

RHYMES

	an	an(t)	or	or	atge	e	e	e	atge
I	an	ant	or	or	atge	e	e	e	atge
II	an	an	or	or	atge	e	e	e	atge
III	an	an	or	or	atge	e	e	e	atge
IV	an	ant	or	or	atge	e	e	e	atge
V	an	an	or	or	atge	e	e	e	atge
VI	an	an	or	or	atge	e	e	e	atge
VII						e	e	e	atge

METER

10	4	6	4	6'	6	6	6	6'

Corrected Readings

(1) *degr'aver.* A: *degra aver* (+1).
(1) *tal[a]n.* A: *talen;* cf. *talen, -an* (PD); rhyme calls for *-an.*
(46) *[lor dan].* A: *follatge;* I, K, d: *lor dan.*
(47) *prei[a]n.* A: *preion.*
(54) *proez' e.* A: *proeza e* (+1).

Bertran Carbonel

Dieus fes Adam et Eva carnalmens

Two manuscripts: *P, R. BEdT* 82.37.
Major editions: Jeanroy, "'Coblas'" (167); Routledge, *Bertran Carbonel* (155–56).

Bertran Carbonel served as a judge at Grasse (Alpes-Maritimes) from 1250 to 1254 (Paden, "Bertran Carbonel"). He wrote poetry including a collection of *coblas* 'stanzas,' individual, free-standing stanzas such as this one, which had become a recognized genre late in the twelfth century. The word *cobla* also meant 'stanza' in the sense of one stanza among several that constitute a song.

Marriage was a subject of controversy. Ascetic spirits found that conjugal sex must be sinful because spouses could not avoid having pleasure. Bertran Carbonel took a more tolerant position: since God created Adam and Eve, commanded them to increase and multiply (Gen. 1.28), and commanded Noah and his sons to do the same (Gen. 9.1), He must have approved of procreative married sex.

P, fol. 59v; variants from *R*, fol. 112r, col. 1.

Dieus fes° Adam e Eva carnalmens°,	made; in the flesh
ses tot pechat°, l'un ab° l'autr'[a]jostar°.	without any sin; with; marry
E[n] totz aqels° qe d'els° fes° derivar°	in all those; them; he made; descend
Dieus volc° fos faiz° carnals ajostamens°.	wanted; to be made; carnal union
5 *E pos° Adam fon° d'aqest mon° raiziz°*	then; was; of this world; root
(senes° razis, arbres non es floriz),	without
per q'°amans fins° ni amairiz complida°,	so; a true lover; completed female lover
qan s'ajostan°, non pecan° ses fallida°.	they marry; do not sin; without doubt

(1–2) *Dieus fes . . . [a]jostar*. 'God made [them] join' in procreative marriage.

(1) *Diéus*. Masc. nom. sg.

(1) *fes*. Pret. 3 sg. of *faire*.

(1) *Adam*. Obl. sg.; cf. identical nom. in v. 5. Names often do not decline (*Old Occitan* 287–88).

(1) *carnalmens*. Adverb modifying *[a]jostar* (v. 2).

(2) *[a]jostar*. 'To join with' (*ab*), 'marry' (*DOM*).

(4) *volc*. Pret. 3 sg. of *voler*.

(4) *fos*. Past subj. 3 sg. of *éser*.

(4) *faiz*. Past part. masc. nom. sg. of *faire*.

(5–7) *pos . . . per q'*. 'Since . . . therefore' (redundant); *q'* is a reduced form of *que*.

(5) *fon*. Pret. 3 sg. of *éser*.

(5–6) *raizís . . . razíz*. Nom. sg. and obl. sg., respectively (invariable).

(6) 'Without a root, a tree has not [ever] blossomed.' If the world (human society) was to flourish like a tree, it had to have a root; its root was Adam.

(6) *árbres*. Masc. nom. sg.

(6) *floríz*. Past part., masc. nom. sg., of *florir*.

(7) 'So [I say] that when a true [male] lover and a completed [female] lover marry, they do not sin.'

(7) *amans fins*. Masc. nom. sg. of *aman fin*.

(7) *complída*. Fem. past part. of *complir*. The canon lawyer Gratian, who wrote in the 1140s, argued that marriage was initiated by consent but completed (*perfectum*) by consummation; see *Decretum* 27.2.39 (Werckmeister 185). An *amairiz complida* was a lover and a wife.

(8) *ajóstan*. Pres. indic. 3 pl. of *ajostar*.

(8) *pécan*. Pres. indic. 3 pl. of *pecar*.

Form

One stanza of eight lines.

SCHEME

a	b	b	a	c	c	d	d

RHYMES

ens	ar	ar	ens	iz	iz	ida	ida

METER

10	10	10	10	10	10	10'	10'

Corrected Readings

(2) *autr'[a]jostar*. P: *autre jostrar*; R: *autraiustar*.

(3) *E[n]*. P, R: *e*.

Quan vei les pratz verdesir

One manuscript: *W. BEdT* 461.206.
Major editions: Mölk; Rieger (628–39); Bec (195–99); Gambino (207–15).

Troubadour chansonnier *W* was composed in northern France, perhaps near Arras (Pas-de-Calais), between 1254 and circa 1280. As *W* presents this poem, several rhymes mediate between Occitan and French, evoking Occitan for an intended French audience (see the note on rhymes below). The effect is that of an interlanguage. Some words are French (see glosses). Preceding editors have attempted to reconstitute an archetypal Occitan version that may never have existed. This edition presents the text with minimal corrections.
 The poem is entered in *W* below a blank staff (lines without notes).

W, fol. 198v, col. 1.

I

Quan vei° les praz° verdesir°	when I see; meadows; turn green
et pare[i]s° la flor° granea°,	appears; flower; blooming
adonques° pens° et consir°	then; I think; I reflect
d'amors qu'ainsi° m'a'legrea°.	this way; has made me happy
5 *Per un pou non° m'a tuea°;*	*per un pou non*, almost; has killed
tan soën° souspir°	so often; I sigh
c'ainc non vi° tan for colea°	because I never saw; so strong a hit
senes colp ferir°.	without striking a blow
A, e, i°!	(onomatopoeia for a sigh)

(1) *vei*. Pres. indic. 3 sg. of *véire*.
(1) *les*. OFr.; Oc. *los*, definite article, masc. obl. pl., 'the.'
(2) *paré[i]s*. Pres. indic. 3 sg. of *paréiser*.
(2) *granéa*. Merges Oc. *granáda* with OFr. *grenée*, past part. fem. of Oc. *granar* and OFr. *grener*.

(3) *pens.* Pres. indic. 1 sg. of *pensar.*

(3) *consir.* Pres. indic. 1 sg. of *consirar.*

(4–5) *legréa … tuéa.* Fem. The speaker is a woman.

(4) *m'a'legréa.* That is, *m'a alegréa.* Merges Oc. *alegráda* with OFr. *alegrée*, past part. fem. of Oc. *alegrar* and OFr. *alegrer.*

(5) *pou.* OFr.; Oc. *pauc* 'a little bit.'

(5) *tuéa.* Merges Oc. *tuáda* with OFr. *tüée*, past part. fem. of Oc. *tuar* and OFr. *tüer.*

(6) *souspir.* Pres. indic. 1 sg. of *sospirar.*

(7) *c'ainc non vi.* 'Because I never saw.'

(7) *vi.* Pret. 1 sg. of *véire.*

(7) *for.* Form before a consonant; usually *fort.*

(7) *coléa.* Merges Oc. *coláda* with OFr. *colée* 'blow to the neck' (*col*).

II

10 *Tota nuit° souspir et veill°*   all night; I lie awake
    et tressal° tot endormia°   I shiver; deeply asleep
    per oc car° ve[j]aire° m'es   because; it seems to me
    que.l meus amis se resia°.   is waking up
    A, De[us]! Seri[a]° garia°   I would be; healed
15   *s'ensi° devengues°*   this way; it happened
    una nuit par escaria°   by fate
        qu'a me s'en vengues°.   he came
              A, e, i!

(10) *Tota.* Oc.; OFr. *tote.*

(10) *nuit.* OFr.; Oc. *noch.*

(10) *véill.* Pres. indic. 1 sg. of *velhar.*

(11) *tressál.* Pres. indic. 1 sg. of *tresalhir.*

(11) *endormía.* Merges Oc. *endormida* with OFr. *endormie*, past part. fem. of *endormir.*

(12) *per oc car.* Equivalent to *per o car.*

(13) *resía.* Equivalent to *resída*, pres. indic. 3 sg. of *residar* (reflexive).

(14) *Serí[a].* Conditional 1 sg. of *éser.*

(14) *garía.* Merges Oc. *garída* with OFr. *garíe*, past part. fem. of *garir.*

(15) *devengués.* Past subj. 3 sg. of *devenir.*

(16) *par.* OFr.; Oc. *per.*

(16) *escaría.* Merges Oc. *escarída* with OFr. *escaríe.*

(17) *vengués.* Past subj. 3 sg. of *venir.*

III

    Domna° qui[.n] amor s'aten°   a lady; gives heed to
20 *ben de[u]° aver fin coraje°;*   must; a sincere heart
    tal n'i a qu'ades° la pren,   at once
    puis° la laissa° per folaje°;   then; leaves; out of frivolity
    maiz eu l'en ten° fin corage   have for him
        ensi° lealment°   *ensi … c'*, so … that; loyally

25 *c'ainc dosna° del mieu parage°*   *ainc ... non*, never; a lady; of my rank
      non ou fiz° tant gent°.   did so; so nobly
        A, e, i!

---

(19) *[.n].* That is, *en.*
(19) *atén.* Pres. indic. 3 sg. of *atendre.*
(20) *dé[u].* Pres. indic. 3 sg. of *dever.*
(21) 'There is such [a man] who takes her at once.' Some men would do so.
(22) *láissa.* Pres. indic. 3 sg. of *laisar.*
(23) *l'.* Equivalent to *li.*
(23) *ten.* Pres. indic. 1 sg. of *tener.*
(25) *c'.* That is, *que.*
(25) *dosna.* Merges OFr. *dosne* with Oc. *domna.*
(26) *fiz.* Pret. 3 sg. of *faire*, vicarious; repetition of *ten.*

IV

      Dosna qui amic° non a   a lover
      ben si gart° que mais no° n'aia°,   should take care; never; to have one
30 *qu'amors pon° ui e demag°.*   stings; today and tomorrow
      Ni tan ni quan non° s'ap[a]ia°;   *ni tan ni quan non*, never; it is content
      senes colp° fai mort°, et plaia°   without a blow; a dead man; a wound
          tal° ja non garra°   such that; it never will be cured
      per nul mege° que j[a]° n'aia,   by any doctor; ever
35   *se mors° non lo.i da.*   death
            A, e, i!

---

(29) *gart.* Pres. subj. 3 sg. of *gardar.*
(29) *áia.* Pres. subj. 3 sg. of *aver.*
(30) *pon.* Pres. indic. 3 sg. of *pónher.*
(30) *demág.* More often *deman.*
(31) *ap[á]ia.* Pres. indic. 3 sg. of *apagar* (reflexive).
(32) *fai.* Pres. indic. 3 sg. of *faire.*
(33) *garrá.* Fut. 3 sg. of *garir.*
(32–34) 'And a wound such [that] it will never be cured by any doctor that [she] will ever get.'
(35) 'Unless death gives him' (*lo*, a doctor) 'to her' (*i*).
(35) *da.* Pres. indic. 3 sg. of *dar.*

V

      Messagier°, levaz° matin°   messenger; get up; early
      et vai° m'en la gran jornaa°,   go; a long day's journey
      la chançon° a mon amic   my song
40 *li portaz° en sa contraa°;*   take; country

digas° li que mol° m'agraa°   tell him; very much; it pleases me
     quan membres° del song°   I remember; song
qu'el mi dist° quan m'ot° baisaa°   he sang to me; had; kissed me
     soz mon paveillon°.   in my tent
45   *A, e, i!*

(37) *leváz.* Imperative 2 pl. of *levar* or unusual spelling for 2 sg. *lévas* (in view of 2 sg. later).
(38) *vai.* Imperative 2 sg. of *anar.*
(38) *jornáa.* Merges Oc. *jornada* with OFr. *jornee.*
(40) *portáz.* Imperative 2 pl. of *portar* or unusual spelling for 2 sg. *pórtas.*
(40) *contráa.* Merges Oc. *contráda* with OFr. *contrée.*
(41) *dígas.* Imperative 2 sg. of *dire.*
(41) *mol.* Usually *molt.* Cf. *for/fort* (v. 7).
(41) *agráa.* Merges Oc. *agráda* with OFr. *agrée,* pres. indic. 3 sg. of Oc. *agradar* and OFr. *agreër.*
(42) *membrés.* Past subj. 1 sg. of *membrar.*
(42) *song.* Equivalent to *son.*
(43) *dist.* Pret. 3 sg. of *dire.*
(43) *ot.* OFr.; Oc. *ac,* pret. 3 sg. of *aver.*
(43) *baisáa.* Merges Oc. *baizáda* with OFr. *baisiée,* past part. fem. of Oc. *baizar* and OFr. *baisier.*

VI

Dins° ma chambre encortinaa°   into; curtained chamber
     fu° il a larron°,   he came; like a thief
dins° ma chambre ben doraa°   in; gilded
49   *fu° il en prison°.*   he was; in [love's] prison

(46) *chambre.* OFr.; Oc. *cambra.*
(46) *encortináa.* Merges Oc. *encortináda* with OFr. *encortinée,* past part. fem. of Oc. *encortinar* and OFr. *encortiner.*
(47) *fu.* Pret. 3 sg. of *éser* 'to go' ("se rendre," PD).
(48) *doráa.* Merges Oc. *dauráda* with OFr. *dorée,* past part. fem. of Oc. *daurar* and OFr. *dorer.*
(49) *fu.* Pret. 3 sg. of *éser* 'to be,' the usual meaning.

Form

Five *coblas singulars* of nine lines and one *tornada* of four. The scheme changes: there are two rhymes in stanzas I–IV but three in stanzas V–VI. Some lines assonate instead of rhyming: *éill/es* (vv. 10, 12), *in/ic* (vv. 37, 39). The refrain (indicated in the scheme by a capital letter) does not repeat at the end of the *tornada.*

SCHEME 1

a	b	a	b	b	a	b	a	C

RHYMES 1

I	ir	ea	ir	ea	ea	ir	ea	ir	a, e, i
II	éill	ía	es	ía	ía	es	ía	es	a, e, i
III	en	aje	en	aje	age	ent	age	ent	a, e, i
IV	a	áia	ag	áia	áia	a	áia	a	a, e, i

SCHEME 2

a	b	a	b	b	c	b	c	D

RHYMES 2

V	in	áa	ic	áa	áa	ong	áa	on	a, e, i
VI					áa	on	áa	on	

METER

7	7$'$	7	7$'$	7$'$	5	7$'$	5	3

Note on Rhymes

Some rhymes delete an intervocalic -*d*- from Occitan to produce quasi-French:

by merging Oc. -*ada* with OFr. -*ee*, they produce -*éa* (stanza I);
by merging Oc. -*ida* with OFr. -*ie*, they produce -*ía* (stanza II); and
by merging Oc. -*ada* with OFr. -*ee*, they produce -*áa* (stanzas V and VI).

These deletions reflect the normal development of Lat. -*t*- between vowels, which became -*d*- in Oc. but was deleted in OFr. For example, Lat. *vitam*, Oc. *vida* > OFr. *vie* 'life.'

Corrected Readings

(2) *pare[i]s*. W: *pareus*; Gambino reads *parens* (?).
(11) *tot endormia*. W: *tote endormia*.
(12) *ve[j]aire*. W: *veraire*.
(14) *De[us]*. W: *Dex* (*-x* = abbreviation for -*us*).
(14) *Seri[a] garia*. W: *com seri garia*; Mölk: *com serai garia*; Gambino: *com seria garia* (+1).
(19) *qui[.n] amor*. W: *qui amor*.
(20) *de[u]*. W: *de*.
(31) *ap[a]ia*. W: *apia*.
(33) *garra*. W: *garria*.
(34) *j[a]*. W: *je*.

Peire Cardenal
Vera vergena Maria

Two manuscripts: *C, T. BEdT* 335.70.
Major editions: Lavaud (232–38); Oroz Arizcuren (362); Riquer, *Trovadores*
(3: 1502–04); Vatteroni (2: 821–31).

Peire Cardenal was born in Le Puy-en-Velay (Haute-Loire). He became a
cleric and a court poet in the service of Raymond VI of Toulouse, then Jaume I
of Aragon. He left seventy compositions, among them several that are critical of
unworthy clergy, and this prayer to the Virgin. His *vida* says he lived to be about
a hundred (*BT* 335–36). He was active as a poet from 1204 to 1271.

An initial in chansonnier *C* has been excised, leaving a lacuna that affects
stanzas III and IV. This edition supplements *C* by drawing on *T.* Text from *T* is
in square brackets [ ], as is the refrain when *C* abbreviates it.

C, fol. 288r, cols. 1–2, and *T*, fols. 109r, col. 2–109v, col. 2.

P. Cardenal

I

Vera° vergena° Maria,	true; virgin
vera vida°, vera fes°,	life; faith
vera vertatz°, vera via°,	truth; way
vera vertutz°, vera res°,	power; creature
5 *vera maire°, ver'amia°,*	mother; friend (lover)
ver'amors, vera merces°,	mercy
per ta vera merce sia°	let it be
qu'eret° en me tos heres°.	choose an heir; your heir

    De patz°, si.t plai°, dona, traita°,   for peace; please; intercede
10 *qu'°ap to filh° me sia faita°.*   that; with your son; it be made

---

(7) *sía.* Pres. subj. 3 sg. of *éser*, expressing a wish.
(8) 'That your heir' (Christ) 'choose me as his heir' (grant me salvation).
(8) *erét.* Pres. subj. 3 sg. of *eretar*.
(8) *herés.* Nom. sg. of *eré*.
(9) *plai.* Pres. indic. 3 sg. of *plazer*.
(9) *traita.* Imperative 2 sg. of *traitar*. The speaker uses 2 sg. (*tu*) for the Virgin throughout.
(10) *faita.* Past part. fem. of *faire*.
(10) In the refrain in *C*, the poet prays for peace between Christ and himself. In *T*, he prays for peace between Christ and *nos* 'us,' humanity (see the corrected readings below).

II

    Tu restauriest° la follia°   atoned for; madness
    don° Adam fon° sobrepres°,   by which; was; overtaken
    tu yest° estela° que guia°   are; a star; guides
    los passans° d'aquest paes°,   those passing through; this region (life)
15 *e tu yest l'alba° del dia°*   dawn; day
    don° lo tieus filhs° solelhs° es,   of which; your son; sun
    que.l calfa° e clarifia°,   who warms it; brightens
    verais°, de dreitura° ples°.   true; righteousness; full
    De patz, [si.t plai, dona, traita,
20 *qu'ap to filh me sia faita.]*

---

(11) *restauriést.* Pret. 2 sg. of *restaurar*.
(12) *fon.* Pret. 3 sg. of *éser*.
(12) *sobreprés.* Past part. of *sobreprendre*.
(13) *yest.* Pres. indic. 2 sg. of *éser*.
(13) *guía.* Pres. indic. 3 sg. of *guiar*.
(14) *passáns.* Pres. part. masc. obl. pl. of *pasar*.
(16) *filhs.* Nom. sg. of *filh*.
(16) *solélhs.* Nom. sg. of *solelh*.
(17) *calfa.* Pres. indic. 3 sg. of *calfar*.
(17) *clarifía.* Pres. indic. 3 sg. of *clarifiar*.
(18) *verais, ples.* Masc. nom. sg. of *verai, plen*; both modify *solelhs* (v. 16).

III

    Tu f[ust° nada° de Suria°,   were; born; Syria
    gentils°] e pau[ra° d'arnes°,   noble; but poor; attire
    umils° e pu]ra° e p[ia°   humble; pure; gentle
    en fatz°, en ditz°, ez en pes°;]   deeds; words; thoughts
25 *faita° [per tal maistria°—*   made; such skill
    ses° totz] mals, [mas ab° toz bes—   without; with

tan fust° de] douss[a° paria°

that you were of such; gentle; company

per que Dieus en] tu se [mes°.
De patz, si.t plai, dona, traita,
30 *qu'ap to filh me sia faita.]*

that God put himself

---

(21) *f[ust*. Pret. 2 sg. of *éser*.
(21) *náda*. Past part. fem. of *náiser*.
(21) *Suría*. The Holy Land including Lebanon, home of the Bride in the Song of Songs (4.8).
(22) *gentíls] e pau[ra*. *E* = adversative 'but.'
(25–28) *faita [per tal maistría … tan fust de] douss[a paria per que per que Dieus en] tu se [mes*. 'Made with such skill … [that] you would be of so gentle company that God put himself in you.'
(27) *fust*. Past subj. 2 sg. of *éser*.
(28) *mes*. Pret. 3 sg. of *metre*.

IV

Aq[uel° que en te se fia°
ja] no.l c[al° autre defes°,
qe, si tot°] lo m[on° peria°,
aquel° non° peria°] ges;
35 *quar als tieus precx° s'umilia°*
l'auzisme°, a cuy que pes°,
e.l tieu filhs non contraria°
ton voler° neguna ves°.
De patz, si.t plai, dona, traita,
40 *[qu'ap to filh me sia faita]*

he who; trusts
doesn't care about; [any] other protection
although; world; perished
he; *non … ges*, not at all; would perish
at your prayers; becomes humble
highest one; whomever it may displease
disobey
your wish; at any time

---

(31) *fía*. Pres. indic. 3 sg. of *fiar*.
(32) *c[al*. Pres. indic. 3 sg. of *caler* (impersonal).
(33) *pería*. Pres. subj. 3 sg. of *perir*; subj. after *si tot*.
(33) *m[on*. Obl. for subject.
(34) *pería*. First conditional 3 sg. of *perir*, usually *periria* or *perria*.
(35) *s'umilía*. Pres. indic. 3 sg. of *umiliar* (reflexive).
(36) *pes*. Pres. subj. 3 sg. of *pezar*.
(37) *contraría*. Pres. indic. 3 sg. of *contrariar*.

V

David, en la prophetia°
dis°, en un salme° que fes°,
qu'al destre° de Dieu sezia°–
del rey° en la ley° promes°–
45 *una reÿna° qu'avia°*
vestirs° de var° e d'aurfres°;

his prophecy
said; psalm; he made
right hand; was sitting
king; law (Bible); promised
queen; who had
garments; vair (squirrel fur); orphrey

tu yest elha, ses falhia°,   no doubt
non o pot vedar° plaides°.   deny; quibbler
De patz, si.t plai, dona, traita,
50 *[qu'ap to filh me sia faita];*

---

(42) *un salme.* "Astitit regina a dextris tuis in vestitu deaurato, circundata varietate" 'A queen stood on your right hand in gilded garments, wrapped in colorful attire' (Ps. 44.10; my trans.).

(42) *dis.* Pret. 3 sg. of *dire.*

(42) *fes.* Pret. 3 sg. of *faire.*

(43) *sezía.* Imperfect 3 sg. of *sezér.*

(44) *promés.* Past part. of *prométre.*

(45) *reÿna.* Subject of *sezia* (v. 43).

(45) *avía.* Imperfect 3 sg. of *aver.*

VI

qu'al latz° de Dieu estas°, traita   side; stand
52 *que.m sia patz de luy faita*

(49–52) 'Please, lady, intercede for peace, that it be made for me with your son; [you] who stand at the side of God, intercede, so that peace be made for me with him.'

(51) *estas.* Pres. indic. 2 sg. of *estar.* The psalm reads "astitit" (see v. 42 note).

Form

Five *coblas unissonans* of ten lines and one *tornada* of two. The last two lines in the stanza are a refrain, indicated in the scheme by capital letters.

SCHEME
a b a b a b a b C   C

RHYMES
ía es ía es ía es ía es áita áita

METER
7' 7 7' 7 7' 7 7' 7 7'   7'

Corrected Readings

(5–6) *ver'amia, / ver'amors.* C: *vera mia vera mors.*

(9–10) *De patz, [si.t plai], dona, tra[i]ta, / qu'ap to filh me sia faita.* T: *de patz donna sitz plas tracta / c'ab ton fil nos sia facta.*

(12) *Adam.* C: *Adā;* T: *Adamps.*

(19–20) Partially excised in *C,* given here as in stanza I; *T: donx paz donna siz plaz tracta / c'ap ton fil nos sia facta.*

(21–30) Lacunae in *C* supplemented from *T.*

(24) *en fatz, en ditz. T: e fatz et en diz* (+1).

(29–30) As in stanza I; *T: de patz donna sitz plas tracta / ab ton fil nos sia facta.*

(31–34) Lacunae in C supplemented from T.

(33) *m[on. T: mon.*

(34) *peria. T: penria.*

(36) *a cuy.* C: *as cuy; T: a cui.*

(40) *[qu'ap to filh me sia faita].* C: *etc.;* T: *c'ap ton fil nosiatz facta.*

(50) *[qu'ap to filh me sia faita].* C: *etc.;* T: *c'ab ton fils nos sias facta.*

Quan lo rossinhols s'escria

One manuscript: *C. BEdT* 461.203.
Major editions: Riquer, *Trovadores* (3: 1697); Chaguinian (193–94).

The Occitan *alba* 'dawn,' a song of the meeting or parting of lovers at break of day, flourished in the thirteenth century. The manuscript containing this one was compiled in Narbonne in the fourteenth; we have no other way to date or locate the poem. It may have been intended as a single stanza (a *cobla* as genre), as it stands in the manuscript.

The lovers resemble birds, as do Paolo and Francesca, who seem light (*leggieri*) as they are carried by the wind of *Inferno* (5.75).

C, fol. 383v, col. 2.

Albas ses titol
albas. Nom. and obl. pl. of *alba* 'dawn song.'
ses. 'Without.'
titol. 'Title'; (in manuscript) rubric, attribution.
The heading introduces three anonymous *albas*. This is the first one.

Quan lo rossinhol° s'escria°	nightingale; calls
ab° sa par° la nueg° e.l dia°,	with; his mate; by night; by day
yeu suy ab ma bell'amia	
jos° la flor°	under; flower
5 tro° la gaita° de la tor°	until; watchman; from the tower
escrida°, "Drutz°, al levar!	calls; lover; get up!
Qu'ieu vey° l'alba	I see
e.l jorn° clar°!"	day; bright

(1) *lo rossinhól.* Obl. sg. for the subject.

(1) *escría.* Pres. indic. 3 sg. of *escridar* (reflexive).

(4) The lovers are like birds in a garden.

(6) *escrída.* Equivalent to *escria* (v. 1). The watchman calls like the bird.

(6) *Drutz.* Masc. nom. (vocative) sg.

(6) *al levar.* Imperative infinitive.

(7) *vey.* Pres. indic. 1 sg. of *véire.*

Form

One stanza of eight lines.

SCHEME

a a a b b c d c

RHYMES

ia ia ia or or ar alba ar

METER

7' 7' 7' 3 7 7 3' 3

Corrected Reading

(3) *bell'amia.* C: *bella mia.*

Dante Alighieri
Tam m'abelis vostre cortes deman

Piacenza, Biblioteca Comunale, MS 190. Written in 1336; the oldest of the nearly eight hundred manuscripts of *The Divine Comedy*. With reference to Firenze, Biblioteca Nazionale Centrale, Fondo Nazionale II.1.36.
Purgatorio 26, vv. 140–47. Major editions: Singleton, *Purgatorio* (1: 288 and 2: 647–48); Durling and Martinez, *Purgatorio*.

Dante wrote *Purgatorio* about 1310. Canto 26 describes the highest circle of this realm, reserved for sinners who were lustful but repented. There the pilgrim encounters the spirit of the poet Guido Guinizelli (who died in 1276) and greets him as his poetic father. Guido points forward to another shade, calling him a "miglior fabbro del parlar materno" 'better craftsman in the mother tongue' (*Purgatorio* 26.117; my trans.). Then Guido disappears.
    Dante ceremoniously asks the second shade his name. He answers, speaking in Occitan, that he is Arnaut Daniel. He borrows words and phrases from poems by the real Arnaut Daniel and other troubadours.[vi] The eight lines constitute an Occitan *cobla*, the genre of poems consisting of one stanza that developed in the late twelfth century. By composing it, Dante made himself an Occitan troubadour (Wells, "Cobbling" 171–72).

Piacenza, MS 190, fol. 59r, col. 1, with reference to Firenze, MS II.1.36, fol. 64r, col. 2.

Tam m'abelis° vostre cortes deman°	pleases me; courteous request
ch'ieu non [me] puos° ne vuoil° a vos	I can; want; conceal myself
cobrire°.	

    vi. Cf. "Tan m'abellis l'amoros pessamens," the first line of a song by Folquet de Marselha (*BEdT* 155.22), quoted by Dante in *De vulgari eloquentia* (2.6.6). At v. 3, cf. *Ieu sui Arnautz qu'amas l'aura* 'I am Arnaut, who pile up the wind,' by Arnaut Daniel himself (see no. 18, v. 43). For more, see Smith.

Ie fui° Arnaut, che plor° e va[u]° cantan°;
consiros° vei° la passada follor°,
5 *e vei giausen° lo jor° ch'esper° denan°.*
Ara° [v]os pre[c]° per achella valor°
che [v]us guida° [al son° de l']escalina°,
sovegna° vos a temps° de ma dolor°!

was; weep; walk; singing
worried; I see; my past folly
rejoicing; day; I await; ahead
now; I pray you; by that merit
guides you; to the top; stair
remember; a while; my pain

(1–2) *tam ... ch'*. 'So much ... that,' *ch'* = *che.*
(1) *tam.* Normally *tan;* the *-m* anticipates *m-.*
(1) *abelís.* Pres. indic. 3 sg. of *abelir* with inchoative *-is* (*Old Occitan* 167).
(1) *deman.* Obl. sg. for subject of *abelis.*
(2) *puós.* Pres. indic. 1 sg. of *poder.* Merges Oc. *puósc* with It. *pósso.*
(2) *vuóil.* Pres. indic. 1 sg. of *voler.*
(2) *cobríre.* Merges Oc. *cobrir* with It. *coprire.* Rhymes with It. *disire, dire* (*Purgatorio* 26.137 and 139); makes a full hendecasyllable (see the section on form below).
(3) *fúi.* Pret. 1 sg. of *éser.*
(3) *Arnaut.* Obl. sg. for predicate complement. Names never followed declension consistently.
(3) *plor.* Pres. indic. 1 sg. of *plorar.* Anticipates *consiros* (v. 4).
(3) *va[u].* Pres. indic. 1 sg. of *anar.*
(3) *cantán.* Pres. part. of *cantar.* Anticipates *giausen* (v. 5).
(4) *véi.* Pres. indic. 1 sg. of *véire.*
(5) *giausén.* Pres. part. of *jauzir* 'to rejoice.' Cf. It. *giausire,* thirteenth century (Battaglia 6: 771).
(5) *espér.* Pres. indic. 1 sg. of *esperar.*
(6) *pre[c].* Pres. indic. 1 sg. of *pregar.*
(7) *guida.* Pres. indic. 3 sg. of *guidar.*
(7) *son.* Variant of *som* 'top' (Appel, *Provenzalische Chrestomathie* 306).
(7) *escalína.* Oc. *escala* with suffix *-ina,* added to nouns with little change of meaning (Adams 236–38). Rhymes with It. *affina* (*Purgatorio* 26.148). Cf. It. *scalena,* thirteenth century (Battaglia 17: 762).
(8) *sovégna.* Pres. subj. 3 sg. of *sovenir* (impersonal); *sovegna vos* (imperative), remember!
(8) *a temps.* "Pour un certain temps" (*PD*).

Form

Eight lines in *terza rima,* the rhyme scheme of the *Comedy.*

SCHEME

a   b   a   c   a   c   d   c

RHYMES

an   ire   an   or   an   or   ina   or

METER

10   10'   10   10   10   10   10'   10

In Occitan the meter is counted as ten syllables masculine or feminine; in Italian as eleven (the hendecasyllable), including a final unstressed syllable that may be cut short. The *Comedy* is written in hendecasyllables. As counted in Italian, verses 2 and 7 are full hendecasyllables; the other lines are truncated.

Corrected Readings

(2) *non [me] puos.* Piacenza, MS 190: *non puos* (−1).
(3) *plor.* Piacenza, MS 190: *ploro* (+1) 1 sg. pres. indic. of Lat. *plorare*, to weep.
(3) *va[u].* Piacenza, MS 190: *va,* pres. indic. 3 sg. of Oc. *anar.*
(4) *la passada.* Piacenza, MS 190: *laspassada.*
(6) *Ara [v]os.* Piacenza, MS 190: *ara.us* (−1).
(6) *pre[c].* Piacenza, MS 190: *preu.*
(7) *che [v]us.* Piacenza, MS 190: *che us* (*ch'us,* −1?).
(7) *[al son de l']escalina.* Piacenza, MS 190 reads *ses fe freg ses calina* (first *ses* expunctuated?), which makes no sense. Corrected from Firenze, MS II.1.36.

Non puesc mudar non plainha ma rancura

One manuscript: f. BEdT 461.177.
Major editions: Meyer (118); Zufferey; Gambino (155–66).

An unknown poet complains of a *gran malautia* 'great disease' (v. 28) that has driven him into exile on an island (v. 11). Perhaps he has withdrawn to a leper colony. Several French poets of the thirteenth century, stricken by leprosy, composed *congés* 'leave-takings' as they prepared to leave the world (for editions of these, see Ruelle).

f, fol. 40r.

I

*Non puesc mudar° non plainha° ma
   rancura,°*
seinher° Austor, car est° de mon estaje°,
car m'es camjat° mon joy e m'aventura°,
   [-aje]
5 *et ai perdut° tot solas° e deport°,*
et ai perdut luy° que sueill° amar fort,
et ai perdut la vostra compainhia°.
*Mort°, car non m'ausis°? Fas° gran
   vilania°!*

keep from; bemoaning; rancor

lord; since you are; standing
has changed; destiny

I have lost; comfort; amusement
him (her); I used to
your company
death; kill; you do; villainy

(1) *puésc.* Pres. indic. 1 sg. of *poder.*
(1) *pláinha.* Pres. subj. 1 sg. of *plánher. Non* is redundant after *non puesc.*
(2) *séinher.* Nom. (vocative) sg. of *senhór.*
(2) *Austór,* (9) *Astór.* The individual cannnot be identified. The name corresponds to Lat. Eustorgius.
(2) *est.* Pres. indic. 2 pl. of *éser,* usually *etz.*

(3) *es.* Pres. indic. 3 sg. of *éser.*
(3) *camjat.* Past part. of *camjar.*
(3) *mon joy.* Obl. sg. for the subject of *es camjat.*
(4) A line that rhymed in *-aje* is missing.
(5) *ai.* Pres. indic. 1 sg. of *aver.*
(5) *perdut.* Past part. of *perdre.*
(6) *luy.* May refer to either gender (*DOM*).
(6) *suéill.* Pres. indic. 1 sg. of *soler.*
(8) *ausís.* Pres. indic. 2 sg. of *aucire.*
(8) *Fas.* Pres. indic. 2 sg. of *faire.*

II

Amixs° n'°Astor, fort m'es greus° e
   salvaje°,   friend; sir; it is very dire; cruel

10 fort engoisos° ez estrainh° a suf[erre]° painful; terrible; to suffer
qu'ieu en Embiers° aia pres° ostalage°; Embiez; have taken; lodging
meravil° mi car tot vieu° no.m soterre° I am amazed; alive; bury
                      myself

o car non soy° tan lueinh° d'aquest pays° go; so far; from this country
ves calque part°, que ja mais res° no.m anywhere; anyone; would see
   vis°,

15 vo° sufrir m'er°, vueilha o non qu'ieu sia, where; I will have to suffer
los mals° qu'ieu trai° tro que° la mort misfortunes; bear; until; kills
   m'ausia°.

---

(11) *Embiers.* Embiez, an island in the Mediterranean off Toulon (Var).
(11) *áia.* Pres. subj. 1 sg. of *aver.*
(11) *pres.* Past part. of *prendre.*
(12) *meravíl.* Pres. indic. 1 sg. of *meravilhar* (reflexive).
(12) *soterre.* Pres. subj. 1 sg. of *sotzterrar; -e* is a support vowel for the double consonant.
(13) *soy.* Pres. indic. 1 sg. of *éser* 'to go' ("se rendre," *PD*).
(14) *ja mais . . . no.* 'Never.'
(14) *vis.* Past subj. 3 sg. of *véire.*
(15) *vo.* Equivalent to *o.*
(15) *er.* Fut. 3 sg. of *éser; sufrir m'er,* literally, 'it will be for me to suffer.'
(15) *vuéilha o non qu'ieu sía.* 'Whether or not I want to be [there].'
(15) *vuéilha, sía.* Pres. subj. 1 sg. of *voler, éser,* respectively. Subj. expressing uncertainty.
(16) *trai.* Pres. indic. 1 sg. of *traire.*
(16) *ausía.* Pres. subj. 3 sg. of *aucire;* subj. after *tro que.*

III

Qu'ieu am° donnas sueill aver compainhia with
ez am clergues°, am jent° ben enseinhada°; clerics; people; taught
ar me soy mes°, car non truop° autra via°, put; I find; another alternative
20 ab una res° qu'es del segle° triada°; person; world; separated

qu'ieu solïa° portar° solas° am l[atz]°,	I used to; wear; shoes; laces
rauba d'esta[m], fos uvern ho est[atz],	
aras mi ven° portar solas de vaca°,	befalls me; cowhide
ez° estauc pres° com fa ors° a estaca°.	and; I am caught; bear; stake

(17) *am.* Equivalent to *ab.*

(18) *enseinháda.* Past part. fem. of *ensenhar.*

(19) *mes.* Past part. of *metre.*

(19) *truóp.* Pres. indic. 1 sg. of *trobar.*

(20) *triáda.* Past part. fem. of *triar.*

(21–23) 'I used to wear shoes with laces, clothing of thin wool, winter or summer; now I wear shoes of cowhide.' Elegant slippers vs. rustic boots.

(21) *solïa.* Imperfect 1 sg. of *soler.* The sense of the imperfect is like that of pres. indic. *suéill* (vv. 6, 17).

(21) *solás.* Usually *sotlars* (OFr. *solers*).

(22) *fos.* Past subj. 3 sg. of *éser.*

(22) *uvern ho est[atz].* Case usage is inconsistent because declension is obsolete: *uvern* is obl. sg. for predicate nominative; *estatz* is nom. sg.

(23) *ven.* Pres. indic. 3 sg. of *venir.*

(24) *ez.* Equivalent to *e* before a vowel.

(24) *estauc.* Pres. indic. 1 sg. of *estar.*

(24) *fa.* Vicarious. 'I am caught as a bear is [caught] at a stake.' Bearbaiting, "[t]he practice of setting dogs to fight against a bear, which has been chained or tethered by the neck or leg, as a form of entertainment" (see "Bear-baiting, *N.*, Sense 1.a").

IV

25 *Qu'ieu solïa chantar per alegr[age]°*	merriment
e per midons° qu'ieu tant amar solïa,	milady
mas aras chant e proë° mon damnage°	show; suffering
car ieu soy pres de tan gran malautia°!	by so great a disease
A mi que° cal°, qu'ieu n'ai lo cor° perdut?	what; does it matter; heart
30 *A Jezu Crist n'ai l'esperit° rendut°;*	soul; given
lo mals qu'ieu trai e la grieu° penedensa°	heavy; penance
vueil° tostens mais° sufrir, ez am temensa°.	I agree; forevermore; fear

(27) *proë.* Pres. indic. 1 sg. of *proar;* final *-e* is an unusual first person marker (*Old Occitan* 25).

(29) *cal.* Pres. indic. 3 sg. of *caler* (impersonal).

(29) *cor.* He has lost a man or a woman (*luy*, v. 6) and a lady (v. 26) to death, and the company of Austor, still living (v. 7).

(30) *rendút.* Past part. of *rendre.*

(32) *vuéil.* Pres. indic. 1 sg. of *voler.*

(32) *ez am teménsa.* 'And [I agree to bear it] with fear.'

Form

Four *coblas singulars* of eight lines.

SCHEME

a	b	a	b	c	c	d	d

RHYMES

I	ura	aje	ura	aje	ort	ort	ia	ia
II	aje	erre	age	erre	ys	is	ia	ia
III	ia	ada	ia	ada	atz	atz	aca	aca
IV	age	ia	age	ia	ut	ut	ensa	ensa

METER

10'	10'	10'	10'	10	10	10'	10'

Note on Declension

The function of *-s*, which earlier marked the masculine nominative singular, is no longer recognized. It is replaced by the oblique singular in nominative functions: *mon joy* (v. 3), *estrainh* (v. 10), and *uvern* (v. 22). The *-s* becomes part of the root in oblique functions: *greus* (v. 9), *ab una res* (v. 20), and *lo mals* (v. 31).

Corrected Readings

(8) *Fas. f: ben fas* (+1).
(10) *suf[erre]. f: sufrir* rhyming with *soterre* (v. 12).
(21) *l[atz]. f: luy* rhyming with *est[atz]* (v. 22), itself corrected.
(22) *esta[m]. f: estainh* 'tin.'
(22) *fos. f: Fort fos* (+1).
(22) *est[atz]. f: estieu* rhyming with *l[atz]* (v. 21), itself corrected.
(25) *alegr[age]. f: alegrier* rhyming with *damnage* (v. 27).

The Queen of Mallorca
Ez yeu am tal qu'es bo e belh

One manuscript: *VeAg*. Parramon 295, no. 92.1.

Major editions: Cluzel (369–73); Alberni, *Cançoner* (1: 501–02). Alberni, "Poemet" gives a normalized text with variants for verses 1–13 from a Catalan translation of the *Decameron* written in 1429.

The queen in question has been identified as one of the two wives of Jaume III of Mallorca. His first wife, Constança of Aragon, probably died in 1346. He married the second, Violant de Vilaragut, in 1347. He was obliged to leave her frequently, traveling to his scattered holdings in France as he resisted the incursions of Pere IV of Aragon. After Pere captured Mallorca, Jaume sold Montpellier to Philip VI of France. Using funds from the sale, he outfitted a fleet and invaded his former kingdom. He died in battle there in 1349.

The poem is a *descort*, a genre that expressed the lover's anguish by irregular versification. The two stanzas follow an identical scheme more than halfway through but then diverge; the second is two lines longer than the first (see the section on form below). At the end of the stanzas, *Ffrança* (stanza I) is a slant rhyme with *guirença* (II) and *pença* (III). The *tornada* echoes stanza II imperfectly. If these are licenses, they may be laid to the nonprofessional poet, a queen in troubled times, and the principle of irregularity that governs the genre.

Lyric poets in Catalonia expressed themselves in Occitan from the thirteenth to the fifteenth centuries. This poem, like others, was intended to be in Occitan and plainly is, despite its occasional Catalanisms (see glosses).

VeAg, fols. 49r–v.

La Reÿna de Mallorques
Reÿna. Queen.
Mallórques. Mallorca, the largest of the Balearic Islands.

I

Ez° yeu am° tal° qu'es bo e belh,	and; I love; such [a one] (one)
e suy gaya° co.l blanch [auz]elh°	merry; white bird
que per amor cria° son chant;	calls out
e suy senyora° e capdelh°,	lady (female lord); I rule
5 *e sell° qu'eu am no s'en apelh°,*	the one (he); complain
car sus totes° suy mils° aman,	above all [women]; more loving
que xausit° ay° lo pus° presan°	chosen; I have; most; prized
e.l mils° del mon°, e l'ame tan°	best; world; I love him so
quez en pensan° lo cuey° veser°	in thought; I think; I see him
10 *e car tener°;*	hold him dear
e cant° no's ver°,	when [I realize that]; true
un desesper° me fer° tan gen°,	despair; strikes; so gently
cant lo say° lay°, ves° Ffrança.	I realize; [that he is] there; near

(1) *Ez.* Creates an effect of ongoing conversation.
(2) *gaya.* Fem. of *gay.*
(2) *blanch [auz]élh.* In Catalonia the *colom xarel·lo* 'white dove' is all white. The *colom collaret* 'collared dove' is white except at the neck (Alcover).
(3) *cría.* Pres. indic. 3 sg. of *criar.*
(4) *capdélh.* Pres. indic. 1 sg. of *capdelar.*
(5) *apélh.* Pres. indic. 3 sg. of *apelar* (reflexive).
(6) *tótes.* Cat. Cf. Oc. *totas,* fem. obl. pl. of *tot.*
(7) *xausít.* Cat. spelling of Oc. *cauzit,* past part. of *cauzir* (Cat. *escollir*).
(7) *ay.* Pres. indic. 1 sg. of *aver.*
(7) *presán.* Pres. part. of *prezar* (passive meaning).
(8) *áme.* Pres. indic. 1 sg. of *amar* with sporadic final *-e,* originally a support vowel (Appel, *Provenzalische Chrestomathie* xxii; *Old Occitan* 25). Cf. *am* without *-e* (vv. 1, 5, 18).
(9) *pensán.* Pres. part. of *pensar.*
(9) *cuéy.* Pres. indic. 1 sg. of Oc. and Cat. *cuidar.*
(9) *vesér.* Oc. *vezer,* Cat. *veser* (modern *veure*).
(12) *fer.* Pres. indic. 3 sg. of *ferir.*
(13) *say.* Pres. indic. 1 sg. of *saber.*

II

L'anyoramen° e.l gran desir	sorrow
15 *qu'yeu ay per vos me cuyd'alcir°,*	nearly kills me
mon dolç° senyor° e car;	gentle; lord
e bien liey° poray° tost° morir	perhaps; I will be able; soon
per vos, qu'yeu am tant e desir°,	I desire
si breu° de çay° no.us vey° tornar°,	soon; here; I see; return

20 *que tant me tarda° l'abressar°*   I am so impatient for; embracing
    e.l raysonar°   conversation
    e tota res°;   everything
e cant me pens° que.us n'etz anatz°   I think; you have gone away
    e no tornats°,   return
25   *e quan lunyat° vos etz°,*   how far away; you are
desesperatz° caix° viu° mon cor°;   in despair; nearly; lives; my heart
    per pauch no° mor°   *per pauch no*, almost; I die
    si breu no n'ay° guirença°.   I don't get; a cure

---

(14) *anyoramén.* Cat. *enyorament*, Oc. *enojamen.*
(15) *cuyd'.* That is, *cuída*, pres. indic. 3 sg. of *cuidar* + infinitive, almost the same meaning as the infinitive alone.
(15) *alcir.* Oc. and Cat. *aucir.*
(16) *senyór.* Used by wives of their husbands.
(17) *poráy.* Fut. 1 sg. of *poder.*
(18) *desír.* Pres. indic. 1 sg. of *dezirar.*
(19) *bréu.* Oc. and Cat. *en breu* 'soon.'
(19) *vey.* Pres. indic. 1 sg. of *véire.*
(20) *tarda.* Pres. indic. 3 sg. of *tardar* 'to be slow' (impersonal); *me tarda* 'I am impatient.'
(20) *abressar.* Cat. *abraçar*, pronounced [əβɾəzá] in the Balearics (Alcover); Oc. *abrasar/abraisar* (*DOM*) 'to embrace'; as a noun, 'embracing.'
(21) *raysonar.* Oc. *razonar*, Cat. *raonar* 'to speak'; as a noun, 'conversation.'
(23) *pens.* Pres. indic. 1 sg. of *pensar* (reflexive).
(23) *anatz.* Past part. masc. nom. sg. of *anar.*
(24) *tornats.* Pres. indic. 2 pl. of *tornar.*
(25) *lunyat.* Past part. of Oc. *lonhar/lunhar*, Cat. *llunyar.*
(25) *etz.* Pres. indic. 2 pl. of *éser.*
(26) *desesperatz.* Past part. masc. nom. sg. of *dezesperar*; modifies *mon cor.*
(26) *víu.* Pres. indic. 3 sg. of *víure.*
(27) *mor.* Pres. indic. 1 sg. of *morir.*

Tornada

Merce°, mairits°, que suffr'° en pas°   mercy; husband; I suffer; peace
30 *los mals que.m dats°; e donchs°*   the pains you give me; so; come
    tornats°,   back
    que nulh° tresor°   *nulh ... no*, no; treasure
    no val° un cor   is worth
    que per vos mor°   dies
    ab° amorosa° pença°.   with; loving; thought

---

(29) *mairits.* Nom. (vocative) sg. of *marit* (see the corrected readings below).
(29) *suffr'.* That is, *suffre*, pres. indic. 1 sg. of *sofrir.*
(29) *pas.* Or *patz*, rhyming with *tornats.*
(30) *dats.* Pres. indic. 2 pl. of *dar.*
(30) *tornats.* Imperative 2 pl. of *tornar.*
(32) *val.* Pres. indic. 3 sg. of *valer.*

(33) *mor.* Pres. indic. 3 sg. of *morir.*
(34) *amorosa.* Fem. of *amoros.*

Form

Two stanzas differing in structure (13 lines, 15 lines) and a *tornada* (as it is identified in the MS) of six. The manuscript does not divide the two stanzas. This edition does so according to their internal structure.

SCHEME

I	a	a	b	a	a	b	b	b	c	c	c	d	e		
II	a	a	b	a	a	b	b	b	c	d	d	c	e	e	f
III										d	d	e	e	e	f

RHYMES

I	elh	elh	ant	elh	elh	an	an	an	er	er	er	en	ansa		
II	ir	ir	ar	ir	ir	ar	ar	ar	es	atz	ats	etz	or	or	ensa
III										as	ats	or	or	or	ensa

METER

I	8	8	8	8	8	8	8	8	8	4	4	8	6′		
II	8	8	6	8	8	8	8	4	4	8	4	6	8	4	6′
III										8	8	4	4	4	6′

Note on Declension

Oblique forms in nominative functions: masculine *bo e belh* (v. 1), *anyoramen . . . desir* (v. 14), *lunyat* (v. 25), *mon cor* (v. 26), *nulh tresor* (v. 31).

Corrected Readings

(2) *co.l blanch [auz]elh. VeAg,* Alberni, *Cançoner* (1: 501): *col blanch solelh* 'like the white sun' (?); *Decameron* (qtd. in Alberni, "Poemet" [347]): *com lauzel* (−1); Cluzel: *co.l blanch oselh* (cf. Cat. *aucell/ocell,* Alcover); Alberni, "Poemet" (364): *co.l blanch auzel.*

(29) *mairits.* So *VeAg,* Alberni, *Cançoner* (1: 502); Cluzel: *mairitz*; Alberni, "Poemet" (346): *m'aiats* 'Have mercy on me,' motivated by the assumption that troubadours cannot have sung about married love. For that belief see Pagès: "Il est peu conforme aux pratiques de l'amour courtois qu'un mari ait été l'amant de sa femme" (208). Cluzel responds cogently: "Est-il rationnel de voir toujours et systématiquement dans une oeuvre lyrique médiévale un simple exercice de style et de versification? Pour nous, cette attitude découle d'une de ces 'légendes érudites' dont on a parlé. Conservons donc la leçon: *mayritz = maritz*; elle s'accorde parfaitement avec l'inspiration générale du poème" (371). The debate is an object lesson in the futility of the concept of so-called courtly love.

For up-to-date links to manuscripts available online, see Wells, *Trobaretz*.

CHANSONNIERS

Manuscripts containing the poems are referred to by the following sigla. Those on parchment have sigla in uppercase; those on paper, in lowercase. Those used as base or consulted for this book are given with URLs where available. For well-informed, frequently divergent opinions about the date and location of these manuscripts, see Hebbard.

A   Rome, Biblioteca Apostolica Vaticana, Vaticani latini 5232. Thirteenth century, Italy (Brunel, *Bibliographie* 94, no. 325).
    Color: digi.vatlib.it/view/MSS_Vat.lat.5232.
    Base of nos. 18, 19, 23. Consulted for nos. 12, 15.
B   Paris, Bibliothèque nationale, fonds français 1592. Thirteenth century, Provence (Brunel, *Bibliographie* 46, no. 152) or end of thirteenth century to beginning of fourteenth, Italy (Camps 11–12).
C   Paris, Bibliothèque nationale, fonds français 856. Fourteenth century, Narbonne (Brunel, *Bibliographie* 43, no. 143; Camps 9–10).
    Color: gallica.bnf.fr/ark:/12148/btv1b8419246t.
    Black and white: gallica.bnf.fr/ark:/12148/btv1b9059111m.
    Base of nos. 16, 20, 26, 27. Consulted for nos. 4, 5.
D   Modena, Biblioteca Estense Universitaria, α R.4.4. Part 1, circa 1254 (Pillet and Carstens xii; Zinelli 86); part 2, thirteenth to fourteenth centuries, Italy (Brunel, *Bibliographie* 91–92, no. 314).
    PDF download of complete manuscript, color: bibliotecaestense
    .beniculturali.it/info/img/mss/i-mo-beu-alfa.r.4.4.html.
    Alternative available at the *Internet Archive* without downloading, color: archive.org/details/i-mo-beu-alfa.r.4.4/page/n5/ mode/2up.

Base of nos. 5, 8, 11, 14, 15.

Dc   In *D*, part 2, fols. 243–60.

E   Paris, Bibliothèque nationale, fonds français 1749. Fourteenth century, Biterrois (Brunel, *Bibliographie* 48, no. 156; Camps 13–4). Color: gallica.bnf.fr/ark:/12148/btv1b6000801v. Base of no. 4. Consulted for no. 5.

F   Rome, Biblioteca Apostolica Vaticana, Chigiani L.IV.106. Fourteenth century, Italy (Brunel, *Bibliographie* 97, no. 337).

G   Milan, Biblioteca Ambrosiana, R 71 sup. Fourteenth century, Italy (Brunel, *Bibliographie* 91, no. 311). Color: ambrosiana.comperio.it/opac/detail/view/ambro:catalog :91073. Alternative color: digitallibrary.unicatt.it/veneranda/ 0b02da8280051bf4. Diplomatic edition: Carapezza. Base of nos. 12, 13.

H   Rome, Biblioteca Apostolica Vaticana, Vaticani latini 3207. Fourteenth century, Italy (Brunel, *Bibliographie* 93, no. 321).

I   Paris, Bibliothèque nationale, fonds français 854. Thirteenth century, after 1273, Veneto (Brunel, *Bibliographie* 43, no. 142; Camps 8–9). Color: gallica.bnf.fr/ark:/12148/btv1b8419245d. Black and white: gallica.bnf.fr/ark:/12148/btv1b9059105w. Base of no. 22.

K   Paris, Bibliothèque nationale, fonds français 12473. Thirteenth century, after 1273, Veneto (Brunel, *Bibliographie* 53, no. 179; Camps 14–15). Color: gallica.bnf.fr/ark:/12148/btv1b60007960. Base of no. 9.

Ka   Udine, Biblioteca Arcivescovale, codici fragmentari I, 265. Thirteenth century, Italy (Brunel, *Bibliographie* 100, no. 348).

L   Rome, Biblioteca Apostolica Vaticana, Vaticani latini 3206. Fourteenth century, Italy (Brunel, *Bibliographie* 93, no. 320).

M   Paris, Bibliothèque nationale, fonds français 12474. Fourteenth century, Naples, from a Venetian exemplar (Brunel, *Bibliographie* 53, no. 180; Camps 15–16). Color: gallica.bnf.fr/ark:/12148/btv1b6000427q. Base of nos. 10, 17.

N   New York, Morgan Library, M819. Fourteenth century, Italy (Brunel, *Bibliographie* 4, no. 11), or 1260 to 1275, Venice or Padua (Canova Mariani 75).

N^2 Berlin, Staatsbibliothek, Phillipps 1910. Sixteenth century, Italy (Brunel, *Bibliographie* 2, no. 4).

O   Rome, Biblioteca Apostolica Vaticana, Vaticani latini 3208. Fourteenth century, Italy (Brunel, *Bibliographie* 94, no. 322).

P   Florence, Biblioteca Laurenziana, Plutei XLI.42. Copy completed in
     1310 by Petrus Berzoli de Gubbio (Brunel, *Bibliographie* 84, no.
     290).
     Color: mss.bmlonline.it/s.aspx?Id=AWOIe_39I1A4r7GxMIEg&
     c=Provincialium%20poetarum%20Carmina%20et%20
     alia#/book.
     Alternative color: teca.bmlonline.it/ImageViewer/servlet/
     ImageViewer?idr=TECA0000492171&keyworks=plut.41
     .42#page/1/mode/1up.
     Base of nos. 21, 24.
Q   Florence, Biblioteca Riccardiana, 2909. Fourteenth century, Italy
     (Brunel, *Bibliographie* 90, no. 306).
R   Paris, Bibliothèque nationale, fonds français 22543. Fourteenth
     century, Languedoc (Brunel, *Bibliographie* 56, no. 194; Camps
     17–18).
     Color: gallica.bnf.fr/ark:/12148/btv1b60004306.
     Base of nos. 6, 7. Consulted for no. 24.
S   Oxford, Douce 269. Circa 1300, Italy (Brunel, *Bibliographie* 9, no. 26).
     Selected folios, color: digital.bodleian.ox.ac.uk/objects/c6e3d99f
     -c135-40e6-bd51-85b0f9a62902/.
     Diplomatic edition: Shepard.
     Consulted for no. 21.
Sg   Barcelona, Biblioteca de Catalunya 146. Fourteenth century, Catalo-
     nia (Brunel, *Bibliographie* 13, no. 36).
T   Paris, Bibliothèque nationale, fonds français 15211. Fifteenth century,
     Italy (Brunel, *Bibliographie* 56, no. 191) or fourteenth century
     (Camps 16).
     Color: gallica.bnf.fr/ark:/12148/btv1b6000798t.
     Base of no. 26.
U   Florence, Biblioteca Medicea Laurenziana, Plutei XLI.43. Fourteenth
     century, Italy (Brunel, *Bibliographie* 85, no. 291).
V   Venice, Biblioteca Marciana, Francesi Appendice Codici XI. Thir-
     teenth and fifteenth centuries, Catalonia and Italy (Brunel, *Biblio-
     graphie* 100, no. 351).
VeAg Barcelona, Biblioteca de Catalunya, 7–8. Fourteenth to fifteenth cen-
     tury, perhaps 1423 to 1432, Catalonia (Brunel, *Bibliographie* 12,
     no. 35; Alberni, *Barcelona* 49–53).
     Color: mdc.csuc.cat/digital/collection/manuscritBC/id/118818.
     Ultraviolet: mdc.csuc.cat/digital/collection/manuscritBC/id/
     119553.
     Base of no. 30.
W   Paris, Bibliothèque nationale, fonds français 844. French chansonnier
     M. Thirteenth century, 1254 to circa 1280 (Aubrey, *Music* 40),
     northern France, perhaps Artois (Brunel, *Bibliographie* 42, no.
     139; Camps 7–8).

Color: gallica.bnf.fr/ark:/12148/btv1b84192440.
Black and white: gallica.bnf.fr/ark:/12148/btv1b90096376.
Base of no. 25.

a   Florence, Biblioteca Riccardiana, 2814. Copied in 1589 by Jacques
Teissier de Tarascon (Brunel, *Bibliographie* 89, no. 305).

a^1 Modena, Biblioteca Estense Universitaria, γ N.8.4.11–13 = Càmpori
Appendice 494, 427, 426. Copied in 1589 by Jacques Teissier
de Tarascon (Brunel, *Bibliographie* 92, no. 315).
Color: bibliotecaestense.beniculturali.it/info/img/mss/i-mo-beu
-gamma.n.8.4.11–13.html.

b   Rome, Biblioteca Apostolica Vaticana, Barberiniani 4087. Sixteenth
and eighteenth centuries, Italy (Brunel, *Bibliographie* 96, no.
335).

c   Florence, Biblioteca Medicea Laurenziana, Plutei XC inf. 26. Fifteenth
century, Italy (Brunel, *Bibliographie* 85, no. 292).

d   Paper supplement to *D*, fols. 262–346. Sixteenth century, Italy
(Brunel, *Bibliographie*, 91–92, no. 314).

e   Rome, Biblioteca Apostolica Vaticana, Barberiniani 3965. Eighteenth
century, Italy (Brunel, *Bibliographie* 95, no. 331).

f   Paris, Bibliothèque nationale, fonds français 12472. Fourteenth
century, Provence; perhaps first half of the century, Arles
(Camps 14).
Black and white: gallica.bnf.fr/ark:/12148/btv1b6000800f.
Base of no. 29. Consulted for no. 21.

g   Rome, Biblioteca Vaticana, Vaticani latini 3205, appendix. End of
sixteenth century, Italy (Pillet and Carstens xxviii; Brunel, *Biblio-
graphie* 93, no. 319).

z   Bologna, Archivio notarile. Thirteenth century, Italy (Brunel, *Biblio-
graphie* 83, no. 286).

OTHER MANUSCRIPTS

Clermont-Ferrand, Bibliothèque communautaire et interuniversitaire (Biblio-
thèque du Patrimoine), MS 201. Ninth or tenth century (Bischoff 261) or
late tenth century (Lauranson-Rosaz 246).
Color: overnia.bibliotheques-clermontmetropole.eu/media-dam/
CLERCO/biblioth/PDF/4_Sciences_et_arts_MS_201_0005.pdf.
Base of no. 1.
Firenze, Biblioteca Nazionale Centrale, Fondo Nazionale II.1.36. Fourteenth
century.
Color: www.danteonline.it/english/codici_frames/codici_nav.asp?img=
231/Img/064R.
Consulted for no. 28.
London, British Library, Harley MS 2750. Circa 1000 to 1025, Germany.

Color: www.bl.uk/manuscripts/FullDisplay.aspx?ref=Harley_MS_2750.
Base of no. 2.

The British Library was the victim of a major cyberattack in October
2023. At the time of writing, services are being gradually restored,
but it is impossible to access Harley MS 2750. It is hoped that the
manuscript will become available again soon. Several facsimiles of
this folio have appeared previously (see headnote to no. 2).

Paris, Bibliothèque nationale, fonds latin 1139. Eleventh to thirteenth century,
Limoges (Bibliothèque nationale de France).
Color: gallica.bnf.fr/ark:/12148/btv1b6000946s.
Base of no. 3.

Piacenza, Biblioteca Comunale, MS 190. Copied in 1336; the oldest manu-
script of Dante's *Divine Comedy*.
Available at *dante online*, black and white: www.danteonline.it/english/
codici_frames/codici.asp?idcod=607.
Base of no. 28.

Adams, Edward L. *Word-Formation in Provençal*. Macmillan, 1913. *HathiTrust*, catalog
    .hathitrust.org/Record/001217627?.
Alberni, Anna. *Barcelona, Biblioteca de Catalunya, VeAg (7 e 8)*. Mucchi, 2006. Intavulare I, 11.
———[*filed as* Anna Alberni Jordà]. *El cançoner Vega-Aguiló (BC, mss. 7 i 8): Estructura i
    contingut*. 2003. U of Barcelona, PhD dissertation.
———. "El poemet de la Reina de Mallorca: Assaig de restauració textual i mètrica." *Medio-
    evo romanzo*, vol. 33, no. 2, 2009, pp. 343–68. With two facsimiles.
Alcover, Antoni Maria. *Diccionari català-valencià-balear*. 2nd ed., Alcover, 1968–69. 10 vols.
    L'Institut d'Estudis Catalans and La Institució Francesc de Borja Moll, dcvb.iec.cat.
Anglade, Joseph. *Grammaire de l'ancien provençal*. Klincksieck, 1921. *HathiTrust*, catalog
    .hathitrust.org/Record/001802959?.
Appel, Carl, editor. *Bernart von Ventadorn: Seine Lieder*. Niemeyer, 1915. *HathiTrust*, babel
    .hathitrust.org/cgi/pt?id=mdp.39015005580181&view=1up&seq=423&q1=tristan.
———, editor. 1930. *Provenzalische Chrestomathie*. 6th ed., Georg Olms Verlag, 1971.
Ashbery, John. "Farm Implements and Rutabagas in a Landscape." *Poetry Foundation*, www
    .poetryfoundation.org/poems/47763/farm-implements-and-rutabagas-in-a-landscape.
Asperti, Stefano. *Bibliografia elettronica dei trovatori*. Version 2.5, Sapienza Università di
    Roma, Dipartimento Studi greco-latini, italiani, scenico-musicali, 2012, www.bedt.it
    /BEdT_04_25/id_testo_incipit.aspx.
Aubrey, Elizabeth. *The Music of the Troubadours*. Indiana UP, 1996. Music: Scholarship and
    Performance.
———. "The Music of the Troubadours: An Online Companion." Paden, *Old Occitan*,
    pp. 578–81.
Auden, W. H. "Paysage Moralisé." *University of Toronto Faculty of Arts and Science*, ian.artsci
    .utoronto.ca/paysage.html.
Avalle, D'Arco Silvio. *Cultura e lingua francese delle origini nella "Passion" di Clermont-Ferrand*.
    Riccardo Ricciardi, 1962.
Battaglia, Salvatore. *Grande dizionario della lingua italiana*. Unione tipografico-editrice tori-
    nese, 1961–2002. 21 vols.
"Bear-baiting, N., Sense 1.a." *Oxford English Dictionary*, Oxford UP, Sept. 2023, https://doi
    .org/10.1093/OED/1021424916.
Bec, Pierre, editor. *Chansons d'amour des femmes-troubadours: Trobairitz et "chansons de
    femme."* Stock, 1995.

Benson, Larry D., editor. *The Riverside Chaucer.* 3rd ed., Houghton Mifflin, 1987.

The Bible. Latin Vulgate Version. *Catholic Bible Online,* catholicbible.online/vulgate.

Bibliothèque nationale de France, Département des Manuscrits. Description of Latin 1139. *Archives et manuscrits,* archivesetmanuscrits.bnf.fr/ark:/12148/cc59066k.

Bischoff, Bernhard. *Anecdota novissima: Texte des vierten bis sechzehnten Jahrhunderts.* Hiersemann, 1984.

Bishop, Elizabeth. "Sestina." *All Poetry,* allpoetry.com/poem/8493577-Sestina-by-Elizabeth-Bishop.

Blackburn, Paul. *Proensa: An Anthology of Troubadour Poetry.* Edited by George Economou, U of California P, 1978.

Bond, Gerald A., editor. *The Poetry of William VII, Count of Poitiers, IX Duke of Aquitaine.* Garland, 1984. Garland Library of Medieval Literature 4A.

Boucherie, Anatole, editor. *Le dialecte poitevin au XIII᷉ siècle.* Pedone Lauriel, 1873. *Google Books,* www.google.com/books/edition/Le_dialecte_poitevin_au_XIIIe_siècle /pG1fAAAAcAAJ?hl=en.

Boutière, Jean, et al. *Biographies des troubadours: Textes provençaux des XIII᷉ et XIV᷉ siècles.* 2nd ed., Nizet, 1973.

Bruckner, Matilda Tomaryn, et al., editors. *Songs of the Women Troubadours.* Garland, 1995. Garland Library of Medieval Literature 97A.

Brunel, Clovis. *Bibliographie des manuscrits littéraires en ancien provençal.* Droz, 1935.

———, editor. 1926–52. *Les plus anciennes chartes en langue provençale: Recueil des pièces originales antérieures au XIII᷉ siècle.* Reprint ed., Slatkine, 1973. 2 vols. in 1.

Camps, Jean-Baptiste. *Les manuscrits occitans à la Bibliothèque nationale de France.* 2010. École Nationale Supérieure des Sciences de l'Information et des Bibliothèques, Diplôme de Conservateur des Bibliothèques dissertation.

Canova Mariani, Giordana. "Il poeta e la sua immagine: Il contributo della miniatura alla localizzazione e alla datazione dei canzonieri provenzali AIK e N." *I trovatori nel Veneto e a Venezia: Atti del Convegno Internazionale, Venezia, 28–31 ottobre 2004.* Antenore, 2008, pp. 47–76.

Carapezza, Francesco, editor. *Il canzoniere occitano G (Ambrosiano R 71 sup.).* Liguori, 2004.

Chaguinian, Christophe, editor. *Les albas occitanes: Étude et édition.* Musical transcription and study of the melodies by John Haines. Champion, 2008. Classiques Français du Moyen Âge 156.

Chailley, Jacques. *L'école musicale de Saint-Martial de Limoges jusqu'à la fin du XI᷉ siècle.* Livres Essentiels, 1960.

Chambers, Frank M. *An Introduction to Old Provençal Versification.* American Philosophical Society, 1985.

Chiarini, Giorgio, editor. *Il canzoniere di Jaufre Rudel.* Japadre, 1985.

Cluzel, Irénée, editor. "Princes et troubadours de la maison royale de Barcelone-Aragon." *Boletín de la Real Academia de Buenas Letras de Barcelona,* vol. 27, 1957–58, pp. 321–73.

Cooper, G. B. "Free Verse." *The Princeton Encyclopedia of Poetry and Poetics,* edited by Roland Greene, 4th ed., Princeton UP, 2012, pp. 522–25.

Crocker, Richard L. "Versus." *The New Grove Dictionary of Music and Musicians,* edited by Stanley Sadie, 2nd ed., vol. 26, Grove's Dictionaries, 2001, pp. 504–05.

Durling, Robert M., editor. *Petrarch's Lyric Poems: The Rime Sparse and Other Lyrics.* Harvard UP, 1976.

Durling, Robert M. and Ronald L. Martinez, editors. *Dante: The Divine Comedy: Inferno.* Translated by Durling, Oxford UP, 1996.

———. *Dante: The Divine Comedy: Paradiso.* Translated by Durling, Oxford UP, 2011.

———. *Dante: The Divine Comedy: Purgatorio.* Translated by Durling, Oxford UP, 2003.

Eusebi, Mario, editor. *Arnaut Daniel: Il sirventese e le canzoni.* All'insegna del pesce d'oro, 1984.

Gambino, Francesca, editor. *Canzoni anonime di trovatori e "trobairitz."* Edizioni dell'Orso, 2003.

Gaunt, Simon, et al., editors. *Marcabru: A Critical Edition.* D. S. Brewer, 2000.

Gillingham, John. *Richard I.* Yale UP, 1999.

Gouiran, Gérard, editor. *L'amour et la guerre: L'oeuvre de Bertran de Born.* Publications U de Provence, 1985. 2 vols.

Grafström, Åke. *Étude sur la morphologie des plus anciennes chartes languedociennes.* Almqvist and Wiksell, 1968.

Guida, Saverio, and Gerardo Larghi. *Dizionario biografico dei trovatori.* Mucchi, 2014.

Haines, John. *Medieval Song in Romance Languages.* Cambridge UP, 2010.

Hebbard, Elizabeth Kinchen. *Manuscripts and the Making of the Troubadour Lyric Tradition.* 2017. Yale U, PhD dissertation. *ProQuest*, proquest.com.

Hilty, Gerold. "Les plus anciens monuments de la langue occitane." *Cantarem d'aquest trobadors: Studi occitanici in onore di Giuseppe Taviani*, edited by L. Rossi, Edizioni dell'Orso, 1995, pp. 25–45.

Jackson, Raych. "A Sestina for a Black Girl Who Does Not Know How to Braid Hair." *Poetry Foundation*, www.poetryfoundation.org/poetrymagazine/poems/146235/a-sestina-for-a-black-girl-who-does-not-know-how-to-braid-hair.

Jeanroy, Alfred, editor. "Les 'coblas' de Bertran Carbonel." *Annales du Midi*, vol. 25, no. 98, 1913, pp. 137–88.

Jensen, Frede. *The Syntax of Medieval Occitan.* Niemeyer, 1986. Beihefte zur Zeitschrift für romanische Philologie 208.

———, editor. *Troubadour Lyrics: A Bilingual Anthology.* Peter Lang Publishing, 1998.

Kay, Sarah. "Derivation, Derived Rhyme, and the Trobairitz." *The Voice of the Trobairitz: Perspectives on the Women Troubadours*, edited by William D. Paden, U of Pennsylvania P, 1989, pp. 157–82.

Keelan, Claudia, translator. *Truth of My Songs: Poems of the Trobairitz.* Omnidawn, 2015.

Kehew, Robert, editor. *Lark in the Morning: The Verses of the Troubadours, A Bilingual Edition.* Translated by Ezra Pound et al., U of Chicago P, 2005.

Klein, Otto. *Die Dichtungen des Mönchs von Montaudon.* Elwert, 1885.

Lauranson-Rosaz, Christian. "Le bréviaire d'Alaric en Auvergne: Le *Liber legis doctorum* de Clermont (MS 201 [Anc. 175] de la B.M.I.U. de Clermont-Ferrand)." *Le bréviaire d'Alaric: Aux origines du Code civil*, edited by Michel Rouche and Bruno Dumézil, P de l'U de Paris-Sorbonne, 2008, pp. 241–76.

Lavaud, René, editor. *Poésies complètes du troubadour Peire Cardenal (1180–1278).* Privat, 1957.

Lazar, Moshé, editor. *Bernard de Ventadour, troubadour du XIIᵉ siècle: Chansons d'amour.* Klincksieck, 1966.

Lazzerini, Lucia. "A proposito di due 'Liebesstrophen' pretrobadoriche." *Cultura neolatina*, vol. 53, 1993, pp. 123–34.

———. *Letteratura medievale in lingua d'oc.* Mucchi, 2001.

Leclanche, Jean-Luc, editor. *Robert d'Orbigny: Le conte de Floire et Blanchefleur.* Champion, 2003. Champion Classiques.

Lee, Charmaine. "Le canzoni di Riccardo Cuor di Leone." *Atti del XXI Congresso Internazionale di Linguistica e Filologia Romanza: Centro di studi filologici e linguistici siciliani, Università di Palermo, 18–24 settembre 1995*, edited by Giovanni Ruffino, vol. 6, Niemeyer, 1998, pp. 243–50.

——. "Nota sulla 'rotrouenge' di Riccardo Cuor di Leone." *Rivista di studi testuali*, vol. 6–7, 2004–05, pp. 139–151.

Lepage, Yvan G. "Richard Coeur de Lion et la poésie lyrique." *Et c'est la fin pour quoi sommes ensemble: Hommage à Jean Dufournet: Littérature, histoire et langue du Moyen Âge*, Champion, 1993, pp. 893–910.

Levy, Émil. 1909. *Petit dictionnaire provençal-français*. 4th ed., Carl Winter, 1966.

Levy, Emil, and Carl Appel. *Provenzalisches Supplement-Wörterbuch, Berichtigungen und Ergänzungen zu Raynouards Lexique Roman*. Reisland, 1894–1924. 8 vols. *HathiTrust*, catalog .hathitrust.org/Record/001802943?.

Lightbown, Ronald W. *Medieval European Jewellery, with a Catalogue of the Collection in the Victoria and Albert Museum*. Victoria and Albert Museum, 1992.

Mélanges de langue et littérature occitanes en hommage à Pierre Bec. Université de Poitiers, Centre d'Études Supérieures de Civilisation Médiévale, 1991.

Meneghetti, Maria Luisa. *Le origini delle letterature medievali romanze*. Laterza, 1997.

Meyer, Paul, editor. 1871. *Les derniers troubadours de la Provence, d'après le chansonnier donné à la Bibliothèque impériale par M. Ch. Giraud*. Reprint ed., Slatkine, 1973.

Mölk, Ulrich. "Quan vei les praz verdesir." *Mélanges de langue et littérature occitanes en hommage à Pierre Bec*, pp. 377–84.

Oroz Arizcuren, Francisco J., editor. *La lírica religiosa en la literatura provenzal antigua*. Diputación Foral de Navarra, Institución Príncipe de Viana, 1972.

Ovid. *The Art of Love, and Other Poems*. With a translation by J. H. Mozley. Harvard UP, 1962. Loeb Classical Library.

Paden, William D. "Before the Troubadours: The Archaic Occitan Texts and the Shape of Literary History." *De sens rassis: Essays in Honor of Rupert T. Pickens*, edited by Keith Busby et al., Rodopi, 2005, pp. 509–28.

——. "Bernart de Ventadour le troubadour devint-il abbé de Tulle?" *Mélanges de langue et de littérature occitanes en hommage à Pierre Bec*, pp. 401–13.

——. "Bertran Carbonel, troubadour et juge." *Revue des langues romanes*, vol. 117, 2013, pp. 417–23.

——. "Declension in Twelfth-Century Occitan: On Editing Early Troubadours, with Particular Reference to Marcabru." *Tenso*, vol. 18, nos. 1–2, 2003, pp. 67–115.

——. *An Introduction to Old Occitan*. Modern Language Association of America, 1998. Introductions to Older Languages 4.

——. "The System of Genres in Troubadour Lyric." *Medieval Lyric: Genres in Historical Context*, edited by Paden, U of Illinois P, 2000, pp. 21–67.

Paden, William D., and Frances Freeman Paden. "Swollen Woman, Shifting Canon: The Birth of Occitan Poetry." *PMLA*, vol. 125, no. 2, 2010, pp. 306–21.

——, translators. *Troubadour Poems from the South of France*. D. S. Brewer, 2007.

Paden, William D., et al., editors. "The Poems of the *Trobairitz* Na Castelloza." *Romance Philology*, vol. 35, Aug. 1981, pp. 158–82.

Paden, William D., Jr., et al., editors. *The Poems of the Troubadour Bertran de Born*. U of California P, 1986.

Pagès, Amédée. "Les poésies lyriques de la traduction catalane du Décaméron." *Annales du Midi*, vol. 46, no. 183, 1934, pp. 201–17.

Parramon i Blasco, Jordi. *Repertori mètric de la poesia catalana medieval*. Curial Edicions Catalanes, Publicacions de l'Abadia de Monserrat, 1992. Textos i estudis de cultura catalana 27.

Pasero, Nicolò, editor. *Guglielmo IX, Poesie*. S.T.E.M.-Mucchi, 1973.

Pattison, Walter T., editor. *The Life and Works of the Troubadour Raimbaut d'Orange*. U of Minnesota P, 1952.

Perugi, Maurizio, editor. *Arnaut Daniel: Canzoni*. Edizioni del Galluzzo, 2015.

Pickens, Rupert T. "Jaufré Rudel et la poétique de la mouvance." *Cahiers de civilisation médié-vale*, vol. 20, no. 80, 1977, pp. 323–37.

——, editor. *The Songs of Jaufré Rudel*. Toronto: Pontifical Institutute of Mediaeval Studies, 1978.

Pignon, Jacques. *L'évolution phonétique des parlers du Poitou (Vienne et Deux-Sèvres)*. 2 vols. Artrey, 1960.

Pillet, Alfred, and Henry Carstens. 1933. *Bibliographie der Troubadours*. Niemeyer.

Pope, M[ildred] K. *From Latin to Modern French with Especial Consideration of Anglo-Norman: Phonology and Morphology*. Manchester UP, 1934.

Pound, Ezra. *Poems and Translations*. Edited by Richard Sieburth, Library of America, 2003.

——. "Sestina: Altaforte." *Poetry Foundation*, www.poetryfoundation.org/poems/53967/sestina-altaforte.

——. *The Spirit of Romance*. New Directions, 1968.

Preminger, A., et al. "Sestina." *The Princeton Encyclopedia of Poetry and Poetics*, edited by Roland Greene et al., 4th ed., Princeton UP, 2012, pp. 1296–97.

Purcell, Sally. *Provençal Poems*. Carcanet Press, 1969.

Raby, F. J. E., editor. *The Oxford Book of Medieval Latin Verse*. Clarendon Press, 1959.

Rieger, Angelica, editor. *Trobairitz: Der Beitrag der Frau in der altokzitanischen höfischen Lyrik: Edition des Gesamtkorpus*. Niemeyer, 1991. Beihefte zur Zeitschrift für romanische Philologie 233.

Riquer, Martín de, editor. *Arnaut Daniel: Poesías*. Quaderns Crema, 1994.

——, editor. *Los trovadores: Historia literaria y textos*. Planeta, 1975. 3 vols.

Rohlfs, Gerhard. *Le gascon: Études de philologie pyrénéenne*. 2nd ed. Niemeyer, 1970. Beihefte zur Zeitschrift für romanische Philologie 85.

Roncaglia, Aurelio. "La tenzone tra Ugo Catola e Marcabruno." *Linguistica e filologia: Omaggio a Benvenuto Terracini*, edited by Cesare Segre, Alberto Mondadori, 1968, pp. 202–54.

Rosenberg, Samuel N., and Hans Tischler, editors. *Chansons des trouvères: Chanter m'estuet*. Livre de Poche, 1995. Lettres Gothiques.

Rosenstein, Roy S. "Translation." *A Handbook of the Troubadours*, edited by F. R. P. Akehurst and Judith M. Davis, U of California P, 1995, pp. 334–48.

Routledge, Michael J., editor. *Bertran Carbonel: Les poésies*. AIEO / U of Birmingham, 2006. Association Internationale d'Études Occitanes 6.

——, editor. *Les poésies du Moine de Montaudon*. Publications du Centre d'Études Occitanes de l'U Paul Valéry, 1977.

Ruelle, Pierre, editor. *Les congés d'Arras (Jean Bodel, Baude Fastoul, Adam de la Halle)*. PU de Bruxelles, 1965.

Schultz-Gora, Oskar, editor. *Provenzalische Studien*. Trübner, 1919–21. 2 vols.

Segre, Cesare, editor. *La chanson de Roland*. Droz, 2003.

Selig, Maria, and Monika Tausend, editors. *Dictionnaire de l'occitan médiéval*. Bayerische Akademie der Wissenschaften, 2013–, www.dom-en-ligne.de.

Semrau, Franz. *Würfel und Würfelspiel im alten Frankreich*. Niemeyer, 1910. Zeitschrift für romanische Philologie 23.

Shepard, William P., editor. *The Oxford Provençal Chansonnier*. Princeton UP, 1927.

Singleton, Charles S., editor. *Dante Alighieri: The Divine Comedy: Translated with a Commentary*. Princeton UP, 1970–75. 6 vols. Bollingen Series 80.

Smith, Nathaniel B. "Arnaut Daniel in the *Purgatorio*: Dante's Ambivalence toward Provençal." *Dante Studies*, vol. 98, 1980, pp. 99–109.

Spetia, Lucilla. "Riccardo Cuor di Leone tra oc e oïl (BdT 420,2)." *Cultura neolatina*, vol. 56, 1996, pp. 101–55.

Thomas, Lucien-Paul, editor. *Le "sponsus": Mystère des Vierges sages et des Vierges folles suivi des trois poèmes limousins et farcis*. PU de France, 1951.

Throop, Palmer A. *Criticism of the Crusade: A Study of Public Opinion and Crusade Propaganda*. Swets and Zeitlinger, 1940.

Toja, Gianluigi, editor. *Arnaut Daniel: Canzoni*. Sansoni, 1960.

Vatteroni, Sergio, editor. *Il trovatore Peire Cardenal*. 2 vols. Mucchi, 2013.

Wartburg, Walther von. *Französisches etymologisches Wörterbuch*. Klopp, 1928–. 25 vols.

Wells, Courtney Joseph. "Cobbling Together the Lyric Text: Parody, Imitation, and Obscenity in the Old Occitan *Cobla* Anthologies." *Mediaevalia*, vol. 39, 2018, pp. 143–83.

———. *Trobaretz: Occitan Manuscripts Online*, trobaretz.wordpress.com. Accessed 14 June 2024.

Werckmeister, Jean, editor. *Le mariage: Décret de Gratien, causes 27 à 36: Édition, traduction, introduction et notes*. Éditions du Cerf, 2011.

Werf, Hendrik van der, and Gerald A. Bond, editors. *The Extant Troubadour Melodies: Transcriptions and Essays for Performers and Scholars*. Van der Werf, 1984.

Wilhelm, James J., editor. *The Poetry of Arnaut Daniel*. Garland, 1981. Garland Library of Medieval Literature 3A.

Wolf, George, and Roy Rosenstein, editors. *The Poetry of Cercamon and Jaufre Rudel*. Garland, 1983. Garland Library of Medieval Literature 5A.

Zinelli, Fabio. "Il canzoniere estense [Occitan MS *D*] e la tradizione veneta della poesia trobadorica: Perspettive vecchie e nuove." *Medioevo romanzo*, vol. 34, 2010, pp. 82–130.

Zufferey, François, editor. "La lèpre des textes: À propos d'un troubadour maudit." *Études de lettres*, nos. 2–3, 1987, pp. 133–43.

Numbers refer to poems.

Adam and Eve, 3, 24; Adam, 19, 20, 26
ages of woman and man, 16
alba, 27
architecture, 11 (vv. 41, 42, 43, 46 [on *assái*]
notes), 19 (v. 29 note on *en plaza*)

backgammon, 5
biblical figures: David, 26; Samson and Deli-
lah, Solomon and David, 8. *See also*
Adam and Eve, God, Virgin Mary

chanson de change 7 (vv. 29–30 note), 12 (v. 9
note on *partís*), 16
charm, 1
cobla, 2, 24, 27, 28
coblas doblas, 5, 8, 11 (and *singulars*), 12, 15, 21
coblas singulars, 3, 11 (and *doblas*), 13, 19, 25,
29
coblas unissonans, 4, 6, 7, 9, 10, 14, 16, 17, 18,
20, 22, 23, 26
Crusade, 4, 6, 8 (v. 42 note), 9 (vv. 38–39, 42
notes), 16 (v. 40 note), 21 (vv. 20,
25–27, 39 notes), 22 (vv. 41, 48 notes)

Dante, 17, 18, 19, 27; as Occitan poet, 28
declension in two cases vs. one, see the sec-
tion "Elements of Occitan." *See also* the
note on declension for nos. 1, 2, 29, 30
descort, 30

falconry, 2, 17 (v. 8 note), 18 (vv. 18–19 note)

Gascony, 8 (v. 3 note), 9, 17, 21 (v. 8 note)
gelos (plural), 14 (v. 17)
gender ambiguity, 29
God, 3, 20; sponsor of Crusade, 21 (v. 39
note); interlocutor in a *tenso*, 22

historiated initial in MS *K*, 9 (v. 1 note)

joglar: the word, 8 (v. 44), 11 (v. 49),
16 (vv. 15, 32, 42 note); mentioned,
9 (vv. 37–38 note), 18

lausengier, 12 (v. 42), 13 (v. 35), 14 (vv. 6,
10), 19 (v. 3)
leprosy, 29
love, qualities or symptoms of: (positive)
courtesy, 9; dreams, 6, 7; fidelity, 12;
fin'amor, 19 (v. 27); joy, 4, 6, 7, 10, 11,
12, 14, 15, 18, 19, 20, 22, 23, 25 (vv. 4,
41); mercy, 7 (v. 33), 10, 11, 13, 26, 30;
openness, 15; paradise, 12, 19, 22; plea-
sure, 6, 7; prosperity, 18 vv. 20–21; sex-
uality, 4 (v. 35), 5, 8 (v. 51), 19, 24, 25,
27; sincerity, 13, 15, 23, 25; warmth, 18
(v. 28); (negative) betrayal, 8; death, 10,
12, 13, 18, 23, 25, 30; despair, 30; fear, 4,
5, 13, 19, 23; grief, 6, 10, 11, 12, 13, 14,
23; pain, 2, 10, 12, 13, 19, 23, 25, 30;
sickness, 6 (v. 15 note on *magri[r]á*),
30; suffering, 18 (v. 33), 23, 29 (v. 27);
wakefulness, 25; weeping, 13, 23